# Anthropology
# & the Colonial Encounter

# Anthropology & the Colonial Encounter

Edited by Talal Asad

Ithaca Press: London
Humanities Press: Atlantic Highlands, N.J.

First edition printed & published
by Ithaca Press and Humanities
Press

Reprint 1975 by Ithaca Press
and Humanities Press

© The Authors 1973

*Printed in The United States of America*

ISBN 0-903729-00-8 Library Edition
ISBN 0-903729-01-6 Paperback Edition
U.S.A. ISBN 0-391-00391-7 Paperback edition

# Contents

# INTRODUCTION
## Talal Asad

British functional anthropology began to emerge as a distinctive discipline shortly after the First World War through the efforts of Malinowski and Radcliffe-Brown, but it was not until after the Second World War that it gained an assured academic status in the universities. Compared with the two decades before the Second World War an enormous quantity of anthropological writing was published in the two decades after it. Within this brief period its claim to academic respectability was virtually unchallenged. By 1961 a prominent sociologist could write that "social anthropology is, among other things, a small but I think flourishing profession. The subject, like social work and unlike sociology, has prestige".[1] A few years later a political scientist contrasted social anthropology favourably with sociology, declaring that unlike the latter, but like the other bona fide social sciences, social anthropology "had built up a body of knowledge which cannot readily be described as anything else".[2]

Functional anthropology had barely secured its enviable academic reputation when some serious misgivings began to make themselves felt from within the established profession. In 1961, Leach claimed that "functionalist doctrine [has] ceased to carry conviction".[3] Five years later Worsley wrote his trenchant critique under the signifi-

[1]Donald G. Macrae, *Ideology and Society*, London, 1961, p. 36.
[2]W. G. Runciman, "Sociologese" in *Encounter*, December, 1965, Vol. XXV, No. 6, p. 47.
[3]E. R. Leach, *Rethinking Anthropology*, London, 1961, p. 1.

cant title "The End of Anthropology?" By 1970 Needham was arguing that social anthropology "has no unitary and continuous past so far as ideas are concerned", "Nor is there any such thing as a rigorous and coherent body of theory proper to social anthropology".[4] A year later Ardener observed that, "something has already happened to British anthropology (and to international anthropology in related ways such that for practical purposes textbooks which looked useful, no longer are; monographs which used to appear exhaustive now seem selective; interpretations which once looked full of insight now seem mechanical and lifeless".[5]

The plausibility of the anthropological enterprise which seemed so self-evident to all its practitioners a mere decade ago, is now no longer quite so self-evident. A small minority, apart from the names just mentioned, has begun to articulate its doubts in radical terms.[6]

What has happened to British social anthropology?

At the organisational level nothing very disturbing has happened. On the contrary, the Association of Social Anthropologists flourishes as never before; it holds annual academic conferences whose proceedings are regularly published in handsome hardcover and paperback editions. Monographs, articles and text-books by writers calling themselves anthropologists appear in increasing number. A prestigious series of annual lectures on social anthropology has recently been launched under the auspices of the British Academy. The subject is now taught in more university and college departments than ever; the profession is even negotiating to introduce it as a sixth-form option in schools. Seen in terms of its public activity, there is no crisis in social anthropology.

On the whole, professional leaders of British anthropology are not impressed by alarmist talk about crisis.[7] They would maintain, if pressed, that as the older ideas of social anthropology became exhausted, it was natural that one should turn to fresh sources of supply.[8] So they prefer to talk of increasing specialisation, which

[4]Rodney Needham, "The Future of Social Anthropology: Disintegration or Metamorphosis?" in *Anniversary Contributions to Anthropology*: *Twelve Essays*, Leiden, 1970, p. 36 and p. 37.
[5]Edwin Ardener, "The New Anthropology and its Critics" in *Man* N. S. Vol. 6, No. 3, September 1971, p. 449.
[6]The most interesting of these include Banaji, "Crisis in British Anthropology", *New Left Review*, No. 64, 1970, Copans, "Pour une histoire et une sociologie des études Africaines", *Cahiers des études Africaines*, No. 43, 1971, and Leclerc, *Anthropologie et Colonialisme*, Paris, 1972.
[7]See for example I. M. Lewis, Introduction to *History and Social Anthropology*, London, 1968, p. xv.
[8]It is this line of reasoning that Firth adopts to explain and endorse the

they see as a sign of the intellectual vitality of the profession.[9] And more positively, they affirm that classic functionalist assumptions are still viable.[10]

Yet we would be well-advised not to be too easily persuaded by such bland assurances. After all, it is a tendency of establishment leaders to maintain at least the myth if not the reality of smooth continuity. There can be no doubt that at the ideological level something has indeed "already happened to British anthropology" as Ardener put it, although this event is better seen as a disintegration of the Old Anthropology rather than as a crystallization of the New.

There was a time when social anthropology could and did define itself unambiguously as the study of primitive societies. "The scope of any science", wrote Nadel shortly after the Second World War, "is to obtain and extend knowledge. In social anthropology as it is commonly understood we attempt to extend our knowledge of man and society to 'primitive' communities, 'simpler peoples', or 'pre-literate societies'. . . If an anthropologist asks naïvely why, if we are only interested in studying society writ large, we should turn to primitive cultures rather than our own civilization ... the answer is simply that our own society is not the only one, and its phenomena not the same as those found, or apt to be found, in primitive society".[11] Statements of this kind do not indicate a very sophisticated concern for the definition of a problematic, but they reflected an element of pragmatic truth, and it was this that gave social anthropology a practical plausibility. When Evans-Pritchard published his well-known Introduction to Social Anthropology in 1951, it seemed reasonably clear what the subject was about. "The social anthropologist", he explained, "studies primitive societies directly, living among them for months or years, whereas sociological research is usually from documents and largely statistical. The social anthropologist studies societies as wholes—he studies their oecologies, their economics, their legal and political institutions, their family and kinship organizations, their religions, their technologies,

recent anthropological interest in Marx, in his British Academy lecture *The Sceptical Anthropologist? Social Anthropology and Marxist Views on Society*, London, 1972.
[9]See for example the Introduction by Max Gluckman and Fred Eggan to the first four volumes in the ASA Monographs series.
[10]See for example Social Science Research Council's *Research in Social Anthropology*, London, 1968.
[11]S. F. Nadel, *The Foundations of Social Anthropology*, London, 1953, p. 2.

their arts, etc., as parts of general social systems".[12] The doctrines
and approaches that went by the name of functionalism thus gave
social anthropology an assured and coherent style.
Today by contrast even this coherence of style is absent. The
anthropologist now is someone who studies societies both 'simple'
and 'complex'; resorts to participant observation, statistical techniques, historical archives and other literary sources; finds himself
intellectually closer to economists or political scientists or psycho-
analysts or structural linguists or animal behaviourists than he does
to other anthropologists. To describe this state of affairs in terms of
scholarly specialization is surely to indulge in mystification. The
'cognate disciplines' of politics, economics, etc., have been in existence from long before the classical functionalist phase of social
anthropology. The question that must be asked is, why was it only
comparatively recently that they have been discovered by anthropologists? Why is it, for example, that in 1940 anthropologists could
write: "We have not found that the theories of political philo-
sophers have helped us to understand the societies we have studied
and we consider them of little scientific value";[13] and in 1966: "We
consider that the time is ripe for a dialogue, if not for marriage between anthropology and the other disciplines concerned with comparative politics".[14] What made the time ripe? How was it that the
separate disciplines (economics, politics, jurisprudence, etc.) which
reflected the fragmented self-understanding of bourgeois society,
with its own historical contradictions, were ready to inspire anthropology?
The answer I would suggest is to be sought in the fact that since
the Second World War, fundamental changes have occurred in the
world which social anthropology inhabits, changes which have
affected the object, the ideological support and the organisational
base of social anthropology itself. And in noting these changes we
remind ourselves that anthropology does not merely apprehend the
world in which it is located, but that the world also determines how
anthropology will apprehend it.
The attainment of political independence by colonial, especially
African countries in the late '50s and the early '60s accelerated the
trend, apparent since the war, of socio-economic change, involving

[12]E. E. Evans-Pritchard, *Social Anthropology, London*, 1951, p. 11.
[13]M. Fortes and E. E. Evans-Pritchard, (eds.), *African Political Systems,*
London, 1940, p. 4.
[14]M. J. Swartz, V. W. Turner, A. Tuden, (eds.), *Political Anthropology,*
Chicago, 1968, p. 9.

these countries in the planned development of national networks of communications, electrification and broadcasting; the promotion of education and of rural improvement projects; the shift of political power from 'tribal' leaders to the nationalistic bourgeoisie. Mainly as a consequence of nationalist expectations, scholars began to recover an indigenous history.[15] Some nationalist writers denounced the colonial connections of anthropology. Thus increasingly the larger political-economic system thrust itself obtrusively into the anthropologist's framework, as did the relevance of the past, both colonial and pre-colonial. At another level, mounting criticism of the functionalist tradition in American mainstream sociology contributed indirectly towards the undermining of functionalist doctrine in British social anthropology.[16] Since it had never adequately clarified the distinction between a totalising method (in which the formation of parts is explained with reference to a developing structure of determinations) and ethnographic holism (in which the different 'institutions' of a society are all described and linked one to another);[17] and, since it had in general confused structural determination with simultaneity, concrete developments in the world outside pushed functional anthropology until it collapsed into micro-sociology. So it is that today most anthropologists have chosen to re-orient themselves in relation to a multitude of fragmentary problems—political, economic, domestic, cultic, etc.— at a 'small-scale' level, and have found in this state of fragmentation their sense of intellectual direction provided for them by their relevant 'cognate discipline'. These changes in the object of study and in the ideological supports of social anthropology might by themselves have led to a disintegration of the discipline, but the same post-war period witnessed a significant development in the organisational base of social anthropology which saved it. In 1946

[15]Partly by challenging the functional anthropologist's dogma that only written records could provide a reliable basis for reconstructing history. Cf. J. Vansina's *Oral Tradition, a Study in Historical Methodology*, London, 1965, originally published in French in 1961. The general tendency of functional anthropology was to assimilate indigenous history to the category of myth—i.e. to view it in terms of instrumentality rather than of truth in the classical non-pragmatist sense.
[16]Leading sociologists in America,—e.g. Parsons, Merton, Homans—had always taken an active and sympathetic interest in British social anthropology, and their writings in turn were a source of inspiration and support to functional anthropologists. The attack on American structural-functionalism by such writers as R. Dahrendorf and C. Wright Mills was therefore bound to affect the doctrinal self-confidence of British social anthropology.
[17]That this distinction remains unclear to many anthropologists even today is apparent from the over-confident remarks of Levi-Strauss in his polemic

the Association of Social Anthropologists of the British Commonwealth (ASA) was founded with under 20 members; by 1962 the
membership had risen to over 150, "even though election to membership required normally both the holding of a teaching or a
research post in the Commonwealth and the attainment of either
a post-graduate degree (usually a doctorate) or substantial publications".[18] Once this base was in effective operation, social anthropology as institutionalised practice could dispense with the doctrinal
specificity it had previously insisted on. Professional distinctiveness
could now be maintained through an established network of vested
interests—for which the ASA was a co-ordinating agency—rather
than by any particular doctrines or methods. Anthropology was
now truly a 'profession'.

Ironically, the same forces that were contributing to the ideological dissolution of classical functional anthropology had also
contributed to a strengthening of its organisational base. Thus
Fortes notes that during the Second World War in Britain, "economic, political and especially military necessities aroused a new and
lively public interest in the African and Asiatic dependencies of
Britain and her allies. The plans for post-war economic and social
development in these areas generated under pressure of war-time
experiences included big schemes of research in the natural and
social sciences. The boom in anthropological studies thus foreshadowed began after Radcliffe-Brown had retired from the Oxford chair [in 1946]".[19] It was in the year of Radcliffe-Brown's retirement that the ASA was founded by scholars who were already
members of the long-established but far less exclusive Royal Anthropological Institute. An exclusive 'professional' organisation was
clearly far better placed to exploit the new funding possibilities for
research in the changing power-pattern of the post-war world.

It is not a matter of dispute that social anthropology emerged as
a distinctive discipline at the beginning of the colonial era, that it

against Sartre: "It is possible that the requirement of 'totalisation' is a
great novelty to some historians, sociologists and psychologists. It has been
taken for granted by anthropologists ever since they learnt it from Malinowski". *The Savage Mind*, London, 1966, p. 250. What anthropologists
learnt from Malinowski was ethnographic holism, not the method of
totalisation.
[18]M. Gluckman and Fred Eggan, "Introduction" to *The Relevance of Models
for Social Anthropology*, London, 1965, p. xii. By 1968 the Association
had about 240 members (Social Science Research Council, *Research in
Social Anthropology*, London, 1968, p. 79.)
[19]M. Fortes, (ed.) *Social Structure*, Oxford 1949, p. xiii.

became a flourishing academic profession towards its close, or that throughout this period its efforts were devoted to a description and analysis—carried out by Europeans, for a European audience—of non-European societies dominated by European power. And yet there is a strange reluctance on the part of most professional anthropologists to consider seriously the power structure within which their discipline has taken shape. The typical attitude is well represented by the following passage from Victor Turner's Introduction to Volume Three of *Colonialism in Africa 1870-1960*, (Cambridge, 1971), in which the problem of the relationship between anthropology and colonialism is trivialised and dismissed in the space of two short paragraphs:

It used to be argued by officials of the *ancien régime* that anthropologists, immersed as they were in the specificities of African life, came to accept the structural perspective of their informants, became their spokesmen, and by their words and works impeded the efforts of district and provincial administrators to govern efficiently. Some were even accused by white settlers and European civil servants of being 'Reds', 'socialists' and 'anarchists'. It is now asseverated by African leaders and administrators, down to the district level, that anthropologists before independence were 'apologists of colonialism' and subtle agents of colonial supremacy who studied African customs merely to provide the dominant white minority with information damaging to native interests but normally opaque to white investigation. Thus yesterday's 'socialist' has become today's 'reactionary'. Sir Alan Burns (1957) and Frantz Fanon (1961) are improbably allied.

It is true, of course, that in their personal capacity anthropologists, like everyone else, have a wide spectrum of political views. Some are known 'conservatives'; others lean far to the 'left'. But as professionals, anthropologists are trained, over almost as many years as doctors, to collect certain kinds of information as 'participant observers' which will enable them, whatever may be their personal views, to present as objectively as the current level of their discipline's development permits, a coherent picture of the sociocultural system they have elected to spend some years of their lives in studying, and of the kinds of processes that go on in it. It is their ultimate duty to publish their findings and expose them, together with an exact description of the means by which they were obtained, to the international public of their anthropological colleagues and

beyond that to the 'world of learning'. Eventually, news of their
work and analyses, through their own 'popular' writings or
through citations, résumés (not infrequently bowdlerised) and
digests by non-anthropologists, seeps through to the general
reading public. Time thus winnows their reports and rids them
of much that is biased and 'loaded'. There is no point in special
pleading or tendentious argument; there are professional
standards against which all reports are measured, and, in the
end, the common sense of the common man. (pp.1-2)
But to speak about 'professional standards' and the authority of
'common sense' is surely no less naïve than are wild remarks about
anthropology being merely the handmaiden of colonialism. There
are today no clear-cut standards in anthropology, there is only
a flourishing professional organisation; and the common sense
of Western common man, himself an alienated and exploited
being, is hardly reliable as a critical test of anthropological knowledge. And yet the easy assurance of Turner's remarks is itself an
indication of the kind of commonsense world that the typical anthropologist still shares, and knows he shares, with those whom he
primarily addresses.

We have been reminded time and again by anthropologists
of the ideas and ideals of the Enlightenment in which the intellectual inspiration of anthropology is supposed to lie.[20] But anthropology is also rooted in an unequal power encounter between the
West and Third World which goes back to the emergence of bourgeois Europe, an encounter in which colonialism is merely one
historical moment.[21] It is this encounter that gives the West access
to cultural and historical information about the societies it has
progressively dominated, and thus not only generates a certain kind
of universal understanding, but also re-enforces the inequalities in
capacity between the European and the non-European worlds (and
derivatively, between the Europeanized elites and the 'traditional'
masses in the Third World). We are today becoming increasingly
aware of the fact that information and understanding produced by
bourgeois disciplines like anthropology are acquired and used most
readily by those with the greatest capacity for exploitation. This
follows partly from the structure of research, but more especially

[20]See for example E. E. Evans-Pritchard, op. cit., M. Harris, *The Rise of
Anthropological Theory*, London, 1969, R. Firth, op. cit.
[21]C. Levi-Strauss was one of the first anthropologists to note this important
fact, although he has barely gone beyond noting it. See *The Scope of Anthropology*, London, 1967, pp. 51-2.

from the way in which these disciplines objectify their knowledge. It is because the powerful who support research expect the kind of understanding which will ultimately confirm them in their world that anthropology has not very easily turned to the production of radically subversive forms of understanding. It is because anthropological understanding is overwhelmingly objectified in European languages that it is most easily accommodated to the mode of life, and hence to the rationality, of the world power which the West represents.

We must begin from the fact that the basic reality which made pre-war social anthropology a feasible and effective enterprise was the power relationship between dominating (European) and dominated (non-European) cultures. We then need to ask ourselves how this relationship has affected the practical pre-conditions of social anthropology; the uses to which its knowledge was put; the theoretical treatment of particular topics; the mode of perceiving and objectifying alien societies; and the anthropologist's claim of political neutrality.

The colonial power structure made the object of anthropological study accessible and safe—because of it sustained physical proximity between the observing European and the living non-European became a practical possibility. It made possible the kind of human intimacy on which anthropological fieldwork is based, but ensured that that intimacy should be one-sided and provisional. It is worth noting that virtually no European anthropologist has been won over personally to the subordinated culture he has studied; although countless non-Europeans, having come to the West to study its culture, have been captured by its values and assumptions, and also contributed to an understanding of it.

The reason for this asymmetry is the dialectic of world power. Anthropologists can claim to have contributed to the cultural heritage of the societies they study by a sympathetic recording of indigenous forms of life that would otherwise be lost to posterity. But they have also contributed, sometimes indirectly, towards maintaining the structure of power represented by the colonial system. That such contributions were not in the final reckoning crucial for the vast empire which received knowledge and provided patronage does not mean that it was not critical for the small discipline which offered knowledge and received that patronage. For the structure of power certainly affected the theoretical choice and treatment of what social anthropology objectified—more so in some matters than in others. (We should in any case avoid the tendency found among some critics and defenders of social anthropology of speaking as though the doctrines and analyses labelled 'functionalism' were parts of a highly integrated logical structure.) Its analyses—of holistic politics most of all, of cosmological systems least of all —were affected by a readiness to adapt to colonial ideology. At any rate the general drift of anthropological understanding did not constitute a basic challenge to the unequal world represented by the colonial system. Nor was the colonial system as such—within which the social objects studied were located—analysed by the social anthropologist. To argue that the anthropologist's expertise did not qualify him for considering fruitfully such a system is to confess that this expertise was malformed. For any object which is subordinated and manipulated is partly the product of a power relationship, and to ignore this fact is to miscomprehend the nature of that object.

Clearly the anthropologist's claim to political neutrality cannot be separated from all that has been said so far. Thus the scientistic definition of anthropology as a disinterested (objective, value-free) study of 'other cultures' helped to mark off the anthropologist's enterprise from that of colonial Europeans (the trader, the missionary, the administrator and other men of practical affairs); but did it not also render him unable to envisage and argue for a radically different political future for the subordinate people he studied and thus serve to merge that enterprise *in effect* with that of dominant status-quo Europeans? If the anthropologist sometimes endorsed or condemned particular social changes affecting "his people", did he, in this ad hoc commitment, do any more or any less than many colonial Europeans who accepted colonialism as a system? If he was sometimes accusingly called 'a Red', 'a socialist' or 'an anarchist' by administrators and settlers, did this not merely reveal one facet of the hysterically intolerant character of colonialism as a system, with which he chose nevertheless to live *professionally* at peace?

I believe it is a mistake to view social anthropology in the colonial era as primarily an aid to colonial administration, or as the simple reflection of colonial ideology. I say this not because I subscribe to the anthropological establishment's comfortable view of itself, but because bourgeois consciousness, of which social anthropology is merely one fragment, has always contained within itself profound contradictions and ambiguities—and therefore the potentialities for transcending itself. For these contradictions to be adequately apprehended it is essential to turn to the historical power

relationship between the West and the Third World and to examine
the ways in which it has been dialectically linked to the practical
conditions, the working assumptions and the intellectual product
of all disciplines representing the European understanding of non-
European humanity.

The papers that follow analyse and document ways in which anthropological thinking and practice have been affected by British colonialism, but they approach this topic from different points of view
and at different levels. All but Roger Owen's were presented first at
a Seminar held in Hull in September 1972. Although each contributor has had the opportunity to revise his paper in the light of discussions that were held at the Seminar, no editorial attempt has
been made to impose any unity on them, or for that matter to ensure that together they represent a comprehensive coverage of the
problem. They stand as individual contributions to an argument
that is only just beginning, and in which as yet only a handful of
anthropologists are seriously interested. (It should be noted that in
over a quarter of a century since it was founded, the ASA has never
regarded colonialism as a topic worthy of a conference.)

The group which met wishes to thank the University of Hull for
providing funds and facilities for the Seminar. Most especially, we
wish to thank Ian Cunnison, Head of the Department of Sociology
and Social Anthropology at Hull, without whose active help and
constant encouragement the Seminar would probably not have
taken place. It was he who canvassed Anthropology Departments
in various Universities for possible contributors, and undertook
most of the organisational duties in preparation for the meeting.

March 1973

# Part 1: General Studies

# EMPIRICISM AND IMPERIALISM:
## A REVIEW OF THE NEW LEFT CRITIQUE OF SOCIAL ANTHROPOLOGY
### Peter Forster

The question of the relationship between anthropology and colonialism has been raised in various quarters recently by various writers who declare that they are approaching their subject from the point of view of a left-wing political value-orientation. The differences in scope, origin and perspective of the various writers are considerable, and some limitation on the subject-matter must be imposed. Particular attention will here be focused on three different sources, one British, one *Current Anthropology* Review Article, and one French. The British source will be the articles that have appeared in the *New Left Review*: Goddard[1], Banaji[2], and, to a lesser extent, Anderson[3]. The *Current Anthropology* source will be the symposium on social responsibilities, with contribution from Berreman[4], Gjessing[5], and Gough[6]. The French source will be the recently published book by Leclerc[7], which deals explicitly with the

[1]D. Goddard, "Limits of British Anthropology", *New Left Review*, No. 58 (1969), pp. 79-89.
[2]J. Banaji, "The Crisis of British Anthropology", *New Left Review*, No. 64 (1970), pp. 71-85.
[3]P. Anderson, "Components of the National Culture", *New Left Review*, No. 50 (1968) pp. 3-57. Reprinted in A. Cockburn and R. Blackburn, "Student Power: Problems, Diagnosis, Action", Harmondsworth, Penguin, 1969, pp. 214-284. Page references are to the reprint.
[4]G. D. Berreman, "Is Anthropology Alive? Social Responsibility in Social Anthropology", *Current Anthropology*, Vol. 9 (1968) pp. 391-396.
[5]G. Gjessing, "The Social Responsibility of the Social Scientists", *Current Anthropology*, Vol. 9 (1968), pp. 397-402.
[6]K. Gough, "New Proposals for Anthropologists", *Current Anthropology*,

question of the relationship between anthropology and colonialism from the point of view of 'critical' anthropology; although appearing in France, this latter work has as its prime focus of attention the British school of anthropology. This list is far from exhaustive; however, the positions adopted by the various writers here considered are sufficiently diverse and unfamiliar to mainstream British social anthropology to make it worthwhile to examine their arguments carefully. The basic unity of the critique revolves around discussion of the colonial situation and the place of anthropology within it. Sometimes the focus of attention is British imperialism (Gjessing, Leclerc, Goddard, Banaji, Anderson), sometimes American neo-imperialism (Berreman, Gough). The stand taken may be the theoretical limitations of classic anthropology (Leclerc, Anderson, Goddard, Banaji) or alternatively, a plea for social responsibility, value-awareness, and politically relevant anthropological investigation (Berreman, Gjessing, Gough). Other source-material discussing the general question of anthropology and colonialism, or of the future of anthropology, will be referred to in the text, and some other writers mentioned may well wish to associate themselves with the New Left; however, I have deliberately avoided an unfortunate tendency characteristic of certain recent exercises in 'critical' or 'radical' sociology, of investigating the left-wing credentials of the authors considered before considering their contributions as valid statements of an argument.

The origins of the New Left critique of social anthropology are fairly easy to discern. Politically and historically interest in this kind of introspection stems from the dismemberment of colonial empires which were previously the stamping ground of anthropologists; from the sociological concomitants of 'development' in the Third World; and more recently from the exposure of anthropological work sponsored by the United States Central Intelligence Agency, and the successful passing of a resolution about the Vietnam war at the American Anthropological Association meeting in 1966. Theoretically, the critique forms part of a more general disillusionment with functionalism (a characteristic of radical sociology too); with empiricism, sometimes within the framework of criticisms voiced elsewhere about the lack of comparison in a supposedly comparative science[8], sometimes as part of a general critique of the lack of

Vol. 9 (1968), pp. 403-407.
[7]G. Leclerc, Anthropologie et Colonialisme, Paris, Fayard, 1972.
[8]See particularly E. Leach, Rethinking Anthropology (title-essay), London, Athlone Press, 1961, pp. 1-27.

anthropological theory (Goddard, Banaji); and again, as part of a
general disillusionment with microscopic studies (Gjessing, Gough).
Goddard and Banaji both hold that British social anthropology has
suffered from over-concentration on normative and jural phenomena; Goddard advocates a greater concern with the metaphysical
elements in Durkheim's thought, while Banaji prefers a greater concern with Lévi-Straussian structural anthropology, considering that
its most fruitful aspects have been either ignored or "naturalised"
in British anthropology. Leclerc also, where he puts forward theoretical proposals, suggests that anthropology should avoid the objectification characteristic of its colonial past, and is critical of the
behaviourism and empiricism of British anthropology; he mentions
with approval writers such as Griaule[9], for whom native cosmology
is not to be seen as a mere superstructure: interpretative analysis
is not to be made at the expense of indigenous interpretation. Finally, a common criticism voiced on both political and theoretical
grounds is that classical anthropology has either ignored or taken
insufficient account of the colonial situation. Thus Goddard criti-
cises British anthropology for speaking of "primitive" rather than
"colonised" peoples, and for its lack of a total conception of the
colonial situation. Anderson is critical of Evans-Pritchard for his
lack of attention in *The Nuer*[10] to the colonial situation while at the
same time approving of Leach (*Political Systems of Highland
Burma*[11]) for the incorporation of the colonial situation into his
analysis. Banaji, by contrast, regards Leach as equally culpable in
his lack of attention to the colonial situation. Leclerc suggests that
much British anthropology, especially applied anthropology, was
closely integrated with Indirect Rule. This he suggests prevented
classical anthropologists from seeing the colonial *system* as a political and historical problem. The *Current Anthropology* symposium
here considered is more concerned with neo-imperialism than with
palaeo-imperialism; none the less, Gjessing particularly is critical of
the a-historical (Radcliffe-Brown) or anti-historical (Malinowski)
perspective of classical anthropology in the colonial situation, and
of the functionalist approach which tended to be reformist with
regard to the colonial administration.

Thus as can be expected from a list of issues raised by writers
grouped together as the 'New Left', both political and academic

[9]M. Griaule, *Dieu d'Eau*, Paris, Editions du Chene, 1948.
[10]E. E. Evans-Pritchard, The Nuer, Oxford, Clarendon Press, 1940.
[11]E. Leach, *Political Systems of Highland Burma*, London, Athlone Press,
1954.

issues are raised, the academic issues being primarily raised in the
authors by their political concerns. The academic issues will be the
main concern of this discussion, but the political proposals put forward are suggested by some authors as binding on the anthropological community generally, and as inseparable from the academic
issues, and are too important to be ignored. I do not intend to speak
of the seriousness of purpose of those who espouse the political
views concerned, of the importance of the issues they raise, or of
the validity of the views they hold. The importance of the political
views held by the writers concerned will be taken to be the effect
of these on academic scholarship. This basically resolves itself
around three areas of concern: the question of a value-free social
anthropology and social science generally, and the role of the
anthropologist in society; the concept of relevance; and the concept
of commitment. These, in different ways, are the concern particularly of the Current Anthropology Social Responsibilities Symposium.

The question of value-freedom in social anthropology and the
role of the anthropologist in society are raised particularly by
Berreman and Gjessing, as a response generally to the literature on
responsibility in science, including the sociological literature, and
more specifically to the Vietnam resolution at the AAA, and to the
exposure of anthropological complicity with the CIA. Particularly
in the context of serious political issues of this nature, it is welcome
that the question of a value-free anthropology has been raised, as it
should be in all social science; but if the discussion of the issue is
to have any lasting value, a number of matters need to be clarified.
This is a useful exercise, as it can also be linked up with the general
question of the effect that palaeo-colonialism had on an anthropologist's academic work. Many important issues are raised by the
whole question of what it means to be value-free; these have been
raised many times before by non-anthropologists, but a number of
common confusions remain. Thus, as far as I am aware, no social
scientist has ever suggested that the investigator of society should
have no value-commitments at all, and Weber strongly repudiated
such a suggestion. The issue of value-freedom unfortunately does
tend to submerge different issues which are easily separable. For
a start, the question of value-freedom is frequently confused with
the question of objectivity. In his critique of some tendencies in
radical sociology, Bandyopadhay[12] emphasises the importance of

[12]P. Bandyopadhyay, "One Sociology or Many—some issues in Radical
Sociology", *Sociological Review*, Vol. 19 (1971), 5-29.

PETER FORSTER 27

this distinction, indicating that left-wing ideology has rejected any
suggestion of a value-free social science but has emphasised the
importance of objectivity. In a different context, Maquet[13] has
raised the question of objectivity in specific relation to social anthropology. In the context of the present discussion, to affirm the value
of objectivity would presumably be to agree with the seriously
politically committed writers who plead for a relevant anthropology.
If, for instance, Gough's new proposals for anthropologists are to be
put into practice and thought to make a valuable contribution to
the advancement of socialist revolution, the findings must be objectively valid. The same idea of objectivity would be even more
important to someone with the political commitment of Frank[14],
for instance, in the *Current Anthropology* discussion. If the politically committed and active anthropologist is to put his knowledge
to any use for the revolution, "like the guerrilla doctor who treats
his wounded comrades", what he has to say had better be true.
Likewise, only objectively valid information collected by the CIA
can be considered dangerous; if information available to the CIA is
not objectively valid, it can only work against the interests of its
neo-imperialist policies. Pseudo-subjectivity is a dangerous luxury
for radical anthropologists to engage in, and can be just as misleading as pseudo-objectivity. To examine the limits of objectivity
in science is a very valuable exercise, but the end in view in this
exercise must be to enable the scientist to move from the less objective to the more objective. The issue has also been raised not in
relation to "objectivity" but in relation to "objectification" (Leclerc, p. 196); I shall return to this in considering the *theoretical*
implications of the New Left critique.

A serious issue is raised by a concept which again arises out of
the issues surrounding the idea of a value-free social science,
namely the concept of relevance. Berreman and Gjessing both
suggest that anthropology today is in danger of becoming "irrelevant", and also are heavily critical of the Ivory Tower. A number
of issues again need to be disentangled here, and a number of
questions need to be asked. Firstly if one accepts that anthropology
arose largely out of the needs of colonial administration, anthropology will indeed suffer from a crisis of identity, now that the
colonial empires are dismembered. More generally, however, the ob-

[13]J. J. Maquet, "Objectivity in Anthropology", *Current Anthropology*, Vol 5
(1964), pp. 47-55.
[14]A. G. Frank, *Comment* to Current Anthropology Social Responsibilties
Symposium, *Current Anthropology*, Vol. 9 (1968), pp. 412-414.

vious question of relevance for what? suggests itself. Gough, to her credit, is completely consistent in putting forward counter-proposals to the activities sponsored by the CIA, drawing the anthropological community's attention to these, and declaring her own value-orientation. There is a danger however, present throughout the *Current Anthropology* symposium, of harnessing most or all anthropological research to immediate short-term aims rather than to development of the discipline, and in consigning those who have fundamental theoretical aims in view to the Ivory Tower. In the first place, future generations of scholars might have cause to see research geared to short-term aims as irrelevant, just as applied anthropology that existed in the colonial situation is now thought to be irrelevant. Anthropological research has usually been esoteric, but esoteric subjects can be of fundamental importance to the comprehensibility of history and society and this to my mind has been one of the most valuable distinctive contributions of anthropology to the social sciences generally. Do we for instance consign Gough's work on the Nayar and matrilineal kinship to the scrap-heap on the grounds of 'irrelevance'? Some of these issues are raised in the discussion to the symposium. Klejn, a Soviet contributor, is critical of this approach:

> I agree completely with Gjessing when he holds that social anthropologists should approach the problems of the 'rising nations of the non-Western world' with a view to satisfying the requirements and interests of these nations themselves. I am worried, however, about the implication that we should reduce the aims of social anthropology to such narrowly pragmatic ones. Does this turn out to be the same as Malinowski's functionalism, but inside out—the same pragmatism, merely diverted from the British colonial administration to the local national interests? Of course, it would be much better to have the 'ten anthropologists' continue the job of the 'ten troops'; but I think that to limit thus the aims of our science would benefit neither the science nor the rising nations. General theoretical research is important; we need to know the laws of social life, the lessons of social history[15].

Lewis in the discussion is also heavily critical of the authors' comments on relevance[16]:

[15]L. S. Klejn, *Comment* to Current Anthropology Social Responsibilities Symposium, loc. cit., pp. 415-417.
[16]I. M. Lewis, *Comment* to Current Anthropology Social Responsibilities Symposium, loc. cit., pp. 415-417.

I disagree with Gjessing's diagnosis that social anthropology is 'today in grave danger of becoming irrelevant'. This, indeed, is the exact opposite of what Kathleen Gough's gloomy assessment of the strategic importance ascribed to anthropological research in the United States would suggest...Social anthropology has never been *merely* an aid to enlightened colonial administration, nor should it be viewed now as *merely* an aid to development in new states. When anthropology ceases to have anything of wider interest to say, it deserves to die. Lewis here points to the crucial danger of over-emphasis on relevance. If it leads to nothing more than the reiteration of certain views of society which anyone can hold whether he knows any anthropology or not, there is no point in having any anthropology at all. The issue of fundamental importance is surely the development of the discipline to further the comprehensibility of history and society. In the past, it has frequently been conservatives who have insisted on immediate relevance and immediate practical applicability of the findings of scientists, while those of more radical opinions have defended the value of fundamental academic definition of problems. In the current discussion of relevance, one often finds these positions reversed.

The concept of relevance leads directly to the concept of commitment, or partisanship. As with relevance, so with commitment, the question 'commitment to what?' immediately springs to mind. Are all social commitments acceptable, and if not, why not? In the case of Berreman and Gjessing's suggestions, notions of commitment are expressed which could include any kind of social commitment. In the discussion, Gulick quite reasonably remarks that[17]:

Consider those anthropologists, mentioned by Berreman, who are working professionally for the United States government for the primary purpose of facilitating the militaristic policies of the United States in South-East Asia. They could quite logically claim that they are being professionally responsible to society.

There is an underlying assumption throughout discussion of commitment that political commitment can only be to left-wing ideology. This is surely absurd to anyone who has the slightest degree of political awareness and one could consign the perpetrators of such a myth quite rightly to the Ivory Tower. The papers here considered show quite enough disunity of commitment to the Left, let alone anywhere else, to suggest anything other than that each an-

[17] J. Gulick, *Comment* to Current Anthropology Social Responsibilities Symposium, loc. cit., p. 414.

thropologist can and will choose his own barricades. The real issue is the extent to which anthropologists have the right *qua* anthropologists to make collective commitments. Appeals to truth, humanism, and similar generalised beliefs exclude some commitment but accept most; the arguments for a more precise collective political commitment on the part of the anthropological community generally are not adequately presented in the *Current Anthropology* symposium. Nor does it help the advancement of the discipline to make declarations such as Haber and Haber's "We are not intellectuals above it all who say the truth to whomever will listen or asks: we are *partisans*"[18]. It is surely any academic's right to engage in partisanship, but it is surely also any academic institution's right to insist that its members engage in academic work. The call to subject all academic work to partisanship helps least of all those who sincerely wish to be both scholars and partisans. Further problems arise with partisanship when anthropological investigation in the field is considered. If partisanship is carried on *in the field*, the accessibility of fields of investigation for future scholars is placed in jeopardy, and anthropology is in danger of being associated in the minds of informants with a particular political and social commitment. The well-known association of anthropology with colonial administration is a good case in point; Jaspan, speaking of Hurgronje's research in Sumatra, which was openly associated with colonial ideology, warns that:

> The consequences of partisan commitment almost seventy years ago and at the opposite end of a large island are still to be felt, and have a negative effect, on rapport formation by present day ethnographers. This should, if nothing else, suggest to those who tolerate or justify commitment its unpredicatable consequences for other ethnographers and for the profession as a whole[19].

At the same meeting at which the Vietnam resolution was passed, the AAA expressed criticism of one form of ulterior commitment:

> There...is good reason to believe that some anthropologists have used their professional standing and the names of their academic institutions as cloaks for the collection of intelligence information and for intelligence operations[20].

[18]Quoted in A. G. Frank, op. cit., p. 413.
[19]M. A. Jaspan, "Anthropology and Commitment to Political Causes", *Anthropological Forum*, Vol. 1 (1964), pp. 212-219.
[20]"Statement on Problems of Anthropological Research and Ethics by Fellows of the American Anthropological Association", American Anthropologist, Vol. 69 (1967), p. 382.

The implications of this criticism must be borne in mind for other forms of ulterior motive in the field. Quite apart from moral objections, ulterior use of the anthropologist's position to support colonialism or the CIA is dangerous for the development of the discipline. Still, the anthropologist committed to left-wing ideology must also consider the implications of politically laudable ulterior motives for the development of the discipline as well.

I shall turn now to examine the New Left contribution to theoretical development of anthropology. One can state at the outset that the contributions to this subject at any rate have the ultimate welfare of the discipline in mind and are more worthy of being considered seriously by the profession as a whole. The argument common to them all is that anthropology has suffered *theoretically* from its association with colonialism. Theoretical critiques are presented by Goddard and Banaji, and to a lesser extent by Anderson and Leclerc. Anderson, Goddard and Banaji form a consistent series of critiques and a number of themes reappear in them all. The characteristic feature is the emphasis on the way in which British society gave rise to a distinctively empirical Weltanschauung, eliminating metaphysical elements, at the same time failing to articulate a conception of society as a totality. This criticism is voiced notably in Anderson in relation to British intellectual life as a whole. He stresses the lack of distinctive British sociology and the lack of acceptance of Marxism in Britain. Anthropology, he suggests, is a partial exception, and has been distinguished as a disciplinary tradition from sociology (in a way in which Durkheim, for instance, was not interested). A holistic view, and a functionalist framework, were adopted in the study of colonised peoples. This was also a consensus model, in which even conflict could be seen as producing ultimate cohesion (Gluckman). By excluding the colonial administration from their field of investigation (a good instance being Evans-Pritchard on the Nuer), and by so doing concentrating on fairly safe subjects, British social anthropology during the colonial period suffered *theoretically*. Only after the second World War, and the crisis in the imperial system, was any theoretical advance made, notably by Leach in *Political Systems of Highland Burma*. Leach also stands outside the general empiricism of British academic life in his recognition of Lévi-Strauss and his use of structural analysis of myth. This development is characteristic of the distinctive place of anthropology in the national culture:

> Both traditional functionalism and the structuralism of Leach's later work are anomalies for English empiricism. Anthropology

formed a deviant sector within English culture, because its
application was outside it. The exception here is a corollary of
the rule[21].

This dogma of the New Left Review, the empiricism of British culture, is a feature pervading the general theoretical critique of social
anthropology by both Goddard and Banaji. The focus of the critique is different, but Goddard and Banaji both find British anthropology just as culpable in its over-empiricism as are other aspects of
British intellectual life. British social anthropology is, if anything,
characteristic of British empiricism rather than deviant from it.
Goddard centres his critique on the notion of structure that British
social anthropology has worked with, which is deficient, he argues,
in being identified with the totality of empirically given social relationships in a tribal society. This highly empirical concept was easily
integrated into functionalism by Radcliffe-Brown; no investigation
was made of hidden relations, principles, or forms, or even of the
possibility of constructing models or theories to explain observed
phenomena. As part of the structural-functional framework, a
general normative emphasis and particularly, a jural focus prevailed. The jural focus was derived from Maine, and notably from
Durkheim's *Division of Labour in Society*. It permeated the study
of all custom supported by binding sanctions, and notably, the study
of kinship. This approach, Goddard argues, has severe theoretical
limitations. There is an emphasis on normative facts, but there is
no recognition that normative facts may be shaped by covert, non-
normative "facts", accessible only to critical analysis. Method and
theory completely converge. Durkheim was the main theoretical
inspiration for social anthropology in Britain, but his framework
was highly selectively adopted:

> Durkheim's rationalist, Cartesian mode of analysis of social phen-
> omena, by reducing them to their constituent elements, was
> interpreted uneasily as a 'sociological positivism' and thus
> made to correspond as nearly as possible to the methodological
> conditions of traditional empiricism. The 'metaphysical'
> elements on Durkheim—society as a phenomenon *sui generis*,
> the apparently outrageous analysis of religion—were quietly
> suppressed or conveniently forgotten[22].

Thus British empiricism expressed itself again in British social
anthropology, and the issues central to Durkheim's preoccupations

[21]Anderson, op. cit., p. 268.
[22]Goddard, op. cit., p. 89.

were dismissed or misunderstood. Such is Goddard's explanation for the pervasiveness of empiricism and functionalism in British social anthropology. The dogma of the essentially empiricist character of British thought is again reasserted, in a yet stronger form, by Banaji who concentrates his attention on post-war anthropology, whose roots he traces in the global revolution against colonialism and in the growth of structural anthropology, the second reflecting the first. Some of Goddard's criticisms are reiterated, but the focus of Banaji's critique is primarily on the diachronic variant of functionalism, seen particularly in the work of Leach and Needham, and on the response in British social anthropology to the work of Lévi-Strauss. The argument is not always easy to decode, as the pages of Banaji's article are bespattered with trendy structuralist jargon, but the main strands can be seen as a continued critique of over-empiricism and functionalism, which have continued to be characteristic of post-war British social anthropology. Functionalism was in fact a non-theory, a theory which arose out of the practice of fieldwork, but the practice of fieldwork sometimes found functionalism wanting, Leach's work in Burma being a notable case in point. There was an anti-functionalist response *within* functionalism, from Leach, foreshadowed by Gluckman's response to Malinowski, which still appealed to the idea of a self-stabilising system. This stood in sharp contrast to Lévi-Strauss's opposition to functionalism, which concerned itself with the unconscious nature of collective phenomena and in this way broke sharply from empiricism. There has been a response in Britain to Lévi-Strauss which can be seen as the "naturalisation" of structuralism in accordance with British empiricism. Here we see an argument which corresponds closely to Goddard's assessment of the British reaction to Durkheim. Leach, the main British expositor of Lévi-Strauss, none the less took an over-empiricist model in both *Pul Eliya* and in *Political Systems of Highland Burma.* He distinguished between actors' conscious models and the empirical field so as to conform to the functionalist distinction between rules and behaviour, but it never occurred to him that the anthropologist might perceive a different reality transcending both of these. Needham, for his part, regretted the over-empiricism and lack of theory in British anthropology, but himself applied structuralism only to systems of prescriptive alliance. *Mythologiques* was neglected, and *Les Structures Elémentaires de la Parenté* was misunderstood either as a model or in its entirety. Structuralism, however, Banaji admits, has an ambiguous relation to history, and part of its limited impact on British anthropology

is due to its own limitations. Its focus of attention is quite different
from that of functionalism:

> Structuralism's break with functional anthropology consisted in
> a sharp and deliberate displacement of the entire axis of
> comprehension from the phenomenal space of an immediate
> intuitive encounter with the savage to the noumenal space of
> *pensée sauvage,* established like any code, by the rigorous non-
> intuitive procedures of science[23].

Thus while providing a break from functionalism, structuralism was
uneven and distorted in its impact on British anthropology. British
empiricists have done the same to Lévi-Strauss as they have done in
the past to Durkheim.

Thus the critique of British social anthropology in the New Left
Review can be seen as part of a general critique of empiricist phil-
sophy which is seen as a characteristically British phenomenon. It
remains therefore to consider Leclerc, a French critic of British
social anthropology, who again stresses a critical, Marxist perspective. His approach centres on the relation betwen anthropology and
colonialism, present but peripheral to the British New Left, but the
key problem to Leclerc. Two issues stand out: first, and most important, the relationship betwen functionalism and colonialism;
second, a critical view of the "objectification' characteristics of
British social anthropology (to which structuralism, however, is not
regarded as the automatic answer). Leclerc suggests that functionalist anthropology had no conception of colonialism as a sytem,
and points to the ambiguous use of 'primitive' in anthropological
work. In contrast to the Victorian evolutionists, who *did* have a
conception of colonialism (justifying it), classic functional anthropologists saw colonialism in a neutral manner, as a specific form of
social change. There were schools of applied anthropology, but the
proponents of these supported Indirect Rule and hardly saw the
colonial *system* as a political and historical problem. No total
critique of colonial reality was provided, and functionalism was
unable to provide one. American cultural anthropology was more
anti-colonialist in its interests, and in the 1930-1950 period American anthropologists have been to some degree spokesmen for the
indigenous inhabitants of colonised societies. Ideas of cultural relativism could compete with colonial ideology.

On the question of objectification, Leclerc considers particularly
the reaction of the Third World to classical anthropology. The

---

[23]Banaji, op. cit., p. 82.

sovereign detachment characteristic of classical anthropology has not been characteristic of the African response, where objectification has been criticised. Ethnocentrism has been much more difficult to eradicate than the post-Victorian anthropologists thought. The concepts of acculturation and modernisation have also been criticised for not having given sufficient weight to exploitation and domination. Leclerc does not present any definite new proposals for anthropologists; he recognises the ambiguity of the concept of development, and the fact that some Marxists have supported colonialism. In his theoretical conclusions, however, he does give approval to the kind of anthropological work that is not 'objectifying'. He gives approval to the work of Griaule, Oscar Lewis and Jan Myrdal, but still stresses the importance of scientific investigation. Thus objectification is not to be rejected by the rejection of objectivity; the difficulty of translation of cultures is recognised as problematic, though Leclerc himself does not propose an alternative solution.

Despite the diversity of conclusions in the work here reviewed, a basic unity of concern of the writers here considered can be seen to be the general relationship between anthropology and colonialism. As one can expect, this is likely to be a concern of the intellectual Left and it remains to assess the attention that the discipline as a whole might pay to this critique. The whole concept of development is too ambiguous, from diverse standpoints, to enable one to say retrospectively what anthropologists should have done about the colonial situation. As far as the issues of relevance and commitment are concerned, it can only be stated that the advocates of such stances are putting forward a heavily *empiricist* view of social anthropology. If anthropology is to be geared directly to practical politics, the empirical conclusions are of major importance; structuralism as well as classical anthropology would be ruled out by such an emphasis on relevance and commitment. The British New Left critique, in sharp contrast, takes empiricism as one of its main targets of attack, and Banaji, at any rate, is favourable to structuralism. But although left-wing political value-orientations have led to widely divergent views of anthropology, it remains true that there are important issues to be raised about the relationship between social anthropology and the colonial situation, and the effect that had on the content of discipline during the colonial period. It can be argued that the colonial situation did make for a tendency to concentrate on empirical studies, particularly in Britain where the system of Indirect Rule was adopted. It might also be argued

that the concern for the collection of unfamiliar ethnographic data
might have led some anthropologists to concentrate in their empirical studies on the *traditional* elements of the societies they investigated (though the discipline itself has produced some sharp criticism
of this kind of approach[24]). There is considerable justification for
the view that functionalism and empiricism are closely related,
functionalism (particularly in anthropology) emerging as a non-
theory, as Goddard and Banaji both suggest. The use of the functionalist framework produced a behaviourist, normative focus in
research reports, and by taking inadequate account of actor's definitions of the situation (which may not coincide) ignored the basic
conflicts and power-relationships in society. The latter perspective,
while by no means confined to Marxists, is the perspective that a
Marxist would adopt. The issue of lack of comparison, lack of
theory, and over-empiricism in social anthropology has been raised
before, and a realisation of some of the issues here outlined might
be helpful for those who would like to see a more theoretical anthropology. None the less, if one examines certain trends in so-
called radical sociology, one should be wary of an over-contempt
for the empirical. Bandyopadhyay, criticising some of these tendencies, points to one form which entertains:

> The belief that sociology is not only non-objective, but cannot
> even be empirical, since to treat the enquiry as an empirical
> one is to accept some version of the correspondence theory of
> truth and this would lead to one-dimensional analysis leaving
> out the role of alternative visions or 'utopias' in changing social
> relations. Sociology, if empirical, would be insufficiently
> dialectic![25]

This position, associated notably with the Frankfurt school of sociologists, excludes any kind of integration of theory and empirical
research: this latter problem being one that sociology has grappled
with from its beginnings, and is worthy of investigation in anthropology too. If a non-empirical social science is one extreme position,
then empiricism is the other extreme. It can be seen that an *empiricist* social science is likely to produce a functionalist perspective,

[24]See particularly J. C. Mitchell, "Theoretical Orientations in African Urban
Studies " in M. Banton (Ed.): *The Social Anthropology of Complex
Societies*, London, Tavistock Publications, 1966; A. L. Epstein, *Politics in
an Urban African Community*, Manchester U.P., 1958. M. Gluckman,
"Anthropological Problems arising from the African Industrial Revolution"
in A. Southall (Ed.): *Social Change in Modern Africa*, London, O.U.P.,
1961, pp. 67-83.
[25]Bandyopadhyay, op. cit., p. 6.

empiricism and functionalism frequently being components of the actor's conscious model of his own society. Obviously one can see from Talcott Parsons that not all functionalism is empiricist, but even here, as Mills[26] points out, one can see the easy coexistence in American sociology of Grand Theory and Abstracted Empiricism. Another aspect of functionalism is its a-or anti-historical approach and it is this particularly that made for some of the deficiencies in some anthropological work in the colonial situation: a different matter it should be stressed from sweeping assertions about 'anthropologists ignoring the colonial situation'. As Evans-Pritchard points out, social anthropology has an important part to play in making the history of colonised territories more than just a history of colonial rule in such territories.[27] Social anthropology, like social history and many branches of sociology has made a distinctive contribution to the study of society in its investigation of those affected by the decisions of powerful men: in contrast to history (as an Arts subject), economics, and political science, which have generally been far more concerned with the study of the powerful than with those affected by political decisions. Social anthropology has never regarded the colonised as "irrelevant" and only the colonialists as "relevant": but if their comments on the "irrelevance" of microscopic studies are to be believed, some would seem to prefer to concentrate on the study of colonial rule.

Fortunately there is a tendency in a number of monographs to criticise the leading assumptions of functionalism and to adopt a historical perspective. Leach in *Political Systems of Highland Burma* questions a number of leading functionalist assumptions, notably the equilibrium model, behaviourism, the assumption of homogeneity, and the non-historical approach. Asad[28] in *The Kababish Arabs* is also critical of the equilibrium model and the behaviourist approach, and regards consensus as problematic rather than as given. It is true that studies of this kind are the product of empirical field-work, but this does not invalidate them, and they are clearly integrated into the mainstream of social science. There is no reason, as Banaji seems to suggest, to adopt a structuralist paradigm merely because it is called social anthropology. The fact

[26]Mills, C. Wright, *The Sociological Imagination*, New York, Oxford University Press, 1959.
[27]Evans-Pritchard, E. E. "Anthropology and History" in *Essays in Social Anthropology*, London, Faber and Faber, 1962, p. 64.
[28]T. Asad, *The Kababish Arabs: Power, Authority and Consent in a Nomadic Tribe*, London, Hurst, 1970.

that British scholars have directed their attention to the empirical world and thus produced the most sophisticated corpus of social anthropology does not invalidate their findings. If Durkheim and Lévi-Strauss have been 'naturalised', there is no reason to suppose that this is for the disadvantage of the discipline in its attempt to make sense of aspects of the empirical world.

# THE ANTHROPOLOGIST AS RELUCTANT IMPERIALIST
## Wendy James

Current criticisms of the social anthropology of the colonial period acknowledge that more than a handful of individual anthropologists were of liberal or even radical political outlook. But they usually maintain that this fact is not relevant for analysis of the development of the subject or its place in the colonial situation. The context is represented as fostering an essentially conservative subject, shaped within the same political ideology as colonial domination itself and bolstering its interests to such an extent that the perceptions and problems of even the liberal-radical practitioner were falsely formulated. At best, it might be admitted, in the words for example of Kathleen Gough, that

> Anthropologists in those days seem to have played roles characteristic of white liberals, sometimes of white liberal reformers,
> in other spheres of our society...living closely with native
> peoples, they tended to take their part to try to protect them
> against the worst forms of imperialistic exploitation...

Applied anthropology came into being as a kind of social work and community development effort for non-white peoples.[1]

Not much attention has been paid to the implications of this admission. The dissent indicated among anthropologists is not usually considered important enough to qualify Gough's picture of the subject as the "child of Western imperialism".

But it can be argued that the appearance of a radical element

---

[1] K. Gough, "New Proposals for Anthropologists", *Current Anthropology*, Vol. 9, 1968, 403-7, at p. 403.

among anthropologists is neither unimportant nor irrelevant; on the
contrary that it has been significant for the development of certain
aspects of the subject; and further, that the very existence of social
anthropology in the colonial period constituted a source of potential
radical criticism of the colonial order itself. The occurrence of liberal views within the subject was therefore not an accident; it was entailed by the nature of anthropological research, which by definition
reaches out geographically, linguistically and philosophically beyond
the bounds of received western civilisation in search of alternative
modes of understanding and living. Of course a good deal of trite
and mediocre work has been produced in practice, and the promise
of the anthropological perspective has rarely been fulfilled. But the
critical questioning of the basis of social life implicit in anthropology
has remained at the heart of the subject, and its growth within western culture during the colonial period necessarily constituted a
source of informed critical comment, since it was ideally based upon
experience of life on the reverse side of the colonial coin inaccessible
to most other members of the dominant society. The subject was
not spurned by the earlier generation of nationalist politicians; and
though the structures of Empire have now collapsed and cleared the
way for a more profound critical appraisal, a historical perspective
reminds us of some of the contradictory aspects of the place of
social anthropology in the colonial situation, the arguments it provoked and the resistance it encountered from the very body of official opinion and authority with which it is now sometimes assumed
to have lived in a cosy conspiracy; or at least a web of unspoken
understandings. As an individual, the anthropologist can often appear as a critic of colonial policy, of the philosophy of western
superiority upon which it was based and in terms of which it was
justified; and he was usually at odds with the various administrators,
missionaries, and other local Europeans he had dealings with. He
cannot often be seen unambiguously as a willing agent of colonialism. But he was nevertheless dependent upon colonial authorities for
permission to carry out his studies, and sometimes for material support; and in the inter-war period at least, open political dissent was
scarcely possible within colonial society. An anthropologist who
turned out to be anything more than a mild social embarrassment
could scarcely have been tolerated; and thus, for anthropology to
continue at all, appearances of co-operation had to be kept up.

   The place of anthropology in the colonial situation was in fact
doubly ambivalent. On the one hand, as I have suggested, there was
an ambivalence in relation to official authority, for although anthro-

pology was supposed worthy of support, its personnel and their activities were questionable; and on the other hand, in relation to the
growing nationalist and revolutionary movements, anthropology,
though initially regarded with sympathy, came to appear increasingly conservative. This double ambivalence, in my opinion, explains why social anthropology has been the object of more suspicion, accusation and blame from both sides of the developing
colonial situation than the low number of its practitioners and their
relatively small output would appear to justify. It would also appear
to have had important effects on the growth of the subject, and its
changing emphases. During the period of the twenties and thirties,
there was undoubtedly tension between officialdom and the expanding subject of anthropology, making it natural for there to be a
strong sympathy between the subject and the early development of
nationalism; but later, particularly after the Second World War, the
perspective of nationalist and revolutionary ideologies made anthropology merely a conservative ally of colonial control, itself increasingly liberal and progressive.

This essay draws attention in particular to the inter-war period.
The first part discusses social anthropology as the *problem child* of
the colonial encounter in Africa, the ways in which it constituted a
body of radical criticism and how this was necessarily tempered.
The second part considers the case of Malinowski's arguments from
1929 onwards for the involvement of anthropology in the "changing" African scene, some effects of these arguments on the development of the subject, and some responses to them from representatives of both colonial officialdom and the new African nationalism.

## I

What can "radical criticism" mean in the context of colonial anthropology? Examples of explicit criticism will be considered in the
second part of this essay, but firstly the implicitly critical character
of much anthropological writing should be noted. A large proportion of the anthropology of the inter-war period is clearly partisan;
in its choice of problems, and the very formulation of substantive
analysis, it is often defensive of the weaker societies and cultures;
of the sophistication of their language and thought, and of the
"rationality" of primitive economics, politics, witchcraft, religion
and so on. This defensive position extended on occasion to matters
of native land rights, and treatment of migrant labourers in the new
industrial areas and under the law. This intellectual and moral defence of the rights and dignity of peoples who had previously been

regarded, under the evolutionary racist theories of the nineteenth century armchair anthropologists, as scarcely human, was more than an academic reaction to earlier theories: it was at the same time a gut-reaction to the persistence of these ideas of cultural and racial superiority among the colonial rulers, local white settlers, and in popular opinion back at home. Although colonial anthropologists could rarely be described as radicals in an active political sense, which would have been almost impossible anyway, I believe that much of their work was given direction by radicalism of a moral kind.

For example, in the thirties the problem of witchcraft was discussed a good deal in colonial circles; on the whole it was accepted that natives possessed a different quality of mind, such that apparent irrationalities could scarcely be dealt with reasonably, but only through the application of laws against the practice or accusation of sorcery or witchcraft (see the special number of *Africa*, 1935[2]). The common assumptions of the practical men of the colonies, I would judge, were fairly close to those of armchair anthropologists of a previous generation, concerning the relative nature of thought and rationality in primitive society. Evans-Pritchard's argument in *Witchcraft, Oracles and Magic among the Azande* (1937) was designed at least in part as a criticism and a refutation of such theories; and on another level, it could be seen as an answer to the prejudices over native mentality commonly held by those with colonial experience, which must have been the despair of many fieldworkers. This aspect of Evans-Pritchard's work appears clearly in the following quotations from an early Zande article, *Sorcery and Native Opinion*. The article begins as follows:

> It is important to understand native opinion about black magic, not only for the anthropologist but also for the colonial administrator and missionary, if they wish to show to the peoples whom they govern and teach that they understand their notions about right and wrong. The native does not so much distrust European justice and education as he despairs of the administrator and missionary ever understanding, or attempting to understand, his point of view as expressed in laws and public opinion. This despair springs largely from the handling by Europeans of such matters as sorcery, with which both missionaries and administrators frequently have to deal. The native becomes convinced finally that the European is quite

²*Africa* VIII, No. 4, Oct., 1935.

incapable of seeing the difference between right and wrong,
between the proper use of a cultural weapon fully sanctioned
by public opinion, such as white magic, and a heinous and
cold blooded murder, such as the crime of black magic or
sorcery.[3]
After a careful and detailed exposition of this crucial moral distinction as seen by Azande, and its significance for social and political life, Evans-Pritchard concludes with suggestions as to how
administrators might benefit from understanding such questions.
How far we may wonder could such hints be of much practical use
to administrators? In any case, they scarcely mask the strong tone
of criticism with which the article comes to a close:

> In conclusion, we may address ourselves to those administrators
> and missionaries and doctors whose lives are spent amongst
> primitive peoples in Africa. If, as we think, a public opinion
> which classes some types of magic definitely as base and
> criminal, and others as virtuous and legal, whilst judging yet
> others with an uncertain voice, exists and functions not only
> amongst the Azande of the Nile-Uelle Divide but in many
> other savage communities, it behoves Europeans to be discreet
> in their dealing with it. Upon no other subject are Europeans
> in the tropics generally so ignorant and in no other sphere of
> native life is ignorance more likely to lead to infliction and
> destruction of good institutions. Such activities as those which
> we have described in this essay are, for reason which we have
> set forward, more conformable to preservation than breach of
> the peace, to conserve than subvert stable administration. We
> may well leave the natives to decide between good and evil,
> morality and immorality, right and wrong, crime and law.
> Moreover, the European may well be advised to remember that
> such acts of magic, the performance of which are public enough
> to be brought to the notice of his office and to be proved to
> have taken place, are little likely to be condemned by public
> opinion as illegal or immoral. Lastly, we may all do well to
> reflect that the mind sensitive to tales of sorcery reveals its own
> crudeness, for it has often been shown that when two civilizations
> come into contact the lesser is always accused of sorcery by
> half-studied and ill-formed judgements of the greater.[4]

This is not a position of ultra-relativism, of which colonial anthro-

[3] E. E. Evans-Pritchard, "Sorcery and native opinion", *Africa* IV, 1931,
22-55, at p. 22.
[4] *Ibid.*, pp. 54-55.

pology has (sometimes with justification) been accused. The moral rights of peoples living under colonial administration are defended in terms of universal categories; and the right of the ruling community to a monopoly of moral judgement is sharply questioned.

The practical men, however approving they were in the abstract of lending support to anthropological research, must often have been puzzled and disappointed at what the anthropologists actually produced. They must even on occasion have been resentful of rebukes such as those of Evans-Pritchard in the passages just quoted, where the anthropologist thumbs his nose at the sacred civilising mission. Without doubt a good deal of tension existed: and I consider that some of the characteristic methods and theories of this period were the outcome, not of conspiracy between scholars and officialdom, but on the contrary, of competition and intrigue between them. Impressive claims had to be made by anthropologists for their subject. Because their resources, duties and even rights were so uncertain, and because their work was so often regarded as quaint (in backward areas) or as unnecessary meddling (in central and significant areas), anthropologists were frequently obliged to defend their activities. This could hardly be done on metaphysical grounds, or in terms of a conviction of political or moral obligation; the lines of defence were rather of a kind more likely to appeal to colonial officialdom. This is partly why there was such an insistent claim by anthropology to be a proper *science;* for the idea of science carries great respectability. Science represented to the crude colonial mind a great achievement of the modern west, and the idea of its application to native peoples, as objects, was promising. (Interestingly enough, literature in anthropology of the kind which I have suggested is motivated by moral radicalism often emphasizes the *scientific* character of native thought). Thus it was good tactics for anthropologists to put forward the claim that their subject, at least the modern variety, was a dispassionate, scientific and important study of the variety of social forms, which deserved the respect and facilities granted to other sciences, like tropical medicine or geology, and like them had to be based on first-hand investigation. It was also prudent for them to add that, of course, it was a study which could yield valuable information for administrators and planners, who indeed would scarcely avoid serious mistakes without the benefit of its expert advice. This double claim gave anthropologists the advantage of being able to stress their practical value when approaching potential sponsors, and nevertheless to resist requests for direct assistance on the grounds that their subject was essentially an abstract science, from which practical men would have to draw their own conclusions. The separation of the objective scientist from the committed feeling man can thus be viewed as part of the strategy of colonial anthropologists in calming any suspicions of their personal motives which might damage their claims for official support and facilities. The following passage from Firth's conclusion to *We, the Tikopia* (1936) illustrates some of the relevant emphases of the time:

A last word may be said about one practical aspect of anthropological study. In revulsion from the mere folklorist attitude of antiquarian anthropology, science today is in danger of being caught up by practical interests and made to serve them, to the neglect of its own problems. Social anthropology should be concerned with understanding how human beings behave in social groups, not with trying to make them behave in any particular way by assisting an administrative policy of a proselytizing campaign to achieve its ends more easily. The scientist gives generalizations regarding the nature of the working of institutions; it is not his duty to affix ethical values to them, nor by conniving at such an ethical evaluation to pave the way for their modification. Missionary, government officer and mine manager are free to use anthropological methods and results in their own interests, but they have no right to demand as a service that anthropology should become their handmaid. Nor can the standards which they invoke—'civilization', 'justice', 'the sanctity of human life', 'Christianity', 'freedom of the individual', 'law and order'—be regarded as binding; the claim of absolute validity that is usually made for them too often springs from ignorance, from an emotional philanthropy, from the lack of any clear analysis of the implications of the course of action proposed, and from confusion with the universal of what is in reality a set of moral ideas produced by particular economic and social circumstances.

This is not to say that the scientist himself may not have his own personal predilections based on his upbringing and social environment, his temperamental disposition, his aesthetic values. He may regard the culture of a primitive, half-naked set of people in an island of the Solomons as a pleasant way of life, giving expression to the individuality of its members in ways alien to western civilization; he may regard it as something he would like to see endure, and he may strive to preserve it in the face of ignorance and prejudice, pointing out the probable results of interference with ancient customs. This he does as a man; his attitude is part of his personal equation to life, but it is not implicit in his scientific study. The greatest need of the social sciences today is for more refined methodology, as objective and dispassionate as possible, in which, while the assumptions due to the conditioning and personal interest of the investigator must influence his findings, that bias shall be consciously faced, the possibility of other initial assumptions be realised and allowance be made for the implications of each in the course of the analysis.[5]

But how successful were these pleas for acceptance and support on the basis of the claim of anthropology to be trustworthily objective and useful? Some doubt is thrown on the extent to which this argument carried much weight in a post-war article by Evans-Pritchard on applied anthropology. His argument is defensive of pure research, and very critical of the lack of interest on the official side:

Mr. Sol Tax remarks...that although he had spent some ten years in research into the social anthropology of the Chiapas and Guatemala Indians no one had ever asked his technical assistance in solving the social problems of the region. Other anthropologists have experienced the same thing. Professor Seligman once told me that in all the years he had worked in the Sudan or on Sudanese problems he was never asked once for his advice and that the only time he volunteered it in connection with the rain-makers of the Nuba Hills, it was not taken. During the fifteen years in which I worked on sociological problems in the same region I was never once asked my advice on any question at all.[6]

Evans-Pritchard ends with an appeal. The Colonial Office and Colonial Governments should understand that:

Much as we would like to help them, with our present limited resources research in social anthropology is only kept going and certainly does not keep pace with the deterioration of the primitive field, so that they cannot expect us to turn aside from our scientific research and teaching to investigate their practical problems and advise on their policies. If they want qualified men to assist them they must create posts in the colonies which will attract them...Colonial administrations do not expect to have the services of doctors, botanists, geologists and engineers without

[5] E. E. Evans-Pritchard, "Applied Anthropology", *Africa* XVI, 1946, 92-8, p. 97.
[6] R. Firth, *We the Tikopia*, 2nd ed. 1957, pp. 487-88.

giving them appointments on their establishments. Why should they expect the services of anthropologists on different terms?[7] The question remains as to why anthropology had not been accepted more wholeheartedly by the colonial authorities. Some indication of the answer is implied in that part of Evans-Pritchard's article where he discusses his Libyan work. He contrasts his pre-war position in the Sudan with his position in Cyrenaica in the early nineteen-forties, where he was a full member of the British Military Administration, as Tribal Affairs Officer, with access to official documents, and entitled to play a part in policy-making. The significant feature of this contrast between his status in the Sudan and Libya lies perhaps in the fact that the Italians had recently been ousted by the British when he was in Cyrenaica: and thus a critical anthropological study of native affairs would reflect on the Italians, rather than on his sponsoring authority. With such a conjunction of interests between his sponsors and himself, it was possible for Evans-Pritchard to write a book of unusually committed characters *The Sanusi of Cyrenaica* (1949) in its treatment of an anti-colonialist national movement and its clearly anti-Fascist sympathies, is in itself an answer to naïve radical criticisms of anthropology. In the older colonies, the anthropologist was rarely so trusted as to have access to archival materials and policy discussions which would be necessary for a historically significant study. One may well ask whether it would have been realistic to expect anthropologists to write books openly critical of any of the forms of colonial rule under which they worked.

The contradictory positions assumed simultaneously by the colonial anthropologist, that he is extremely useful to administration and at the same time that he must be free to pursue his specialist interests, arise out of the profound paradox of the subject in relation to its sponsoring authorities. Relatively peaceful and progressive colonial rule in the inter-war period was prepared to permit and even encourage field-working anthropologists to carry out personal investigations of a direct kind which had scarcely been possible previously, at least in the Old World. The "sociological" character of their work increased steadily, and with it a greater awareness of the relevance of the overall economic and political situation. The anthropologist of this period, more than the missionary, and more than the bush administrator, found himself speaking not only of, but for, the local populations he knew well. He tended more than others to

[7]*Ibid.*, p. 98.

know the common man, and to bypass the local chiefs and dignitaries. There was little possibility of a European traveller knowing the people intimately in the pre-colonial period: contacts in the nineteenth century for example, between the classic explorers and the local populations of Africa, were usually with kings and chiefs, or otherwise with servants and runaway slaves. The situation of a lone European living for months or years in an ordinary village without a retinue was only possible when benevolent colonial administration was well-established. And yet the situation of such study was often so demanding in personal as well as intellectual terms that a commitment to something stronger than data-gathering was surely required. The collection of facts from the grass-roots level of society in the industrial West has frequently grown out of, or resulted in, a radical orientation; and anthropological fieldwork in the Malinowskian tradition shared this character to some extent in relation to the colonial regimes. The colonial period thus paradoxically opened the way for the creation of a body of literature that itself reflected criticism upon the prevailing situation and the political philosophy which justified it. I see, therefore, the colonial anthropologist as a frustrated radical: and his claims to scientific status, the separation of his work from any apparent moral or political views, and the avowal of its practical usefulness, as largely determined by the need to make a convincing bid for the survival and expansion of his subject.

## II

All these sides of the dilemma are clear in Malinowski's efforts, from the late nineteen twenties to the end of his life, to extend the scope of scientific anthropology to embrace the study of social and cultural change in Africa. Indeed his dilemma is more complex; for whereas in the early thirties, he was arguing that scientific study was uninvolved and therefore of use to administration, his sympathies for developing African nationalism sharpen with time and in his later writings he comes to argue that scientific research must be politically committed. Malinowski's writings on Africa are not in themselves a major contribution to the subject; but he was a most influential teacher, and his interest in the expansion of social anthropology into the area of modern African problems led to a large number of studies in this field by his students. The significance of his views is therefore greater than his actual published writings might suggest, for it is implicit in the work of others, particularly in the direction of "social change" and so forth. However "practical"

and administratively useful these studies might claim to be, and
however conservative some later studies of this type turned out to
be, it was the radical sympathies of Malinowski and his undoubted
desire to shake up the placid colonial establishment which originally
pushed anthropology in this direction.

An article of Malinowski's in 1929 on "Practical anthropology"[8]
marked the beginning of a debate on the question of the usefulness
of anthropology, and a long series of defensive articles by anthropologists which continued until well after the war. Many were published in *Africa,* journal of the International African Institute (founded 1926). One of the Institute's main aims was "the closer association of scientific knowledge and research with practical affairs", and
a good deal of applied anthropology was encouraged and supported.
In spite of this supposed collusion of anthropology and practical
affairs, the tone of the debate which followed Malinowski's initial
provocative contribution suggested underlying frictions. Malinowski's own previous work had been on the "traditional" community
of the Trobriand Islands in Melanesia, but in his 1929 article he is
staking out a much wider claim for the subject and its relevance.
He challenges the practical men who dismiss the subject, and recommends it to their notice in terms they are likely to find acceptable.
He emphasises that it is politically unbiased, and therefore scientific;
and highly useful and up-to-date, since it is concerned with changing conditions. The modern "functional" type of anthropology is
contrasted in these terms with old-fashioned antiquarianism, of
whose usefulness the practical men were justifiably sceptical. I think
that by "functional" in this context Malinowski meant little more
than "sociological", as against the approach of what he had referred
to elsewhere as the "dusty museum-moth". He writes:

The Institute stands in the first place for the practical application
of scientific knowledge. It can reach on the one hand various
Colonial interests in their practical activities, while at the same
time has at its disposal the knowledge of theoretically trained
specialists.

I think that in the very combination of practical and theoretical
interests lies the proper task of the Institute. There is a gap
between the theoretical concerns of the anthropology of the
schools on the one hand, and practical interests on the other.

The gap must be bridged over, and in doing this the Institute
can make itself very useful.

[8] B. Malinowski, "Practical Anthropology", *Africa* II, 1929, 22-38.

The practical man is inclined to pooh-pooh, ignore, and even to resent any sort of encroachment of the anthropologist upon his domain. On the other hand it is not always easy to advise the colonial administrator or missionary just where to find the anthropological information he requires. Now I think that the gap is artificial and of great prejudice to either side. The practical man should be asked to state his needs as regards knowledge on savage law, economics, customs, and institutions; he would then stimulate the scientific anthropologist to a most fruitful line of research and thus receive information without which he often gropes in the dark. The anthropologist, on the other hand, must move towards a direct study of indigenous institutions as they now exist and work. He must also become more concerned in the anthropology of the changing African, and in the anthropology of the contact of white and coloured, of European culture and primitive tribal life...

It is then the thesis of this memorandum that there exists an anthropological No-man's land; that in this are contained studies of primitive economics, primitive jurisprudence, questions of land tenure, of indigenous financial systems and taxation, a correct understanding of the principles of African indigenous education, as well as wider problems of population, hygiene and changing outlook. Scientific knowledge on all these problems is more and more needed by all practical men in the colonies. This knowledge could be supplied by men trained in anthropological methods and possessing the anthropological outlook, provided that they also acquire a direct interest in the practical applications of their work, and a keener sense of present-day realities.[9]

Under the heading "Scientific control of colonial administration" he continues:

By the constitution of the Institute all political issues are eliminated from its activities. This can easily be done by concentrating upon the study of the facts and processes which bear upon the practical problems and leaving to statesmen (and journalists) the final decision of how to apply the results.

There follows a general statement of support for the concept of indirect rule; but unless anyone should think that anthropologists are politically biased in any way instead of being objective scientists, he adds:

[9]*Ibid.*, pp. 22-23.

But whether we adopt in our practical policy the principle of direct or indirect control, it is clear that a full knowledge of indigenous culture in the subjects indicated is indispensable. He then defends the usefulness of functional anthropology (as against the earlier antiquarianism) for such questions as political organisation, law, language, land tenure, economics, and the changing native. His article ends with a plea for assistance from the IAI for promoting work in the "modern Functional School of Anthropology".

The following year, 1930, two replies appeared in *Africa*. The first by Major Ruxton, formerly Lt. Governor of Southern Provinces, Nigeria, was sympathetic to Malinowski's claims, indeed strengthening them for applied anthropology:

As there is a distinction between the pure and the applied chemist, so there should be one between the pure and applied anthropologist. The latter cannot exist without the former, but it is the latter who is required to advise on the practical work of administration, and the Institute can do much to evolve him. As the field of work of the pure anthropologist is that of yesterday, so that of the applied anthropologist should be today, preferably tomorrow.[10]

But the second reply from P. E. Mitchell then provincial commissioner in Tanganyika, and later Governor of Kenya etc., was extremely sceptical of the usefulness of anthropology, unless the subject could enable the "practical men" of the colonies to carry out their jobs better:

Professor Malinowski...writes...as an anthropologist, and he proposes that the anthropologist shall record the facts and the 'practical' man draw his deductions therefrom. How many anthropologists would agree that a division into anthropologists and practical men is satisfactory is open to doubt: but as I am certainly not an anthropologist I hope that I may speak for the practical man.

As Malinowski points out, anthropologists have largely occupied themselves with the past, or at least with the passing; and they have developed a technique of their own in recording and discussing in particular the curious or quaint in primitive societies. Thus if an inhabitant of a South Sea Island feels obliged on some ceremonial occasion to eat his grandmother,

[10]F. H. Ruxton, "An anthropological no-man's land", *Africa* III, 1930, 1-12, at p. 2.

the anthropologist is attracted to examine and explain the
ancient custom which caused him to do so: the practical man,
on the other hand, tends to take more interest in the grandmother...

Practical men are concerned first with making secure life and
property and with the complex administrative arrangements
which modern economic life demands and they are of all men
least likely to underrate the importance of accurate knowledge.
They certainly endorse the view that any organisation, for
example the Institute, which assists them to that knowledge,
must be of value in proportion to the efficiency of the service
that it renders, and invaluable if it reaches that point of efficiency
where the correctness of its statements of fact can be taken
for granted and be made generally known. But that is the
difficulty.[11]

He goes on to criticise the length of time taken by anthropologists
and missionaries for their work to be completed—it is often out of
date when it appears and has little bearing on the future; and the
minute detail of anthropological observations, which makes the
study of large areas out of the question. He compares the anthropological specialist to the laboratory scientist, and asks where is the
general practitioner, who can tackle important and urgent problems
when needed.

As Malinowski implies, the anthropologist has in the past been
mainly interested in the ancient and the curious: he has
studiously pursued knowledge of primitive mankind, and has
occupied himself little, if at all, with the present and future.
His method has been built up to serve his purpose; his
technique is that of the laboratory and what he has been disposed to call his field-work has been the field-work of a
collector for a museum. But now he is waking up to the splendid
prospects of service to mankind which the science to which he
has devoted himself holds out, and is casting round for the
means of applying to practical things the knowledge which he
possesses, or feels confident that he can acquire; and he stands
a little dismayed before a world which hurries past him and
seems to care little for the help which he can give.

Now it seems to me that the main difficulty lies in this, that the
anthropologist is disposed to look out at the busy world from
his laboratory window; and when he offers help, it is in terms

of laboratory methods. He must learn to come down into the street and join in the life which he desires to influence if he is to play the part which he wishes to play, and which I am confident he can play with great profit especially to all those who are struggling with the complex problems of twentieth-century colonisation in East Africa.[12]

He suggests there is a need for the trained "general practitioner" as well as the laboratory specialist; such men do exist, but not in an organised body, or with organised training. In this category of "general practitioner" Mitchell includes all the practical men of the colonies: and not merely administrators and missionaries, but traders and commercial men—in fact one presumes he means the whole of the expatriate community, perhaps even the European housewife. Mitchell certainly makes it clear what sort of use he reckons ought to be made of social anthropology in the interests of colonialism—but how many anthropologists of that time, let alone now, would agree with him? In explaining what he means by a general practitioner of social problems, he writes:

> For example, the planter who is engaged in working out a practi-
> cal and just relation between white employer and native
> labourer is, in this sense, a general practitioner. By organising
> these men, by helping them to realise the community of
> interests which they have, but infrequently understand, by
> mobilising them in fact, the Institute can perform a function of
> the highest value...by harnessing in the service of our common
> humanity those who are intimately concerned, because they
> are a part of it, in the life of the countries in which they live.
> This is to my mind the direction in which effort should be made
> rather than the projection of the laboratory worker into the
> field, into the turmoil of everyday life, into an atmosphere of
> which he has had no experience and which he cannot be
> expected to understand.

Social anthropology is dismissed as purposeless unless made to serve the interests of practical colonialism:

> In the relation of man with man and race with race; in those com-
> plexities which we call 'the State' or 'Government'; in the
> many-sided economic life of our modern world; in all that goes
> to make up the great problems of our time; in all this the
> acquisition of knowledge is a well-developed science, but in its
> pursuit we have rather overlooked the means of applying our

[12]*Ibid.*, p. 220.

knowledge when we have acquired it. As I see it, its acquisition and application should be complementary branches of the same activity. Obviously the latter is impossible without the former: but the former if not followed by the latter is purposeless.

> If anyone has had the patience to read this far, he will I hope have reached the same conclusions as the writer, that the true practical anthropology is that which devotes itself to enlisting and organising, as the complement of the scientific worker, those practical men, and there are many, who are ready to serve the community in which they live; at times we shall have urgent need of this specialist, but we must not, for that reason, forget the family doctor.[13]

It is clear from Mitchell's article what kind of anthropology the colonial establishment would like to have seen—a real tool of imperialism. But anthropologists were not on the whole prepared to play this part. Later in the same year (1930) Malinowski published a reply to Mitchell in the same journal. In this he defends anthropology from the suggested close co-operation with practical men; he argues its essential requirement of independence as an objective science; and to my mind at least, this claim stems from a refusal to side unambiguously with the colonial attitude. He starts by bemoaning the mechanisation and over-rapid "progress" of the modern world, which is due to science. He admits that traditional anthropology represented an escape from this, but grants that it has to change, and become of use to the science of progress. He regrets this, however, and writes:

> And now, after twenty years of anthropological work, I find myself, to my disgust, attempting to make the science of man into as bad and dehumanising an agency to man as physics, chemistry, and biology have been for the last century or so denaturalising to nature. In short, I am attempting to make anthropology into a real science, and science inevitably has to introduce uniformity and rationalisation into the phenomena with which it deals.[14]

So that is Malinowski's opinion of the kind of anthropology that the colonial establishment would like to see. But he goes on to explain that of course anthropology will change: and that the new functional method will be both scientific and of use to the practical man. He complains that Mitchell's criticisms are out of date, that they

[13]*Ibid.*, p. 223.
[14]B. Malinowski, "The rationalization of anthropology and administration", *Africa* III, 1930, 405-29, at p. 406.

may apply to antiquarian anthropology but not to the modern functional school; and that Mitchell has attacked anthropology on imaginary grounds—for example the reference to eating grandmothers in the South Seas, which Mitchell says should be called murder and dealt with accordingly. Malinowski suggests that even such judgements are not always unambiguous, and that right and justice may not all be on one side:

Fortunately or unfortunately, the custom, born in the imagination of Mr. Mitchell, does not really exist, so the functional anthropologist need not concern himself very much about it. But the practical man, who very often on equally imaginary grounds cries 'Murder' and hangs a native, might thereby provoke some other natives to retaliate and then we should have a punitive expedition in which the 'practical man' himself would act as the murderer. Mr. Mitchell's example is imaginary, but unfortunately I could quote numerous cases from the South Seas in which the practical man, having 'regretfully' and unintelligently violated native customs by the mere right of his ignorance and moral zeal, has brought whole native tribes to grief. Let Mr. Mitchell read the report of the Goaribari massacres in New Guinea; the history of 'black-birding' in the South Seas; or even the data referring to the repatriation of the blackbirded Kanakas to the Melanesian homes; for that matter, the antecedents of any of the numerous punitive expeditions in the South Seas. Africa is not my special field, but I have a vague idea that 'punitive expeditions', wholesale massacres of natives by whites, strange retaliations in the names of 'justice', 'prestige', and 'the white man's honour' did also occur in the Dark Continent, and that it is not only the coloured African there who deserves the title of 'murderer', nor is it the white European who should use such terms of abuse as marks of his own racial superiority.[15]

The mounting intensity of Malinowski's criticism finds more specific expression in relation to the problems of land tenure, which Mitchell suggested could not be dealt with realistically because of the length of time a full anthropological survey would take. Malinowski reminds Mitchell of the method of science:

Precision, thoroughness and accuracy do not consist in a blind and pedantic accumulation of useless evidence, but in a critical selection of the relevant by crucial tests. It is this spirit of

[15]*Ibid.*, p. 411.

relevancy as against mere accumulation, of critical selection as against groping in the dark, that the scientific anthropologist might bring to the assistance of the man who has a practical interest in the control of human affairs.

My critic confidently affirms that 'the only method which can be called practicable is that of question and answer and daily observation of the lives of the people'. Has this method, unaided by any guiding theoretical principles, given such brilliant results? In the matter of land tenure, for instance, do we know this subject in a satisfactory manner in any part of Africa? Why is it that such serious blunders in the framing of policy have been made as the individualising of land tenure in Uganda, which avowedly led to the greatest difficulties; or the haphazard methods of dealing with this question in West Africa, which brought into being committees and commissions, the results of which could not even be published? Was the question of land tenure studied in South Africa and a wise policy laid down by the practical men who were settling and organising that country? Let Mr. Mitchell look for the answer in the *Report of the Natives' Land Commission, 1916.*

And again, why is it that the fundamental principles of British land policy in Africa have not been laid down in any consistent manner? The decisions of the Judicial Committee of the Privy Council regarding the native rights to land are contradictory. In Southern Rhodesia it was held that natives had really no rights to their land whatever. On the other hand, in Nigeria the Privy Council ruled that the rights in land were vested in the natives. What is more important for the present argument, however, is that the judgement was based on an admission of ignorance, since it was held that 'it was really a matter of conjecture to say what the rights of the original "natives" were'. Their Lordships' decision further stated that:

'The estimation of the rights of aboriginal tribes is always inherently difficult. Some tribes are so low in the scale of social organisation that their usage and conceptions of rights and duties are not to be reconciled with the institutions or the legal ideas of civilised society. Such a gulf cannot be bridged. It would be idle to impute to such people some shadow of the rights known to our law, and then to transmute it into the substance of transferable rights of property as we know them'.

Hence the Judicial Committee plainly regard the question of native land tenure as both beyond the scope of practicable

inquiry and below the dignity of legal recognition. On the
contrary, I maintain that there is no people 'so low in the scale
of social organisation' but have a perfectly well-defined system
of land tenure. It is absurd to say that such a system 'cannot
be reconciled with the institutions or the legal ideas of civilised
society'. To reconcile the two is precisely the task of Colonial
statesmanship.[16]
Malinowski also heaps criticism upon Mitchell's conception of there
being a community of interests between all practical men in the colonies—including commercial men—which he invited the anthropologist to join and to advise; he takes this to be the "central miscon-
ception" of Mitchell's argument.

Why have these men not yet organised themselves nor achieved
any singularly constructive results? Let us look more closely at
the possibilities of team-work done by missionaries and settlers,
administrators and journalists, engineers and recruiters. And
here I should like to ask why does Mr. Mitchell not include
among them the native African, 'savage' and detribalised alike;
or the West Coast lawyer; or the black expert in yellow
journalism; and incidentally also the East Coast Indian? They
are also actors in the play; they also, no doubt, share in the
'community of interests'. Why does the idea of harmonious
co-operation between them appear hardly plausible? Because
we know that these groups, far from having any 'community'
of interests, are divided by profound, indeed irreconcilable,
differences. And why, again, is this the case? Because they have
deeply-rooted personal interests at stake, which cannot possibly
be brought into harmony with each other. And this is not because
of any lack of goodwill or of knowledge. The dissensions
involved far transcend any intellectual effort or emotional
adjustment; they cannot be bridged over by mere goodwill.

The whole life-work of, say, an economic exploiter on the one
hand and a missionary on the other, develops in either case
an entirely different type of bias in the individual. The one has
vested his capital, his life-interest, and his work in some venture,
which may fail or succeed according as to whether he can secure
an adequate supply of native labour. However much he may
sympathise with the natives, he is bound to have more sympathy
with his wife and children, with his dream of success and
constructive enterprise, with the belief, shared by industrialists

[16]*Ibid.*, pp. 414-5.

and financiers, that a maximum production of wealth is an
unqualified blessing for the world at large...

To speak of a 'community of interests' between the recruiter
and the missionary, or between the Indian trader and the white
settler, is a travesty of facts. Above all, I doubt whether the
idea of 'the planter who is engaged in working out a practical
and just relation between white employer and native labourer'
is not a sporadic phenomenon. On every question, whether it
be land tenure and native reservations or the political power
of tribal authorities, there must crop up deep-seated differences
of opinion, influenced, not merely by self-interest, greed, or
ruthless rapacity on the one side, and mawkish sentimentalism,
wrong-headed dogma, or false humanitarianism on the other;
but also by the fundamental assumptions as to what is good for
the native and for the white man, and what is the aim of African
development. And these assumptions are bound up with the very
existence of the several classes of African workers, classes
which, again, differ profoundly...[17]

As though feeling that he might have gone too far, for these passages are surely very strong words for 1930, Malinowski then soberly
insists on the responsibility of administrators for the decisions they
must take, although anthropologists can act in an advisory capacity.
He anxiously emphasises that there is overall agreement on this
question. But talk of economic exploiters, the land rights of natives
in Southern Rhodesia, criticism of the Buganda land tenure agreement and so on must be taken as serious evidence of political dissent from colonial policies within the camp of social anthropology.

Malinowski's position is further consolidated during the thirties.
He appears increasingly concerned with political realities, and less
with the need to put up a pleasing case to officialdom. Significantly,
the ideals of scientific integrity are evoked to justify the study of
vital and relevant problems of an economic, political and legal kind
in a review article of 1939. Malinowski is criticising the abstract
"culture trait" approach of Herskovits to problems of change, in
the latter's book *Acculturation* (1938), and recommends instead
British methods, as laid out in *Memorandum XV* of the IAI,
which take political realities into account.

The contact anthropologist has to study the methods of
recruitment and the wage system, the effects of the Colour Bar
legislation and of the anomalous contracts of African labour, as

[17]*Ibid.*, pp. 421-22.

well as of the Pass Laws. He must study these facts scientifically,
objectively, and in relation to each other. He need not in his
scientific work be concerned with any partisan or even practical
issues. But his study will reveal to him that for the present the
Europeans are in a position to dictate the legal and economic
terms. The conditions thus imposed are found to produce definite
effects. Thus, if he studies the budgets of a family dependent
on wages, he will find that the income does not really balance
with expenditure. Scientific field-work reveals that the wages
received by a mine labourer do not compensate the tribal
economy for the total loss caused by his absence. From this it
would be his duty to draw the conclusion that a system which
produces inevitable impoverishment in a native reserve must
lead through malnutrition, disorganization, and demoralization
to gradual demographic decay . . .
    Those of us who advocate "practical anthropology" insist
only on the study of vital, relevant, and fundamental problems.
That such problems affect practical interests directly is not our
fault. That a question does not become less scientific because it
is vital and relevant will only be denied by one who imagines
that academic pursuits begin where reality ends. Professor
Herskovits has never laid himself open to such criticism in his
field-work or in his treatment of actual questions. It is therefore
both regrettable and incomprehensible that he chooses to attack
practical anthropology as a matter of method.[18]
The increasingly political stand taken by Malinowski is an indication of his sympathy for the growing nationalist movements of
Africa. Jomo Kenyatta's presence at Malinowski's seminars in
London in the thirties, and Malinowski's own visits to Africa, where
he called on several of his own students engaged in field-work, must
have opened his eyes to the explosive situation in what had been
peaceful anthropological territory. In his Introduction to Kenyatta's
Facing Mount Kenya (1938) he touches on the dangers of totali-
tarianism; the current spread of political opinion in Africa; and the
question of whether the minority of agitators "will be able to keep
a balanced and moderate view of economic, social and political
issues, or whether by ignoring them and treating them with contempt we drive them into the open arms of world-wide Bolshevism".
He mentions various events which are "uniting the world of

[18]B. Malinowski, "The present state of studies in culture contact: some
comments on an American approach", Africa XII, 1939, pp. 27-47.

coloured peoples against Western influence and above all against Great Britain and the United States", and introduces Kenyatta's book on the Kikuyu people as a salutary eye-opener to the West:

Mr. Kenyatta has wisely refrained from using any such language as appears in my last sentences. He presents the facts objectively, and to a large extent without any passion or feeling. That some of this is contained in his presentation of facts is a help and not a hindrance. For if the present book does nothing more but to help us to understand how Africans see through our pretences, and how they assess the realities of the Dual Mandate, it will be rendering a great service . . .[19]

Whatever may be thought of Kenyatta's book today, it is beyond question that at that time he saw in social anthropology something that could be turned to use as part of the growing nationalist challenge to colonial rule; and his book was regarded both in nationalist and official colonial circles as a highly political document. In his Preface, Kenyatta thanks among others "the members of the Kikuyu Central Association, my comrades-in-arms of the past, present and future" (the Mau-Mau rising was still to come) and goes on:

In the present work I have tried my best to record facts as I know them, mainly through a lifetime of personal experience, and have kept under very considerable restraint the sense of political grievances which no progressive African can fail to experience. My chief object is not to enter into controversial discussion with those who have attempted, or are attempting, to describe the same things from outside observation, but to let the truth speak for itself. I know that there are many scientists and general readers who will be disinterestedly glad of the opportunity of hearing the Africans' point of view, and to all such I am glad to be of service. At the same time, I am well aware that I could not do justice to the subject without offending those 'professional friends of the African' who are prepared to maintain their friendship for eternity as a sacred duty, provided only that the African will continue to play the part of an ignorant savage so that they can monopolise the office of interpreting his mind and speaking for him. To such people, an African who writes a study of this kind is encroaching on their preserves. He is a rabbit turned poacher.

But the African is not blind. He can recognise these pretenders to philanthropy, and in various parts of the continent he is

[19]B. Malinowski, "Introduction" to J. Kenyatta, *Facing Mount Kenya*, 1938, pp. x-xi.

waking up to the realisation that a running river cannot be dammed for ever without breaking its bounds. His power of expression has been hampered, but it is breaking through, and will very soon sweep away the patronage and repression which surround him.[20]

In the body of the book the Kikuyu people are presented as a people who have suffered conquest, subjugation and loss of land; for example:

Since the coming of the Europeans the warrior organisation has been rendered powerless . . . the spirit of manhood in the youth has been almost killed by the imposition of imperialistic rule which restricts people from moving and functioning freely in their own country. The European prides himself on having done a great service to the Africans by stopping the 'tribal warfares' . . . But consider the difference between the method and motive employed in the so-called savage tribal warfares, and those employed in the modern warfare waged by the 'civilised' tribes of Europe, and in which the Africans who have no part in the quarrels are forced to fight . . . It would have been much better for the Africans to continue with their old tribal warfare, which they fought with pride and with the loss of a few warriors, rather than receiving the so-called civilising missions which means the subjugation of the African races to a perpetual state of serfdom.

In the old order of the African society, with all the evils that are supposed to be connected with it, a man was a man, and as such he had the rights of a man and liberty to exercise his will and thought in a direction which suited his purposes as well as those of his fellow-men; but today an African, no matter what his station in life, is like a horse which moves only in the direction that the rider pulls the rein. The harmony and stability of the African's mode of life, in political, social, religious and economic organisations, was based on the land which was, and still is, the soul of the people. The first step which the European civilising missions took to disorganise the Africans in order to exploit and oppress them, especially in South and East Africa, was to take away the best African lands . . .[21]

Other writers who had been trained to some extent by Malinowski were carrying out sociological investigations of a kind which re-

[20]J. Kenyatta, *Facing Mount Kenya*, 1938, pp. xvii-xviii.
[21]*Ibid.*, pp. 211-13.

vealed the hard facts of survival and subsistence in rural areas of
Africa drained of manpower by the developing mining and industrial towns. Audrey Richards' *Land, Labour and Diet in Northern
Rhodesia* (1939) is an outstanding example of this kind of work.
She also confronted the dilemma of why there was suspicion and
non-co-operation between anthropologists and officials, when the
work of anthropologists ought to be practically useful. She contributed to the debate in *Africa* in 1944,[22] with an article which surveys
the previous fifteen years in which there was supposedly a good deal
of development in practical anthropology, but in fact real co-operation and support from the authorities for the subject was disappoint-
ingly small. Among the positive achievements in the subject she
notes the change in focus away from primitive communities: "Most
of Malinowski's pupils, however worked among the larger African
tribes of the greatest political importance and where European
contact had been at its maximum."[23] One might ask whether this
could be one of the reasons why the official attitude was so lukewarm. Certainly, in giving the reasons why she judges that there
had been only very moderate success for the IAI programme of
closer association between research and practical affairs, reflected
in the small number of research posts and the difficulty of financing
research, she refers to suspicion of the social investigator. Both in
such work in Britain, and in Africa,

> The protests do not come from the individual questioned, for
> most people like to talk about themselves and to find that their
> views are considered important . . . The criticisms in both cases
> come from those in authority: the Mayor or the M.P. of the
> English borough, the district commissioner or the missionary
> in Africa. These probably fear disturbances of some kind or other
> as the result of the investigation, and probably feel resentment at
> a stranger making inquiries in an area over which they have
> control.[24]

In a footnote she points out that in South Africa, the Union Government as a wartime measure was refusing permission to anthropologists to enter Native reserves. The article goes on to discuss the
personal misunderstandings and suspicions which dog an anthropologist's fieldwork, and diplomatically gives a reasonable explanation of the (scientific) reasons why the anthropologist "is bound to

[22]A. I. Richards, "Practical anthropology in the lifetime of the International
African Institute", *Africa* XIV, 1944, 289-301.
[23]*Ibid.*, p. 291.
[24]*Ibid.*, p. 293.

lead a life which is very strange in the eyes of other Europeans", having the reputation of "dancing round a tom-tom in a loin-cloth". This is all directed at officialdom; and ends with an implied appeal for greater research support. For earlier in the article Audrey Richards commented that "It looks as though the anthropologist had been advertising his goods, often rather clamorously, in a market in which there was little demand for them",[25] and asked why. The fundamental answer to her question surely would lie in the gulf of serious mutual distrust between at least some brands of social anthropology and the authorities responsible for "good administration".

The debate over the use of anthropology, conducted in the pages of *Africa* for a couple of decades, does not appear to have led to greater understanding. On the contrary, there was in some respects a polarisation of opinion. For example, on the official side, in 1951 Sir Philip Mitchell was able to state his earlier misgivings about anthropology in an even more slighting manner than he had done over twenty years earlier. In a review of Lord Hailey's *Native Administration in the British Territories in Africa*, he writes of the contribution of anthropology as follows:

It has always been a matter of particular difficulty in colonial Africa to ensure that those who are responsible for the initiation of policy or legislation, or for important administrative action or decisions (and in African conditions a heavy responsibility may rest on very young shoulders) should be adequately informed not only of past events and old customs, but of current social, political and economic conditions, in their own country and in others offering useful analogies or experience. There was, especially during the nineteen twenties and thirties, a spate of special reports and investigations; at one time, indeed, anthropologists, asserting that they only were gifted with understanding, busied themselves with enthusiasm about all the minutae (*sic*) of obscure tribal and personal practices, especially if they were agreeably associated with sex or flavoured with obscenity. There resulted a large number of painstaking and often accurate records of interesting habits and practices, of such length that no one had time to read them and often, in any case, irrevelant, by the time they became available, to the day to day business of Government.[26]

[25]*Ibid.*, p. 292.
[26]P. E. Mitchell, review of "Native administration in the British territories in Africa", *J. African Administration* III, 1951, 55-65, at pp.56-57.

This clearly unfair jibe received a sober reply from Schapera,[27] spelling out once more the case for the usefulness of anthropology and suggesting co-operation on the ground between anthropologists and administrators, but protectively retaining the right to investigate esoteric scientific problems. The terms of the debate were thus very close to what they had been for a generation: and this in itself suggests that a fundamental opposition of interest, sympathy and commitment between the camp of colonial officials, on the one hand, and of social anthropologists on the other, had not been overcome.

Indeed, Malinowski's position had hardened even further. His most powerful statements on the need for the work of the social scientist to be politically involved appear in the collection of his writings posthumously edited by Phyllis Kaberry under the title *The Dynamics of Culture Change: an Inquiry into Race Relations in Africa* (1945). There is a markedly more intense tone in these later writings, partly perhaps a sign of increasing disaffection with the apolitical, amoral natural science approach of those influenced strongly by Radcliffe-Brown, and of a deepening personal radical commitment. In the first chapter we read:

There is a moral obligation to every calling, even to that of a scientific specialist. The duty of the anthropologist is to be a fair and true interpreter of the Native . . . In reality, the historian of the future will have to register that Europeans in the past sometimes exterminated whole island peoples; that they expropriated most of the patrimony of savage races; that they introduced slavery in a specially cruel and pernicious form; and that even if they abolished it later, they treated the expatriated Negroes as outcasts and pariahs. . . .

The Native still needs help. The anthropologist who is unable to perceive this, unable to register the tragic errors committed at times with the best intentions, at times under the stress of dire necessity, remains an antiquarian covered with academic dust and in a fool's paradise . . . Research in order to be of use must be inspired by courage and purpose . . .

Shall we, therefore, mix politics with science? In one way, decidedly "yes" . . .[28]

[27]I. Schapera, "Anthropology and the administrator", *J. African Administration* III, 1951, 128-35.
[28]B. Malinowski, *The Dynamics of Culture Change: an Inquiry into Race Relations in Africa*, 1945; edited, with a new Introduction, by P. Kaberry, 1961, pp. 3-4.

Malinowski develops his argument that in the context of Africa, where change is proceeding everywhere, there can be no division between the theoretical and the applied aspects of anthropology. He insists on the need for a broad prospective:

We are dealing with a subject matter which is in flux; the rapidity of change confuses observation and confounds policies. The growth of new unexpected forces and factors, such as African nationalism and the development of autonomous African churches, poses difficulties of description and analysis as well as of policy. In this new work the theoretician and practitioner must take account of wide issues of Western rule, economic as well as imperial; they have to be acquainted with the rudiments at least of economic, legal, and political theory and, with all this, of anthropological method.[29]

In the subsequent chapter he claims that "the whole range of European influences, interests, good intention, and predatory drives must become an essential part of the study of African culture change." It is not merely a question of considering local Europeans as part of an integrated community with the Africans.

The treatment of the complex situation of change as one 'well integrated whole' . . . ignores the whole dynamism of the process . . . Above all, it obscures and distorts the only correct conception of culture change in such areas: the fact that it is the result of an impact of a higher, active culture upon a simpler, more passive one.[30]

The "contact" situation is highly one-sided; in a list of its characteristics in the fifth chapter of the collection, Malinowski notes that Europeans have not given African people instruments of physical power, "firearms, bombing planes, poison gas, and all that makes effective defence or aggression possible". Nor do "we" give instruments of political mastery; nor do we share with them the substance of economic wealth and advantages. "Even when, under indirect economic exploitation as in West Africa and Uganda, we allow the Natives a share of profits, the full control of economic organization remains in the hands of Western enterprise".[31] Nor do we admit of social, political or even religious equality. On the whole we are more generous with spiritual gifts, while withholding wealth, power and independence. And now for the justification of his stand in terms of science:

[29]Ibid., p. 9.
[30]Ibid., p. 15.
[31]Ibid., p. 57.

This argument may be mistaken by the superficial reader as an outburst of pro-Native ranting. It is nothing of the sort. All this is simply a statement of one of the most scientifically relevant factors in culture change as it occurs in parts of Africa. To ignore the fact that there is a selective giving on the part of the Europeans makes for a distortion of evidence, and this is a sin against science.[32]

It is true that Malinowski was afraid of extreme nationalism and the political dangers of its spread, and was not committed to a revolutionary position. But he sketches clearly in these later writings the essential features of the developing political situation, makes plain his own sympathies, and justifies them in terms of the scientist's duty. The colour bar for example "has to be put on the methodological map", because of its theoretical importance in cultural change.

Indeed, the sooner we speak quite freely and openly about it and also with a complete scientific detachment, the better; for the educated Africans are rapidly becoming aware of, and exaggerating, the situation. The African is becoming an anthropologist who turns our own weapons against us. He is studying European aims, pretences, and all the real and imaginary acts of injustice. Such an anthropology is no doubt mutilated and misguided, full of counter-prejudices, and charged with bitter hostility. It is often blind in its intransigence and sweeping in its wholesale indictment. But it cannot be ignored by the man of science; and it would be better if the practical man did not treat it as a joke or as an insignificant and minor excrescence. For on the whole it contains a great deal of truth, and it foreshadows the formation of a public opinion, of a national and racial feeling which, sooner or later, will have to be taken into account by the practical contact agents.[33]

And even more explicitly:

The various movements which have so far appeared have broken down largely because the Natives are not yet ripe for national, well-organized, collective action. By the time, however, when a European power in control may become politically embarrassed and when there is fertile ground for the combination of the Natives from the Lakes to the Cape, such a collective body of opinion may not be an irrelevant factor. The anthropologist

[32]*Ibid.*, p. 58.
[33]*Ibid.*, p. 59.

should have as one of his duties, not to act as a spy, still less as an *agent provocateur*, but to study the growing forces of Bantu nationalism; to insist as all those with knowledge and foresight do, that an improvement in social and, above all, economic conditions, constitutes the only way out of the difficulty; and that no price is too high to pay to prevent inevitable disaster.[34] Malinowski does not face the question of how "inevitable" disaster can be prevented. In positive terms, he merely suggests some liberal reforms, and the need for the continuance of some elements from the traditional past. On these points he could certainly be said to stand close to official colonial policy and practice.

But I have quoted extensively from Malinowski and some of his contemporaries and his pupils, in order to suggest that taken as a whole, his views nevertheless constitute a point of view of greater political perception and radical significance than might at first be thought. Of course Malinowski was not trying to overthrow the system. His students' grants would have soon dried up if that were the case. Of course his activities and writings, and those of his colleagues, were contained within the total colonial situation; how could it have been otherwise? But just as Malinowski himself rejected the concept of the "culture contact" situation as an integrated whole, we must reject the concept of the colonial situation in the inter-war period as an integrated whole. We must recognise that there were developing contradictions, not merely between the administrators and their philosophy of just rule on the one hand, and nascent nationalism and socialism on the other, but between each of these and social anthropology, caught in the middle and constrained from either side.

In the inter-war period, the main constraints were from colonial authority itself. A historical view of the subject should therefore give full weight to the ways in which social anthropology was a vehicle for criticism of that authority.

[34]*Ibid.*, p. 61.

In the preparation of this article, I have been indebted both to discussions at the Hull seminar and to helpful criticism from Natale Olwak Akolawin. Maurice Freedman and Godfrey Lienhardt also kindly read and commented on the manuscript.

# THE COLONIAL FORMATION OF BRITISH SOCIAL ANTHROPOLOGY
## Stephan Feuchtwang

**Preliminaries:** scope, plan and definitions

The subject of this paper is the relation between British anthropologists and their sponsoring institutions. The objective of this paper is to locate the effect on anthropological knowledge of the social conditions of British anthropology as it became an institution, the so-called discipline and profession of social anthropology. I shall not be concerned with the history of social anthropology as a history of knowledge and its production *per se*. I am not going to produce a reading of the frames of reference of social anthropology as part of an ideological practice within the complexity of practices which constitute British society. I am concerned only with one relation in that complex, namely the relation between the material conditions of that ideological apparatus which is social anthropology, as it was formed historically and the knowledge produced in it.

The intentions of the anthropologists and their sponsors are beside the points I will make. I am looking for the effects of an institutional formation, and of a large number of events. That the events should have a combined effect is no reason to think either that it was intended or that I must have direct recourse in explaining it to its being intended.

The plan of this paper is to start from the present and first to think out what are the inevitable effects of the type of sponsorship sought and given for anthropological research, then to analyse the match between anthropologists' actions toward sponsors and the development of anthropological theory, methods and its objects of study. The third and largest part will then recount a history of the formation of the institution of social anthropology as a profession and a discipline, and the concluding part will be a more informed and precise argument of the fit between it and its sponsoring institutions, predominantly those of the British imperial state. From this plan it should be apparent that I do not aim to be empirically conclusive, but rather to put forward an informed argument as a necessary step at the beginning of the neglected work of knowing what social anthropology is and does, is not and does not do.[1]

By 'the discipline' I mean what I take to be the prominent characteristic of British social anthropology, which I think is the seeking of knowledge of total systems or structures from small-scale social units by direct personal observation with as little participation as possible. The broken relation of someone who goes out directly to experience the life of people quite other than himself while at the same time preserving a distance and an ethic of non-interference which maintains that otherness has its counterpart in a theory of total social systems in small social units, to be understood inductively but nevertheless involving reconstruction and isolation from an encompassing system which is analytically ignored. I want to dwell upon this distance, and amplify it, because I think it is the point at which the relation of the discipline to its practical conditions and sponsoring institutions is clearest.

By 'the profession' I mean the establishment of British social anthropology as university department and degree, where it is taught as a mental discipline: the teaching of anthropology, writes Raymond Firth, is more the implanting of a view and method than the imparting of information, ethnographic detail and the 'right' theory.[2]

I want to note here that I will be concerned with that period particularly in which the classics of British social anthropology were

[1]Argumentative initiatives have already been made, it is true, in the *New Left Review*, the first by David Goddard, 'Limits of British Anthropology' (NLR 58, 1969). While the first two paragraphs of his article, which state that anthropological studies in Britain grew up as part of the colonial situation, are also my starting point, he follows them with a critique of British structural-functionalism unrelated to its institutional conditions. Like Jairus Banaji's later article ('Anthropology in crisis', NLR 64, 1970), his critique is made by contrasting British empiricist structuralism with Lévi-Straussian structuralism.
[2]Raymond Firth, 'Aims, methods and concepts in the teaching of social anthropology', in D. Mandelbaum (ed), *The Teaching of Anthropology*, American Anthropological Association, Memorandum 94, 1963.

produced which we still now, in London at least, include in the first
years of indoctrination to social anthropology, namely the late colonial period. Some of the developments of anthropology in the 1960s
included in the latter years of indoctrination have broken with *some*
of the characteristics of the anthropology produced in the late colonial period, but others, in which the one I have isolated are included, are still maintained. Professor M. G. Smith in a seminar on
the history of British social anthropology at University College,
London, in 1971, talked of the break-up of colonial complacency,
and in it the demise of functionalism. How complete, how radical,
is its demise? We still put priority on 'community' studies, on 'exotic' societies, as he himself called them, and on 'preliterate' societies,
a term he also used for the subject matter of anthropology. These
terms, reserving structure from dynamics, repressing history into
code of myth or into moments of equilibrium, are derived from the
products of an anthropology formed as I shall argue in a complex
of colonial attitudes, and surviving reformed in neo-colonial
conditions.[3]

## 1. Three ways in which research cannot help being effected by its sponsors

We live in a political system in which research and teaching are
segregated from applied research, training, and government in institutions called 'academic', a segregation legitimated by an historically founded conventional idea of 'academic freedom'. Social anthropological teaching and research is subject to this segregation
into academic and applied, so much so that the possibility of 'pure'
research is a firm belief and the possibility of its use either ignored,
this ignorance being the 'correct' attitude, or else denied.

(1) Nevertheless, anthropology is thought to be useful by some
agencies, apart from its use as a mental discipline (an ideology).
Many of the funds for social anthropological research are given for
its practical use in multi-disciplinary development projects in Mal-
aysia, for community development in Africa, for public security

[3]For present purposes what I mean by neo-colonial conditions is a global
system of *nations* in relations of economic dependence upon and actual or
potential military subordination to metropolitan nations, and which are to
a large extent successors to *colonial* relations. The rulers of subordinate
nations in this system service these relations if they do not actively break
with them. Most anthropological research is conducted through and
financed by them, or by the metropolitan agencies of the metropolitan
nations, rarely if ever by the nations and movements which have broken
from these relations.

and military intelligence in Thailand, for the training of district
officials in Papua New Guinea. Even supposing that much of the
data of this work is not published, going only into reports or data
banks access to which is restricted, it is still likely to be part of and
informed by the rest of its researchers' contributions to social anthropology and must also to some extnet help them form their ideas of
anthropology as a discipline which they simultaneously or in the
future will conduct and administer. And of the published work
which forms the discipline's ethnographic groundwork we can ask,
with some certainty of its being a substantial question, how much
of it was done on commission, determined not by anthropology
alone but also by the demands of colonial and neo-colonial relations.
(2) On the other hand, contracted research has been distinguished
from academic research and the use of an academic name and place
of study for contracted research called a breach of professional
ethics, especially while the research report is restricted and not
made freely available to the scientific community.[4] The Scarborough
and Hayter ear-marked government funds which financed so much
of area studies, including anthropological study, in Britain after the
second world war, and the Ford foundation which did the same in
the U.S., may have been provided with an idea of the national interests, but the funds were administered by academics in the hope
that this would guarantee an impartial use of the funds for scientific
advancement. Is such a hope realistic?

Are there not, especially as funds begin to flow less easily, lists of
non-academic priorities such as those Lucy Mair mentions as having
existed for the Colonial Social Science Research Council[5] and which
are being worked out by the U.S. Social Science Research Council,[6]
possibly guided by the U.S. government Foreign Areas Research
Co-ordination Group?[7] Do not the academic administrators direct
research toward topics and areas which they know or guess to be
favoured by their sponsors?

[4]This was the gist of many contributions to the discussions of Project
Camelot at the annual meeting of the American Anthropological Association in 1966. I think I am justified in taking examples from U.S. post-war
anthropology because in the first place many British anthropologists at
some timeor other in the research areas themselves, or in Britain and the
U.S.A., are sponsored by U.S. agencies, secondly because I find many a
parallel in the present U.S. relations between profession and sponsors with
the British profession and its sponsors.
[5]Lucy Mair, 'The social sciences in Africa South of the Sahara: the British
contribution', *Human Organisation*, 19: 3, 1960.
[6]According to Dr. Jack Stauder, in a paper on 'The "relevance" of anthro-
polgy' given to a Wenner-Gren Symposium, 1970.

Eric Wolf and Joseph Jorgensen, members of the American Anthropological Association's Ethics Committee, found[8] in the arrangements of university contracts for counter-insurgency work in Thailand an 'ambiguity of motive: is the government soliciting social scientists or is the social science community soliciting government?' The Committee on African Studies, which included anthropologists, in a report to its sponsor the Ford Foundation in 1958 wrote: 'It seems to us most appropriate and desirable to encourage Africanists individually and in their associations, to provide assistance in professional consultation, in training for specific needs, in *designing research* (my emphasis) so as to be useful to government and business.'[9] The American Anthropological Association itself, in its *Fellow Newsletter* 8:1, January 1967, p. 7, reported that it was setting up a committee for liaison between the Association and government agencies 'to suggest *improvements in the use of anthropology* (my emphasis); to strengthen the relations between Government and the profession; to visit agencies to discuss policies and actions with respect to anthropological methods and data, employment, contracts, grants and fellowships.'[10]

As we will see, this academic solicitation, seeking to be useful especially to government, was true of British anthropology in its development from the turn of the century. It is of course possible that there be no disagreement between the professional anthropologists and their sponsors and so no reason for any disavowal of the sponsors' interests since they are the same as or compatible with those freely accepted by the anthropologists. But then surely one is bound to ask whether this arrangement was arrived at by means of anthropological reasoning and work, and not by some other contingent decision. And the answer is that it cannot possibly have been when there is so little, almost no, work done by anthropologists on their own governments' and societies' relations to the external societies they choose to and are paid to study.[11] In fact the only criteria for such agreement that were mentioned in the past in Britain and at

[7]'Presumptive evidence for an inquiry into a military-academic synapse . .' one of whose links is between the FAR Group and the SSRC in the United States is summarised in 'The American Asian Studies Establishment', in *Bulletin of Concerned Asian Scholars*, 3: 3 and 4, 1971.
[8]So they wrote in *New York Review of Books*, 19, Nov. 19, 1970, p. 27.
[9]as quoted in Stauder op. cit.
[10]ibid.
[11]Study of the relationship between them is not entirely absent from social anthropology, but it is not social so much as cultural and is limited to the phenomena of contact itself (culture contact in the past, ethnicity now) not the social system of contact.

present in the U.S. have been deliberately differentiated from anthropological work as such and categorised as the 'Ethical', 'personal' and 'common sense' responsibilities towards the individuals with whom they (we) have worked in the field and towards colleagues in the profession. A self-censorship, a limitation of the discipline, has been exercised. The discipline does not include analysis of its sponsors and its relations to them.

A pure form of this self-censorship, in which no criteria, not even ethical, are offered for the choice of sponsor and the use of research, is the claim that it makes no difference who provides funds so long as the researcher is allowed to conduct the research project he has devised, so he claims, independently, nor is it of scientific or professional concern how the result is used so long as it is accessible to professional colleagues. Such a purist concern, is questionable. Has the discipline in fact developed under its own logic, independently? I shall pose this question in the second part of this paper.

(3) If government funds, or the funds of government-supporting agencies are used and foreign government permission to conduct investigations needed, then the work will be limited according to government diplomatic policy. This in itself must impose contingent limits upon the geographical distribution of ethnographic research, as Kathleen Gough has pointed out.[12] Future funds and future permission for each anthropologist and his successors are determined, furthermore, by whatever is the record of his or her research, publications and reputation in the sponsoring agencies' sources of information. As Wolf and Jorgensen pointed out, academics in Thailand who collaborated in counter-insurgency work feared losing the opportunity for further research if they refused. Of course it is possible to conduct research of one's own and on the side do what pleases sponsors, but the limits within which this can be done need investigation. I am not satisfied with the obvious fact that there is some leeway. Apart from prior geographical limitations there is the restraint on publication of any analysis that might be taken as critical of the sponsor or permission-giver. The professional demand for publication would make it senseless to do work that was not publishable. Any analysis is critical at least in the limited sense that it distinguishes phenomena and representations—such as a particular government policy or project, or an educational programme—from the basis, and finds the consistency and contradiction in an historical system or structure. It can easily be offensive. Has the choice to

[12]Kathleen Gough, 'Anthropology: Child of Imperialism' Monthly Review, April 1968.

STEPHAN FEUCHTWANG                                        77

pursue it regardless of tact and professional considerations often
been taken?

## 2. Has the discipline developed under its own logic?

Take as a point of departure a paper by Peter Worsley entitled
'The End of Anthropology?', given at the 6th World Congress of
Sociology, May 1966. As an anthropologist and from within the
discipline and its theoretical foundations, he found, if I read him
correctly, that three major directions implied in those foundations
had been neglected.

(1) The development of theory of direction, or emergence, has
been avoided. Worsley sees this as an ideological reaction: in avoiding imperialist and racist notions of superiority anthropologists had
for half a century recourse instead to a combination of universalism
and relativism.

But this is also a change consistent, as I will argue in the next
part, with the changed character of late colonial relations. It was in
any case not a change which came about through internal criticism
and reasoned rejection but by means of a process of discrediting the
scientific study of history and of causal explanation in social science
on tangential and external grounds.[13] If evolutionary thought had
engendered the ideology for a reactionary and oppressive politics
and produced untenable theories of race and the mechanistic stages
of progress, this does not mean that a more rigorous approach could
not produce more adequate and tenable evolutionary theories and
theories of large-scale types or modes of social relation. Yet this is
what the founders of British social anthropology in their wholesale
rejection of all causal reasoning in anthropology would have us
believe.

(2) Worsley points out what anthropology could have been doing
as a self-professed science of society whose subject-matter was the
variety of human or social types. It could have been developing an
adequate comparative theory and typology starting with such types
as had already been developed. Instead, a surreptitious evolutionism, unworked and unquestioned except as a matter of fact, has
continued in the dualist vocabulary used to identify anthropology's
subject-matter: primitive/modern, simple/complex. There has been
in British social anthropology no systematic inquiry into and transformation of the concepts of social types such as the hunting-

[13]See R. Makarius' introduction to the French edition of Morgan's *Ancient
Society* (L. H. Morgan, *La Cociété Archaique*, 1971) pp xiv-xxvii, for a
description of this process.

gathering, the pastoral, the hydraulic, the feudal. Where there has
been comparison it has been regional or of types of a single institution (e.g. the family, marriage, descent) or a universal mechanism
(e.g. conflict), never of total social systems.

Totality has been stressed often enough, but never as that of a
type of system, rather as that of a unique society or institution described. Possibly this was to some extent a consequence of the choice
of field out of contingent rather than for scientific reasons. Societies
so chosen at least clustered regionally and so even if the choice of
people to study was not based on a typology and a comparative
theory, that still left regional variation as the grounds for descriptive comparison.

(3) Worsley notes the absence of studies of numerically large and,
to the new state being formed, economically important regions of
the Sudan, one of the principle hunting grounds of British social
anthropology. Instead, minute 'primitive' populations were isolated
in study. Now, if we look at the data provided by historians, we
find that the social systems which anthropologists chose as units of
study were very often parts of much larger social systems, which
might just as well have been the unit of study in a science of social
types. A well known case in point is that of the Tallensi as part of
the Dagomba-Mamprusi-Mossi Tri-dominion and then afterwards,
of course as part of the British colonial system.[14] I doubt that the
larger-scale system was rejected just because a system that size was
not amenable to direct observation. There are other ways of studying a society than the observation of its entirety, indeed even field-
work observation in the British ethnographic tradition is used as the
basis for the description of much more than was actually observed.
The scale of the theory based upon observation and of the concepts
used in description is never in any event confined to that of the observations made. Why should the particular method of study, so-
called participant observation, have been so stressed and celebrated,
and the empiricist ideal—inducing social structure only from what
was known through the senses of the observer[15]—have been given
such currency? Perhaps the method and its stress were and are concomitants of the study of societies as isolates, not a cause.

The poignant distance of the field-work relation, the distance of
the analyst from his own analysis, is conceivably part and parcel of

[14]See R. F. Stevenson, *Population and Political Systems in Tropical Africa*,
    1968, chapter **VI.**
[15]A. R. Radcliffe-Brown, 'The concept of function', in *Structure and
    Function in Primitive Society*, 1951, p. 190.

the distance of the sponsors from that analysis. The distance kept between the people who are the subject-matter of social anthropology and the production of social anthropology itself also fits the field-work method. It fits the *institutional* definition of knowledge as academic and it fits the sponsors' imperial and neo-colonial relations to the same people, as colonial subjects, to be kept in order, put to work and aided, at a distance. The anthropologist studies the peasant, the hunter, the farmer, the labourer. He studies mainly the illiterate. Sometimes he studies the numerate entrepreneurs and the literate minor officials and local notables, even small kingdoms and their courts, but never the imperial, aiding, government-advising or funding agency or boss of the local entrepreneurs and local rulers. Yet it is precisely in the opposite ratio that the readership of the anthropologists' work is ranged.

Literacy has been one of the main criteria of social classification in anthropology and of what is central to its study: preliterate peoples. It has another side in the development of anthropological theory besides defining its subject-matter, and that is the lack of challenge by its subjects, unable to read the finished work. Surely this lack of challenge has encouraged notions of immutable and unconscious structures and left un-raised in social anthropology the question and theory of the state of consciousness and of the internal transformation of society and social production of its own knowledge.

### 3. The formation of British social anthropology

The method employed in writing this history is to generalise from official statements of major institutions of anthropological research, teaching and funding and the writings of professors of anthropology and notable colonial administrators who sponsored anthropologists. I take these to be key instances of British social anthropology because of their co-ordinating functions or, in the case of the professors, their influence as teachers and administrators of social anthropology.

The history of organised anthropology before the second world war was one of very slow development, out of origins in humanitarian reform and political involvement, which were then set aside and distinguished from a 'purely' scientific interest. This separation manifested itself in the duality of the several appeals to government for funds. They met with success only when the colonial governments were forced to engage in policies of major reform leading, after the second world war, to the granting of formal political independence to colonies and to the establishment of social anthropology as a teaching profession in its own right for the first time in several universities in Britain.

In a continuous line of successive institutions, the Royal Anthropological Institute (RAI) can be taken back, as George Stocking has done,[16] to the Aborigines Protection Society, founded in 1838 after parliamentary hearings on the Kaffir wars. The RAI's goals were to pursue an evangelism abroad that would administer the same justice and civilisation in the colonies, as it did at home: 'not to halt European colonisation overseas, but to change its character'. It tended, however, in its history to move toward the study of aborigines 'in the purity of their race' as 'objects of interest in the natural history of man' (as the Society's Fourth Annual Report put it), until members formed, in 1842, a separate body entirely for this purpose, and called it the Ethnological Society of London. Through a combination of medical-anatomical and linguistic-philological approaches its main objective of study was to trace the essential unity of man.

To put them in a larger context, it must be noted that the Aborigines Protection Society and the Ethnological Society of London were in line with one side, in the controversy in Britain reflecting the two sides of the American Civil War. The other side stood, of course, for the natural inferiority of the Negro race and its separate origin. Dissension on these lines, between those tracing a single origin and those tracing several origins of human races, split the Ethnological Society of London itself, and those with the multiple origin theories that favoured slavery and natural aristocracy separated from it and formed, in 1863, the Anthropological Society of London.[17] Its members conducted mainly physical anthropological research, pioneering the measurement of physical types and their classification, and advocated racist policies to colonial administrators while, by contrast, the Ethnological Society of London maintained a 'liberal political orientation'.

But in 1870 the two anthropological societies were reconciled into the single Anthropological Institute of Great Britain and Ireland (now the Royal Anthropological Institute) in which the postulates of original unity and of Darwinian evolution were united with a re-

[16]George W. Stocking Jr., 'What's in a name? The origins of the Royal Anthropological Institute (1937-71)', *Man* 6: 3, 1971. All quotations in this and the next two paragraphs are from Stocking's article.
[17]M. Banton, *Race Relations*, 1967, p. 34, cites its presidential address in favour of slavery.

spect for the careful study of the differentiation of human types. 'Having rejected in the 1840s the left hand of philanthropy, it (organised anthropology in Britain) rejected in the 1860s the right hand of political racism. For the next two decades . . . the Anthropological Institute stayed in the centre of the road. It took for granted the British Empire and the White Man's Burden, but it was not actively concerned with either colonial policy or savage uplift.' (p. 386). It was dependent on its subscriptions for funds. But in the 1890s, as Stocking also notes, this changed. British organisations of anthropology began to petition government sponsorship, and began a long history of attempts to make anthropology attractive to British colonial administrations.[18]

In 1896 the subsection for Ethnology (formed in 1846), of the British Association for the Advancement of Science, with the Anthropological Institute and the British Museum petitioned government for funds and facilities to found an Imperial Bureau of Ethnology, modelled on the American Bureau of Ethnology, the Dutch government's policy of educating its East Indian administrators in ethnology, the ethnological wealth of the Leyden museum, and on the precedent of British Imperial ethnological work already done in reports by colonial administrators and for the Census of India. The aims of the Imperial Bureau were to be two-fold, for science and for colonial administration. The scientific aim, repeated into the present day, was archival, historical, and an academic reason for focusing on small-scale social units and not on large-scale systems, namely to record data from peoples vanishing through contact with Europeans—the aborigines of Australia, Oceania and the East Indies, the so-called tribals of India and tribes of Africa, not the so-called civilisations of the Far East and India, Malaya, Burma, Siam, the Middle East. The administrative aim was to co-ordinate information on the subject peoples for the preparation of colonial administrators so that they would not make anew the mistakes of the past. The only result of this petition was a room in the British Museum for an ethnology section.

Another appeal by the Anthropological Institute, this time with the Folklore Society of Great Britain and Ireland, was made in 1900 to Joseph Chamberlain, Secretary of State for the Colonies, for funds to compile records of the customs of the native people of South Africa who were, to everyone's surprise, not disappearing under

[18]The first part of this history is told by J. L. Myres, 'Anthropology and the State', Presidential address to the Royal Anthropological Institute, JRH 1929.

European contact after all, but whose social organisation was breaking up in an alarming way. The records would help in the difficulties 'of management by a European government' to control the disruption of contact with knowledge of the pre-contact social order. Chamberlain was unresponsive. But in 1908 there was something in the nature of a delayed response to the 1896 appeal, when Wingate invited Oxford and Cambridge anthropologists to train administrators for his newly formed Sudan civil service. In the same year and the next Ridgway, Cambridge professor of anthropology and President of the Anthropological Institute, renewed the 1896 appeal for an Imperial Bureau of Ethnology, to be housed in the Institute, and addressed it to the India and Colonial Offices and then to Asquith the Prime Minister. The appeal[19] was signed by administrators, merchants, bankers, and shipowners. It repeated, in substance, the two aims of the former appeal and added a third, namely to make anthropometric surveys in order to gauge physical improvement and deterioration. There was no concrete response to this appeal either. Anthropology was considered important but not useful by the government. In 1914 there was another minor success; the Australian government began the training in ethnology of administrators of aborigines. In the same year a Royal Commission on Higher Education heard Sir Richard Temple, a fellow of the Royal Anthropological Institute and representative of the Anthropological section of the British Association, recommend the training of colonial service officials in anthropology, more specifically in language and the knowledge of racial characteristics—still apparently the two major concerns of anthropology. For this purpose anthropology departments should be opened in British universities. War put an end to that hope. But British West African colonial administrations had officials trained in anthropology (Meek, Rattray, Talbot) from 1920 onwards, to conduct surveys and reports.

In 1921 Temple went ahead on his own initiative to organise under RAI auspices a Joint Committee on Research and Teaching, representing all anthropologists in British education, in order to collect and publish anthropological information 'for the use of the Imperial services, teachers, misionaries and others'. Money for it came from an appeal fund and a grant from the Rockefeller foundation, not from the British Imperial government. Shortly afterwards, within five years, teachers, missionaries and others, with the

[19]Royal Anthropological Institute Documents A56 and A10: 3.

support of their universities and missionary societies all over Europe, and funded also by the Rockefeller foundation, with in addition the Carnegie foundation, *and* some colonial governments, founded the International Institute of African Languages and Cultures (IAI). Not only did some colonial governments help to finance it, but Lord Lugard, ex-governor of Nigeria, agreed to become head of its Executive Council, 'and it is largely through his influence that British administrations in Africa have given such generous and unswerving support to the Institute from the beginning.'[20]

I think the founding of the IAI is a turning point in the attractiveness of anthropology to colonial administrators. It is important to note the differences between its aims and those of the previous anthropological projects, including Temple's. The practical aims of the latter were to support a simple one-sided, application of imperial rule in the situation of contact, whereas the IAI was founded, among other things, to improve the education of natives 'on modern lines' in the situation of contact,[21] a more complex, two-sided, support of modern (i.e. imperial) rule. Indeed, some of its members may have seen the IAI's activities as a preparation for formal political independence. And the anthropology of the IAI was different. In 1931 it made a five-year plan for itself, based on Malinowski's article, 'Practical Anthropology', published in its journal *Africa* 2:1, 'to study the processes of change in a purely objective scientific way.'[22] Under this plan, studentships were given to colonial administrators and to missionaries to take academic courses, many of them under Malinowski at the London School of Economics, and research fellowships to academic social scientists giving special emphasis to language studies and to culture contact and culture change. Their research was to include direct observation—fieldwork. A Readership had been created at the LSE for Malinowski in 1923 and he chose for it the title *social* anthropology. In these same years Radcliffe-Brown had taken up professorships created for him at the university of Cape Town, and then in Sydney, and in both he was much engaged in training administrators of the natives and conducting projects in applied anthropology.

The functionalist anthropology of Malinowski and Radcliffe-Brown was a wholesale break with the philological, evolutionist, racialist, and historical (diffusionist) anthropology offered in Britain

[20]Rev. E. W. Smith, of the IAI and the RAI, in Memorandum XII of the IAI, 1932.
[21]ibid.
[22]ibid.

84	THE DISCIPLINE AND ITS SPONSORS

until the 1920s. There are grounds for considering the turning point
of the late 1920s as a move either toward an anthropology more
suited to colonial administrative need or else as a change which met
with new colonial administrative needs more than the previous
anthropology could.

In his *African Survey* (pp. 54-61 of the 1957 edition), Lord
Hailey, a key link between colonial administration and the new anthropology, identifies social anthropology with functional, practical
and applied anthropology. He notes that it made a break with the
anthropology of origins and became a kind of knowledge more useful to colonial administration in doing so. The Union of South
Africa from 1925 employed a staff of trained anthropologists in its
administration, and the use of anthropologists to conduct surveys
spread to other British African administrations besides those that
had already used and continued to use anthropological expertise.
Social anthropologists who were commissioned in the 1930s to conduct surveys or make reports, mentioned by Hailey, were I. Schapera in the High Commission Territories of South Africa, M. Read
in Nyasaland, A. I. Richards in Northern Rhodesia and P. J. Peri-
stiany in Kenya.

Education of the colonial subjects and both sides of the phenomena of 'contact' were the main concerns of the Standing Committee on Applied Anthropology which the RAI constituted in 1937.
It was not government sponsored but intended, in its own words[23]
to 'study the problems of culture contact and the application of
anthropological knowledge to the government of subject races' by
means of publication, representation to governments, and personal
contacts with officials. *Man* 1938 contains records of a number of
initiatives taken by the committee: a memorandum to the Australian Prime Minister that the inviolability of reservations be enforced; a deputation including Malinowski and Margaret Read to
the Secretary of State for the Colonies to draw attention to the need
for a better understanding of native opinion and the correct translation of new political institutions into the native words of the territories to be transferred to the Union of South Africa; a suggestion
that anthropological research might, among other things, 'indicate
the persons who hold key positions in the community and whose
influence it would be important to enlist on the side of projected
reforms' and reports on the use of anthropological study for education in colonial development, to point out habits and prejudices

[23]in *Man*, 1937, Article 139.

that might be obstacles to health programmes in East Africa, and to base a sense of citizenship and loyalty to modern institutions 'on the standards of respect for obligation implicit in the native system'. Do not let us forget that the modern institutions, the new political institutions, and the educational programmes were all part of a 'government of subject races'. This independent committee had no truck whatsoever with the contemporary nationalist movements in the colonies, interested though anthropologists were in contact and change, and sensitive to them as they should or must have been.

In the same year the committee sent a deputation to the Secretary of State for the Colonies with a memorandum on 'The place of anthropology in colonial studies'.[24] In the same year, Lord Hailey, from the administrative side, had written in *African Survey*, as cited in the committee's amemorandum: 'The professional anthropologist' should be 'of great assistance in providing Government with knowledge which must be the basis of administrative policy'. One of the advantages to government of a professional anthropologist is, the memorandum mentions, that in investigating such essential subjects as native customary law and land tenure he will not be obstructed as would an investigator known to be connected with the executive side of government. The memorandum suggested a Colonial Research Fund (as had Lord Hailey) and the appointment of between twelve and sixteen research fellows and six and eight lecturers in British universities, who would respectively spend half their time in the colonial field and in training experts—the training, it was stressed, to be general in the first instance, emphasising the totality of social systems. The other half of their time was to be in academia. Research institutes, such as the Rhodes-Livingstone Museum founded two years before, should be established as research bases in the colonies.

The Colonial Social Science Research Council (CSSRC) constituted six years later under the Colonial Development and Welfare Act of 1940 with special provisions for 'the acquisition of knowledge required for implementing projects of social or economic development',[25] followed the recommendations of the RAI committee closely. One of its standing committees was for anthropology and sociology, its first secretary was Raymond Firth, half of the Colonial Research Studies series written by its Colonial

[24]RAI document A57.
[25]Forward by Lord Hailey to HMSO, *A Review of Colonial Research 1940-60*, edited by Sir Charles Jeffries, 1964.

Research Fellows and its members between 1944 and 1962 were by anthropologists, all of whom were later, if not then, teachers of social anthropology and most of whom teach it now. Half of the CSSRC's total allocation of funds went to the establisment of institutes in the colonial territories.

The President of the RAI in this crucial period of the institutionalisation of social anthropology, from the year following the deputation from the committee for applied anthropology to the formation of the Colonial Research Committee in 1942 which planned the CSSRC and which included Lord Hailey and Audrey Richards, of the IAI, was Radcliffe-Brown. His efforts, according to Fortes,[26] laid the basis for the boom in anthropology which was part of the general boom in natural and social science education arising out of the experience of the second world war. His and Malinowski's students filled most of the teaching posts in the university departments of anthropology that were created and expanded in Britain after the war. The Association of Social Anthropologists of the British Commonwealth, membership of which requires 'normally both the holding of a teaching or research post in the Commonwealth and the attainment of either a postgraduate degree (usually a doctorate) or substantial publication' was formed in 1946 with under twenty members, and had grown by 1962 to more than one hundred and fifty.[27]

Whereas until the war social anthropology, that is British structuralism and functionalism, had begun to flourish in certain colonial conditions, the war itself seems to have generalised those conditions enough to have stimulated a qualitative leap into professionalisation under state sponsorship. The war entailed a suddenly increased and widespread need for the *co-operation* of colonial subjects beyond the level required by colonial governments normally concerned to save on the costs of administration. And as we know well it also entailed as an aftermath the intensification of anti-colonial struggles which forced the metropolitan government to adopt a new kind of colonial policy, namely withdrawal from direct rule while endeavouring to ensure co-operation after the retreat.

As a paternal ruler and pragmatic advisor to the British government, Lord Hailey recognised the war to be a watershed in colonial policy. During the war itself he wrote a confidential report (Native

[26]in the preface to M. Fortes (ed), *Social Structure: papers in honour of A. R. Radcliffe-Brown*, 1949.
[27]Max Gluckman and Fred Eggan (eds.) in *The Relevance of models for Social Anthropology*, A.S.A. Monographs 1, 1965, pp. xi-xii.

Administration and Political Development in British Tropical Africa) of an inquiry he conducted in 1939-1940 for the Secretary of State. The war, according to Hailey, saw the ascendancy of the second of two schools of thought. The first was the laissez faire school of thought which had 'little belief that self-government can ever be realised in our African dependencies on any terms which will benefit their populations at large or will avoid prejudice to their connection with Great Britain' (p. 50). The second believed that self-government would enhance the connection. Its 'forces at home and in the dependencies' 'will exert increasing pressure for the extension of political institutions making for self-government, and for the fuller association of Africans with them. The strength of this pressure is likely to be enhanced as the result of the war.' He had already noted (p. 3) that at home, in Great Britain, 'it had been necessary for the State to come to the aid of under-privileged areas or communities. It has become clear that in the Colonies the maintenance of the doctrine that they should be independent of assistance from the British Treasury would condemn some of them to the permanent position of depressed areas.' 'The government must (it is generally felt) exercise a degree of intervention in both the economic and social life of the nation which would not have been accorded to it by an earlier generation. The influence of these ideas has been increasingly felt in the interpretation which the general public now places in its obligations towards the colonial dependencies. It has been reflected in a concrete form in the passing of the Colonial Development and Welfare Act of 1940.'

Lord Hailey was obviously central in the articulation of colonial administration and professional anthropology. Writing from the vantage point of 1944[28] he described colonial development as passing through three stages, the first being introduction of law and order and creation of basic infrastructure for the economic development (i.e. extraction) of natural resources, the second, which he judged had then been reached, being one in which the colonial administration is faced with the 'problem of assisting the indigenous communities to advance their social life and to better their standard of living.' This would lead to the next stage, which he envisaged as the political advance of indigenous peoples. So his practical and effective interest in anthropology coincided with his second stage of colonial development. The anthropology which took his administra-

[28]Lord Hailey, 'The role of anthropology in colonial development', *Man* 44: 5, 1944.

tive interest was not the study of human origins, it was the study of
how societies work.[29] And the societies with which he thought administrators needed most help from anthropologists were not societies where an easily understood and compatible system could be
incorporated easily to colonial rule using native personnel. These,
we may note, were the 'civilisations' and 'despotisms' of the East,
given to another set of academic disciplines and institutions altogether
—namely, Oriental studies. Anthropology could help with another
kind of people and imperial problem, tribal peoples of India and
Africa and the Pacific 'where administrators encountered cultures
which were to them of a novel type, and where they did not find
personnel of a class which they could readily associate with themselves in the formation of the legal administrative institutions of the
country' (i.e. colony).[30]

To sum up the story so far, then, organised anthropology when
finally established as a government sponsored profession was dom-
inantly social anthropology and it was institutionalised at a certain
distance from practical application of knowledge even as it had had
to be as an unsuccessful petitioner of imperial government. Administrators were trained by but not the same as anthropologists. Anthropologists made investigations useful to but not identified with administration.

Lucy Mair, a student of Malinowski who worked on the *African
Survey*, has linked Indirect Rule closely with the pre-war
study of social anthropology in Africa: 'As far as Africa is concerned, it is mainly in colonies governed under the system of Indirect Rule, where the economic policy is to encourage independent
native production, that the study of social anthropology receives
official encouragement.'[31] Indirect Rule is what Lord Hailey and
C. K. Meek, one of the Nigerian government trained in anthropology, referred to as the use of native institutions and personnel for
local government. It is of great interest, then, to see what working
in this system meant to Lucy Mair. 'To me,' she wrote, 'the question
of primary interest is: How should we study an African society in

[29]ibid.
[30]ibid. C. K. Meek wrote much the same about 'the government's attitude
towards anthropological research', namely that it should provide 'data
which would help the government to make the fullest use of native institutions as instruments of local administration'—in his *Law and Authority
in a Nigerian Tribe*, 1937, p. xv.
[31]Lucy Mair (ed.), *Methods of Study of Culture Contact in Africa*, 1938,
(Memorandum XV to the IAI) p. 1.

order to lay down lines of policy which would be oriented not
towards some necessarily vague ultimate ideal, but towards the
solution of specific problems of adaption which have arisen or
may be expected to arise in the near future;[32] This attitude
towards the limitations of applied anthropology[33] is, if it was
general, of great significance. It is in sharp contrast to the anthropology rejected as conjectural history by the functionalists, with
its long-term interest and perspectives. And it is in apparent
contrast with the scientific ambitions of Radcliffe-Brown for a
natural science of society and with the global generalisations
made by Malinowski. Indeed, Malinowski himself criticized
Fortes for being too functionalist, functionalism having been worked out as a method for studying one culture alone 'which through
age-long historical development had reached a state of well-
balanced equilibrium,' whereas contact with Europeans meant disequilibrium, and functionalism had to be applied in a more complex form as 'the search for the Common Measure' determining
new emerging institutions in order to predict and advise on how they
might reach stability.[34] Nevertheless this was a short-term perspective, and governments did not want advice on long-term policy.
Translated into social science this comes out, in Gunter Wagner's
words as accepting as given 'the essentially rigid forces' of change.[35]
   As for the kind and scale of social unit toward which interested administrators would have drawn anthropologists Lord Hailey identified them, in the passage already cited, as 'tribal peoples'. Lord
Lugard gives some more definite indications of what this meant
methodologically in his preface to *A Black Byzantium*, 1942, by S.
Nadel, at that time a government anthropologist of the administration of the Anglo-Egyptian Sudan. Lugard notes that Nadel's
first object was to discriminate between the essential characteristics
of Nupe culture, and the variations from the typical pattern in a
'heterogeneous society divided by gulfs of culture, ethnic extraction,
community and class'. This involved an examination of 'the factors
of social cohesion upon which the claim of a community to rank as
a unit of self-government is based.' 'Since it is the declared policy
of the British Government to help different units of native society

[32]ibid.
[33]She repeated this attitude in fuller form in 1956. 'Applied Anthropology
   and Development Policies', *British Journal of Sociology* 7, 1956, reprinted
   in her *Anthropology and Social Change*, LSE monographs 38, 1969.
[34]In Lucy Mair (ed.) 1938 p. xxxvi.
[35]'The study of culture contact in its practical applications' in Lucy Mair
   (ed.), 1938, p. 105.

to govern themselves in accordance with civilised canons of justice, and of impartiality between rival claims . . . it goes without saying how valuable such an objective study would be to the Administration. We find that, in fact, it has been utilized in conjunction with the researches of District Officers' (p. iv). Not only were the Nupe to be known and kept as a division of sub-units of social cohesion but the Nupe themselves, in fact, were a sub-unit of Fulani overlordship supported by and mediating colonial British rule. The administration was not, of course, interested in the detailed study of the Nupe so much as in the lessons to be drawn for administration of the larger territory of which the Nupe constituted one division.

So anthropology was useful to colonial administration when, in showing how systems of stability and internal cohesion worked (functionalism), it showed them to be small scale tribal divisions of systems. But the founders of functionalism had global perspectives. Radcliffe-Brown's presidential address on applied anthropology to the Anthropology Section of the Australian and New Zealand Association for the Advancement of Science in 1940 is remarkable for its ambitious plan for anthropology to be the theoretical side of the social experiment which was imperialism. It also envisaged the end of imperialism: 'Imperialism is the self-assumed role of controller of other peoples. They will not let this continue indefinitely. In the meantime, let this blind experiment become less blind. Let it become experimental anthropology leading to better knowledge of the control of society and social change in our own societies.' But it was not as a science of social change that social anthropology became famous. It was for its small scale, intensive, timeless ethnographies. Although in his address Radcliffe-Brown defined the task of social anthropology as the formulation of 'the general laws of the phenomena that we include under the term culture or civilisation', the address itself in its references to social anthropological subject matter was restricted to 'primitive peoples', and to references to his own work with African and Papuan tribes, without any construction of social types (such as he could have been building on the basis of Marx and Morgan). And although in the same address he stresses social evolution, it is an evolution towards more complex and higher-order systems. They are systems of integration. Change is reduced to integration, The more encompassing level is that imposed by 'Western administration' in the imperial experiment. Social evolution in this scheme is to be observed and modified by anthropologists, through the training of ad-

ministrators and the advice to administrations, so that it becomes
a controlled process in which some evolve more than others, indeed
in which some evolve the others.

A contemporary article in *Africa* by Malinowski[36]—an expansion
of the earlier one on 'Practical anthropology', written after correspondence and agreement with a former Lieutenant-Governor of
Southern Nigeria—is also ambitious in its vision for the anthropologist, though not quite so visionary as Radcliffe-Brown's. He too saw
anthropology and administration coming together in the long-term
interests of the native: 'One class of men who can and must organise . . . who have to keep their head above the chaos of conflicting opinions and the turmoil of conflicting interests . . . are the administrators. It is their professional and implicit duty to look after
the interests of the natives, who do not and *cannot* (my stress) share
in deciding about their own destinies, though, sooner or later, they
may have to be admitted to some joint councils. The greater his
capacity to foresee the course of events and frame the policies accordingly, the better he (i.e. the administrator) will acquit himself of
his task. And here, in the capacity for looking far ahead, knowledge, statesmanship, and research meet, and they ought to be made
to collaborate.' '. . . in Africa there is one element which is largely
deprived of voice and immature in its own judgment, that is, the
native.' (pp. 432-4). Social anthropology was firmly to be identified
with a paternal authority. Such an identification with colonial administration of course precludes any questioning of it. Lucy Mair
writes of Malinowski's 'pre-occupation with policy' and of 'his conviction that the main purpose of the study of social change was to
enable governments to control it.'[37] Some of the implications of this
stance are brought out in Malinowski's *Dynamics of Culture
Change*, in a chapter on 'Indirect Rule and its Scientific Planning',
in which much of the ideology of present-day development policy
has its franker and more open precedent. Indirect Rule is welcomed
because it means 'the maintenance of as much as is possible of the
Native authority instead of its destruction' (pp. 138-9). The qualification, 'as much as is possible', is presented as a matter of indis-
putable scientific judgment of an inevitable social evolution: 'the
progressive adaption of native institutions to modern conditions.'
The problem for cultural anthropology, he writes, is of finding in

[36]'The rationalisation of anthropology and administration', *Africa* 3: 4,
1930.
[37]In R. Frith (ed.), *Man and Culture*, 1957 p. 241.

the culture of the native compensations for the loss of his military
power, for the substitution of new for the old 'sources of revenue'
and for a new 'native capacity for legislation', but here's the rub,
'leaving the ultimate control in the hands of Europeans.' It means
in addition, finding ways of *avoiding* certain new developments in
the situation of contact, notable among which is the educated native
(who has found voice and judgment) who challenges the colonial
right: the problem, that is, of 'obviating those situations in which
an illiterate chief has to deal with an educated clerk, with educated
commoners, and upstart demagogues' (p. 145). 'The object is to
create in Native authority a devoted and dependable ally, controlled, but strong, wealthy and satisfied' (p. 147). Elsewhere he calls
this process a 'complex experiment' in 'the gradual growth of collaboration' (p. 141). But in later pages Malinowski makes it plain
that what he means by alliance and collaboration is assimilation to
what is unquestionably a superior mode of life: 'If from the outset
it were possible to make quite clear in preaching the gospel of civilisation, that no full identity can be reached: that what are being
given to Africans are new conditions of existence, better adapted to
their needs but always in harmony with European requirements, the
smaller would be the chances of a strong reaction and the formation
of new, potentially dangerous, nationalisms' (p. 160). Such nationalisms are 'sociologically unsound'.

Tutelage and trusteeship were then the slogans of imperial ideology,[38] and Malinowski's chapter on Indirect Rule follows closely
the conclusions of Lord Hailey. The latter in a talk given to the
Royal Institute for International Affairs in December 1938[39], had
praised Indirect Rule not as an efficient means of administration
but as the most efficient educative instrument in the transition to
self-management at a local level. He reminded his audience of the
lessons to be learned from the experience of British rule in what he
called 'the East', in particular the disruptive (i.e. nationalist) effects
of higher education for the colonial subjects, concluding: 'Pru-
dence seems to lie . . . in securing the early association of educated
Africans with our administrative institutions. If we do not do so,
there will inevitably arise a state of tension which, sooner or later,
we shall have to meet by large-scale political concessions. And in
that case, they will not necessarily be made either in the right way,

[38] See for instance Lord Hailey's remarks on 'the tutelary power' in *An
African Survey*, 1938, p. 413.
[39] Published as 'Some problems dealt with in the African Survey' in *International Affairs*, March 1939.

or to the right class, or with the best result for all the people concerned.' The concordance of the two views of the anthropologist and the administrator is plain, though the one is veiled in the language of science, the other in the language of bourgeois paternal rectitude.

Evolution for Malinowski was a matter of culture—forms of behaviour, ceremony and speech and the development of values which he took to be absolute such as survival and, in his latest work, freedom. For Radcliffe-Brown it was a matter of higher-order systems of integration with a strong identification of system with norms and jural order. Divisions in the terms of their science are therefore cultural, customary or jural divisions, and change or contradiction are matters of temporary maladjustment of values and norms in a superior, and global system of civilisation or integration. To identify such divisions, and in this way, was of course much more congruent with imperial administration than to identify competition or contradiction between economic systems or between total political and economic systems, only one of which was the imperial system. To have done the latter would have meant having to choose sides in the application of anthropology. In the former the sides are there, there is still an us and a them. But the choice is loaded with a moral and social justification in the favour of us, and they are the ones divided.

Anthropology, as social anthropology, became important to administration, colonial administration, in the context of retreat from direct coercive rule and in the context of its direction of reforms from above, after it had been involved in what it recognised to be wasteful mistakes or when a need for a response from its subjects arose and was in danger of being thwarted. It may have been directly after a rebellion and its suppression. In the second world war these conditions were generalised. But perhaps the Aborigines Protection Society itself is the prototype, founded as the result of the Kaffir Wars, and much later examples are the commissioning of Evans-Pritchard to study the Nuer after their rebellion and its suppression, and Meek's study after the women's rebellion in Eastern Nigeria.

The present professors of social anthropology, authors of texts much used in teaching undergraduates its foundations, did the research for them in the pre-war, war-time and immediate post-war period. Social anthropology as a discipline was first formulated in the mid 'twenties and became a fully formed profession in the late 'forties. Thenceforth application of anthropology was less simple because imperial relations were no longer colonial, no longer a single political system of administrative apparatuses, and it was advocated less frankly and openly than it had been. Social anthropology was justified to a much more exclusive extent than it had been as a study for its own sake.

But 'theoretical' studies are not, Lucy Mair has remarked[40] of no interest to 'the practitioner of government'. The example she gives of a kind of theoretical study that is of interest to 'administrative officers' is "work of the type that can be described as 'mapping'. Under their (the Rhodes-Livingstone Institute and the East African Institute) auspices what were unknown regions, from the sociologist's point of view, have become areas with well-marked characteristics, about which theoretical generalisation is both possible and profitable, and into which administrative officers, if they wish can now venture with much better guidance than was available to their predecessors." This work, funded by a Colonial Research Grant, was published serially as the Ethnographic Survey of Africa. It was in fact the kind of work, survey work, undertaken by a number of Colonial Research Fellows in the late 'forties with guidance from colonial governments[41]—Firth in West Africa and Malaya, Leach in Sarawak, Richards—in East Africa. And, although administered by academics, the grants were nevertheless guided, as Lucy Mair also notes[42] according to government policy priority lists, so that research institutes and applicants for Colonial Research Fellowships 'know that a project which is on the priority list stands a better chance of a grant than one which is not'.

Nevertheless, at the end of the second world war Evans-Pritchard gave a talk on applied anthropology, published in 1946,[43] in which he distinguished between scientific work and practical advice, the first free of moral values, the second necessarily based on moral values and common sense. Both Ian Hogbin[44] and Lucy Mair[45]

[40]Lucy Mair, 'Social sciences in Africa South of the Sahara', 1960, op. cit. p. 98.
[41]according to HMSO op. cit., p. 61: The second need (i.e. beside mainly demographic data) which the Council (CSSRC) identified was that of assessing priorities amongst the many urgent problems calling for investigation. Here the Council felt that the best guidance was to be obtained from the colonial governments themselves, from personal discussions with colonial officials and by visits of members of the Council or other experts to particular territories.' Such visits included those of A. I. Richards and R. Firth, mentioned in the text.
[42]Lucy Mair, 1960, p. 98.
[43]'Applied Anthropology', Africa, 16: 2, 1946.
[44]In Firth (ed.), Man and Culture op. cit., p. 253.
[45]In 'Anthropology and the underdeveloped territories', a lecture given in

have since then upheld the same distinction, in which the anthropologist is said to bring to matters of policy-making and judgement,
to criticism of a colonial policy specifically, no special knowledge
or responsibility other than that of an unusually well *informed* lay-
man.

Evans-Pritchard urged the anthropologist to 'restrict his research
to scientific problems'. 'We study primitive societies . . . to gain a
better understanding of ourselves' and to teach 'a clearer understanding of the nature of human society in general' (p. 93). He
argued, on the by now familiar lines of dual purpose, for knowledge itself and secondly for expert practical advice, that research
was urgent because of the disappearance of primitive societies and
that more teaching positions in universities and more technical advisory positions in colonial governments be established for anthro-
plogists in order to consolidate the science and also for the ultimate
gain of administration which must depend on the advance of the
science. He himself had filled both the roles of researcher and advisor and saw no incompatibility between the two reporting as advisor (he was Tribal Affairs Officer in the British administration of
Cyreneica during the war) on 'native problems' and making sure
the natives got 'a square deal' 'accommodated to administrative requirements and imperial policy' (p. 96).

Why is there no *scientific* incompatibility with accepting imperial
policy? Was there not, in 1946 and before, the possibility of an
analysis of the imperial system, an analysis which might turn out to
be the basis for criticism of the whole system as such? And why is
Evans-Pritchard still scientifically concerned chiefly with 'the primitive field' (p. 98)? Is that a scientific category, a type of social
system? And if so, is it disappearing any faster than other kinds?
These questions which are a fundamental step to the statements by
which they justified their discipline and its practice, have hardly
been asked even today by the leading social anthropologists. 'Primitive societies' were an administrative and perhaps a cultural fact
within the colonial system, unquestioned until their conversion into
'new nations' was imminent.

Such questions began to surface in 1949, when, as members of
the CSSRC, Evans-Pritchard and Firth contributed an article on
anthropology and colonial government to *Man*[46]. They discussed the
problems of 'a science of which the objectives are still in process of

1950, printed in her *Anthropology and Social Change*, op. cit., p. 40.
[46]Article 179, *Man*, December, 1949.

definition', and they proposed 'some division of function between government anthropologists and those working in collaboration with but not in the service of governments.' They pointed to the theoretical interest of 'colonial affairs as such' and of the 'rapid change' of colonial societies which until then were 'a special type of social order, in which external political dominance and ethnic sectionalisation are marked features'. But, after this promising opening, they summed up the subject at its largest as 'the general processes of Westernisation', and with hopes that the change was towards democracy and meritocracy. From the war until very recently, how little has in fact been written on the colonial system in social anthropology and how absent it is from its teaching syllabi is shown elsewhere in this volume.

Common to all these writers on the use of anthropology seems to have been a strict limitation of its practical analysis—in the size of unit studied and the time-scale of prediction—in contrast with the universalism of their theoretical generalisations and of their moral attitudes. The interests of the subjects of their studies, to whom anthropologists often became attached enough to defend, were left to personal ethics, to a humanitarian, universal morality (of which only Malinowski tried to make a scientific principle) and to predictions and recommendations on the short-term effects of colonial policies. Thus they excluded from rational analysis the transformation of different kinds of social system, and the possibility that the interests of their subjects and the reality of the social forces they represented meant a total riddance of the sponsoring agencies of anthropology. The agents of change were given, not studied. The imperially transformed were studied as structures of ideas or relations that were also empirically there, as natural facts. The contradiction between studying change without studying the system of change itself was resolved by posing change as disintegration and its cure, re-integration. Neither the subject 'colonial affairs as such', nor the methods for its study were cultivated. Instead, the study of social change was relegated to a second-class, impure realm. Applied anthropology was included if at all in the academic discipline as an optional subject, and was thought to be less rigorous, and only in applied anthropology was social change studied.

## 4.  Conclusion

The rejection of history as a science, with the implicit assumption that such a science must accept a determinist ideology, is, in the history of anthropology, the moment in which the combination of inquiry into the original unity of man with the differentiation of racial types becomes a combination of the psychic unity of man with the relativity of cultures and societies, more or less explicitly expressing a now unstudied evolutionary scheme. The new combination fits the needs of British colonial administration for a pragmatic knowledge of its subjects—how we can keep them working so that they administer themselves without disrupting our rule. Origins, history, evolution and diffusion of culture are of no interest to administration until it is forced by its subjects to recognise a history they are making for themselves despite it. But in that case the administration wants a short-term solution. It wants to overcome what, to it, is an obstruction of its own interest in an undisrupted order of its making and of the interests of competitive strategy and exploitation of resources and manpower in which it feels itself in the name of civilisation, trade, the balance of payments, and development, to be, and in fact is, bound to act.

While British anthropology was still diffusionist, colonial administration had to rely on its own officers' intelligence reports among which were some made by government anthropologists. Even so, government anthropologists and district officers before the formulation of British social anthropology, although able to report on language, custom, diet and disease as a series of topics in any one culture, were less able to make social order as such intelligible. Whenever the administration had been unable to use or were unsuccessful in using a diplomatic, political, or legal handle which it could recognise, to maintain order and the boundaries of its rule, such serial and impressionistic reports must have been visibly deficient, since it was the system of law, the secret of order, which it needed to know. An anthropology which could produce such knowledge—and the pre-1950 pride of social anthropology was the knowledge of the political systems and systems of kinship in which societies with little or no central administrative handles were ordered —did in fact replace diffusionist anthropology between the 1920s and the 1940s.

The influence of social anthropology was probably directly practical only in the elements of survey information which it provided. Its colonial formation was not in its success as a useful adjunct to colonial administration as such, but in conforming to an approach which seemed attractive and was no threat to it, or at least not to the reformers and developers in it. To the more reactionary elements in the colonies and in their administrations anthropologists were, no doubt, dangerous intruders. To officials and officers of the colonial services concerned with immediate action anthropologists were woolly, impractical, utopian. But this need not mislead us into thinking that anthropology developed independently of colonial interests. It means that we must specify the colonial interests with which anthropology was most closely identified: it supported the ideology of the welfare state in the depressed (for which read tribal) areas of the colonies. If Lord Hailey was a typical, though prominent, as well as formative sponsor of social anthropology we may see in his writings one way in which anthropology provided this support. His surveys mediated the work of anthropologists to administrative officers. In the war-time report already cited, he drew support from the expertise of sociologists and anthropologists as a generality, their warnings against underestimating the strength of native custom and the integrity of native social structure, in recommending the development of native authorities for local 'self-government'. After the war he published *Native Administration in the British African Territories*, (4 vols 1950-51, and a 5th in 1953 on the High Commission Territories), an expansion of the war-time survey, written 'to meet the need felt by officers of the African Administrations for information regarding the practice followed in areas other than those with which they are personally acquainted'. In these volumes social anthropologists are his chief references for the African political and property systems in all the territories surveyed.

The pre-condition for such problems of administration in which anthropology was needed is the wide-spread establishment of colonial administration itself, which reached its greatest geographical extent for Britain in the years of Joseph Chamberlain and his successors, the point of greatest expansion being reached with the distribution of ex-German empire in 1919.

This is the *prima facie* argument for the existence of an historical relationship between British social anthropology and British colonial administration in those problematic conditions of administration which I have specified above. Evidence of a critical attitude towards colonial administration being a common feature of social anthropologists' writing would not of itself contradict the argument put forward here, if it is true that they rarely, if ever, amounted to an analysis of the administration and of the imperialist system itself. Social anthropologists, I argue, did not analyse colonialism, they reproduced the colonial divide in an inverted form as a colonial 'us' interpreting or representing a colonized 'them'. Criticism commonly amounted to appeals to the given colonial administration for protection from too sudden change which would bring about the disintegration of the social order anthropologically analysed. However well represented, however altruistically, it was done within the system.

Indirect rule in Africa was the mould of British social anthropology. It was itself a formalisation of policy at a high administrative level of the British colonial apparatus by administrators (Lugard and Hailey) whose previous experience and model (both negative and positive) was the Indian empire. The first field work of the founders of British social anthropology was not in Africa either, nevertheless their advice was sought mainly in Africa and sponsorship for training given first and foremost for work in Africa.

Indirect rule gave to anthropologists small-scale cultural formations as units of study to be treated as integrated and complete social systems. These units were studied on the one hand as facts related immediately to universal humanity and on the other hand as matters for recommendations on short-term effects of colonial policy. The interests of the subjects of the units, through which the anthropologist might have analysed himself and the system in which he came to study them, were instead treated as matters of personal ethics or as identical in the long term with the European colonial values of civilisation, modernity, justice, law and order. Anthropologists never applied the test of research to the practical condition of research.

It has been pointed out to me in discussion that it could not have been otherwise. There was no choice of doing otherwise. This is true in the colonies only until the time an anti-colonial movement developed. But in the metropolis this is not so. Long before the period with which we are concerned, both political and theoretical positions had been developed which could expose the historical limitations in which the colonies were held.

That anthropological research *is* used, has its application, is related to practical action, was not denied in the pre-war years. In the post-war decades the regional administrations of the imperial system have been replaced by national governments and the high-level, metropolitan imperial apparatus by a Foreign and Commonwealth Office, a Ministry for Overseas Development and a large number of advisory missions. Social anthropology has become an undergraduate, and will shortly become a sixth-form examination syllabus, and anthropological research is now funded in the main by an internal government body the Social Science Research Council. Though the imperial relations of dominance and dependence remain, the political system has changed. Internal divisions of the system have become national divisions. That anthropology has a use is frequently denied nowadays although the anthropological research of the colonial era is the mainstay of the first years of teaching. This denial is part of a generally held notion that it is possible institutionally to pursue knowledge in abstraction. It is an expression of a more developed institutionalisation of the distance between knowledge and its use, maintained before the war but now expressing an even further removal from direct administration than the indirect rule of the 'twenties, 'thirties and 'forties. It is manifest in the methodological pride of British social anthropology: field-work, in which the derivation of knowledge from a practice is celebrated but that knowledge is rarely returned to or shared with the observed in practice; in which the social scientist's empathy with his subject-matter is celebrated because the subject-matter is after all of the same order as himself, but he must do his utmost to repress his presence.

The effect of the discipline as it has developed has been to atomize and universalise the knowledge of total systems sought. Real participant observation, the comparison of socio-economic types, an historical science of social formation and of the transition between types, and the study of imperialism as a system, these are parts of a social science that could logically have been anthropology, but have not been.

# TWO EUROPEAN IMAGES OF NON-EUROPEAN RULE
## Talal Asad

### I

In order to understand better the relationship between social anthropology and colonialism, it is necessary to go beyond the boundaries of the discipline and of the particular epoch within which that discipline acquired its distinctive character. The descriptive writings of functional anthropology are largely devoted to Africa, are in effect virtually synonymous with African sociology during the twentieth century colonial period. But we need to see anthropology as a holistic discipline nurtured within bourgeois society, having as its object of study a variety of non-European societies which have come under its economic, political and intellectual domination— and therefore as merely one such discipline among several (orientalism, indology, sinology, etc.). All these disciplines are rooted in that complex historical encounter between the West and the Third World which commenced about the 16th century: when capitalist Europe began to emerge out of feudal Christendom; when the conquistadors who expelled the last of the Arabs from Christian Spain went on to colonise the New World and also to bring about the direct confrontation of 'civilised' Europe with 'savage' and 'barbaric' peoples;[1] when the Atlantic maritime states, by dominating the world's major seaways, inaugurated 'the Vasco Da Gama epoch

---

[1] "The Americas were therefore the scene of the first true empires controlled from Europe, and Western imperial theory originated in sixteenth-century Spain." P. D. Curtin, (ed.) *Imperialism*, London, 1972, p. xiv. For further information on this subject, see J. M. Parry, *The Spanish Theory of Empire in the Sixteenth Century*, Cambridge, 1940.

of Asian history';[2] when the conceptual revolution of modern science and technology helped to consolidate Europe's world hegemony.[3] The bourgeois disciplines which study non-European societies reflect the deep contradictions articulating this unequal historical encounter, for ever since the Renaissance the West has sought both to subordinate and devalue other societies, and at the same time to find in them clues to its own humanity. Although modern colonialism is merely one moment in that long encounter, the way in which the objectified understanding of these modern disciplines has been made possible by and acceptable to that moment needs to be considered far more seriously than it has.

The notes that follow constitute an attempt to examine some of the political conclusions of functional anthropology (African studies) and of orientalism (Islamic studies) in order to explore the ways in which the European historical experience of subordinate non-European peoples has shaped its objectification of the latter. I hope that such a comparison will make somewhat clearer the kind of determination exerted by the structure of imperial power on the understanding of European disciplines which focus on dominated cultures. Such an attempt is not without its dangers for someone who is trained in only one of these disciplines, but it must be made if we are to go beyond simplistic assertions or denials about the relationship between social anthropology and colonialism. I should stress that I am not concerned with all the doctrines or conclusions of functional anthropology—or for that matter of orientalism.

What I propose to do in the rest of the paper is to concentrate on two general images of the institutionalised relationship between rulers and ruled, objectified by the functional anthropologist and the Islamic orientalist. As we shall see, the images are very different, for the first typically stresses *consent* and the other *repression* in the institutionalised relationship between rulers and ruled. After sketching in these two images, I shall go on to indicate significant omissions and simplifications that characterise each of them, and follow this up with some more general theoretical observations concerning what they have in common. I shall then turn to the wider historical location of the two disciplines which, so I shall argue in my conclusion, help us to understand some of the ideological roots and consequences of these images.

[2]Cf. K. M. Panikkar, *Asia and Western Dominance*, London, 1959.
[3]Cf. J. D. Bernal, *Science in History*, London, 1965, especially Part 4.

## II

I begin by characterising what I call the functional anthropologist's view of political domination.

In general, the structure of traditional African states is represented in terms of balance of powers, reciprocal obligations and value consensus—as in the following passage by Fortes and Evans-Pritchard:

A relatively stable political system in Africa represents a balance between divergent interests. In [centralised political systems] it is a balance between different parts of the administrative organisation. The forces that maintain the supremacy of the paramount ruler are opposed by the forces that act as a check on his powers; [...] A general principle of great importance is contained in these arrangements, which has the effect of giving every section and every major interest of the society direct or indirect representation in the conduct of government [...] Looked at from another angle, the government of an African state consists in a balance between power and authority on the one side and obligation and responsibility on the other [...] The structure of an African state implies that kings and chiefs rule by consent.[4]

Echoes of the same view are also found in a comparatively recent paper by P. C. Lloyd, "The Political Structure of African Kingdoms":

The political elite represent, to a greater or lesser degree, the interest of the mass of the people. In African kingdoms permanent opposition groups within the political elite are not found [...] A vote is never taken on any major issue, but all concerned voice their interests and the king, summing up, gives a decision which reflects the general consensus.[5]

This, then is the functional anthropological image of political domination in the so-called tribal world: an emphasis on the integrated character of the body politic, on the reciprocal rights and obligations between rulers and ruled, on the consensual basis of the ruler's political authority and administration, and on the inherent efficiency of the traditional system of government in giving every legitimate interest its due representation.

The orientalist's image of political domination in the historic

[4]M. Fortes and E. E. Evans-Pritchard, (eds.), *African Political Systems*, London, 1940, pp. 11-12.
[5]M. Banton, (ed.), *Political Systems and the Distribution of Power*, London, 1965, p. 76 and pp. 79-80.

Islamic world is very different. Here there is a tendency to see the
characteristic relationship between rulers and their subjects in terms
of force and repression on the one side, and of submission, indifference, even cynicism on the other. The following brief quotation
from Gibb's essay "Religion and Politics in Christianity and Islam"
illustrates the kind of view I am thinking of:
> ... [the governor's] administrative regulations and exactions on
> land, industry and persons, and the processes resorted to by
> [their] officers were regarded as arbitrary and without authority
> in themselves, and directed only to the furthering of their
> private interests. In the eyes of the governed, official 'justice'
> was no justice. The only authoritative law is that of Islam;
> everything else is merely temporary (and more or less forced)
> accommodating to the whims of a changing constellation of
> political overlords.[6]

A similar kind of image underlies the following remarks by von
Grunebaum:
> As an executive officer, the [Islamic] ruler is unrestricted. The
> absoluteness of his power was never challenged. The Muslim
> liked his rulers terror-inspiring, and it seems to have been bon
> ton to profess oneself awestruck when ushered into his
> presence [...] [The medieval Muslim] is frequently impatient
> with his rulers and thinks little of rioting, but on the whole he
> is content to let his princes play their game.[7]

The same author, tracing the political theories of Muslim canonical
jurists writes:
> So the requirements of legitimate power had to be redefined with
> ever greater leniency, until the low had been reached and the
> theoretical dream [of a *civitas dei*] abandoned. The believer
> was thought under obligation to obey whosoever held sway, be
> his power *de jure* or merely *de facto*. No matter how evil a
> tyrant the actual ruler, no matter how offensive his conduct,
> the subject was bound to loyal obedience.[8]

He then proceeds, with the aid of further quotations to characterise
what he calls "that disillusionment bordering on cynicism with
which the Oriental is still inclined to view the political life".
    The essential features of this image are to be found in the pion-

[6]J. H. Proctor, (ed.), *Islam and International Relations,* London, 1965, p. 12.
[7]G. E. Von Grunebaum, *Islam, Essays in the Nature and Growth of a
Cultural Tradition,* London, 1955, pp. 25-6.
[8]G. E. Von Grunebaum, *Medieval Islam,* Chicago, 1946, p. 168.

eering works of orientalism at the turn of the last century—as in this
passage by Snouck Hurgronje:

> The rulers paid no more attention to the edicts of the *fuqaha*, the
> specialists in law, than suited them; these last in their turn,
> were less and less obliged to take the requirements of practice
> into account. So long as they refrained from preaching revolt
> directly or indirectly against the political rulers, they were
> allowed to criticise the institutions of state and society as
> bitterly as they liked. In fact, the works on [religious law] are
> full of disparaging judgements on conditions of 'the present day'.
> What is justice in the eyes of princes and judges is but
> injustice and tyranny...Most taxes which are collected by the
> government are illegal extortions...; the legally prescribed
> revenue...is collected in an illegal manner and spent wrongly...
> Muslim rulers, in the eyes of the *fuqaha*, are not the vice regents
> of the Prophet as the first four Caliphs had been, but wielders
> of a material power which should only be submitted to out of
> fear of still worse to follow, and because even a wrongful
> order is at least better than complete disorder...[In fact in
> Islamic history] the people obeyed their rulers as the wielders
> of power, but they revered the ulama [learned men of religion]
> as the teachers of truth and in troubled times took their lead
> from them...In this way, the [religious] law, which in practice
> had to make ever greater concessions to the use and custom
> of the people and the arbitrariness of their rulers, nevertheless
> retained a considerable influence on the intellectual life of the
> Muslims.[9]

So the orientalist's image may be characterised briefly as follows:
an emphasis on the absolute power of the ruler, and the whimsical,
generally illegitimate nature of his demands; on the indifference or
involuntary submission on the part of the ruled; on a somewhat
irrational form of conflict in which sudden, irresponsible urges to
riot are met with violent repression; and, finally, an emphasis on the
overall inefficiency and corruption of political life.

### III

The historical realities, of course, are more complicated than these
views. But the remarkable thing in both cases is the direction in
which the simplification occurs.

[9]*Selected Works of C. Snouck Hurgronje,* edited by G. H. Bousquet and
J. Schacht, Leiden, 1957, pp. 265 and 267.

In Africa, a basic political reality since the end of the nineteenth century was the pervasive presence of a massive colonial power— the military conquest of the continent by European capitalist countries, and the subsequent creation, definition and maintenance of the authority of innumerable African chiefs to facilitate the administration of empire.[10] Everywhere Africans were subordinated, in varying degree, to the authority of European administrators. And although according to functionalist doctrine "Every anthropologist writes of the people he works among as he finds them",[11] the typical description of local African structures totally ignored the political fact of European coercive power and the African chief's ultimate dependence on it.

For example Fortes's *The Dynamics of Clanship among the Tallensi* describes Tale political structure with only a few brief ambiguous references to British rule in the introduction and then again in the final section of the final chapter. Yet in a paper published seven years earlier ("Culture Contact as a Dynamic Process") he had noted that the local District Commissioner among the Tallensi was:

6 miles from a police station, and some 30 miles from a permanent administrative headquarters. The political and legal behaviour of the Tallensi, both commoner and chief, is as strongly conditioned by the ever-felt presence of the District Commissioner as by their own traditions[...] The District Commissioner is in direct communication with the chiefs. To them he gives his orders and states his opinions. They are the organs by which he acts upon the rest of the community, and conversely, by which the community reacts to him.[12]

In spite of all this, Fortes had seen the District Commissioner essentially as a "Contact Agent" between European and native cultures, and not as the local representative of an imperial system. It was this non-political perception of a profoundly political fact which led him to assert that the District Commissioner was *not* regarded "as an imposition upon the traditional constitution from without. With all that he stands for, he is a corporate part of native life in this area".

One might suggest that, in spite of methodological statements to

[10]For a summary of these developments with special reference to East Africa (including the southern Sudan) see chapter 11 of L. Mair's *Primitive Government*, London, 1962.
[11]L. Mair, *op. cit.*, p. 31.
[12]*Methods of Study of Culture Contact in Africa*, International African Institute Memorandum XV, London, 1938, pp. 63-4.

the contrary, functional anthropologists were really not analysing existing political systems but writing the ideologically loaded constitutional history of African states prior to the European conquest. This would certainly help to explain the following remarks by the editors of *African Political Systems:* "Several contributors have described the changes in the political systems they investigated which have taken place as a result of European conquest and rule. If we do not emphasise this side of the subject it is because all contributors are more interested in anthropological than in administrative problems".[13] One reason why developments in indigenous political structures due to European conquest and rule were seen as "administrative problems" by European anthropologists was that real political forces in all their complexity formed the primary objects of administrative thinking and manipulation on the part of European colonial officials. Yet the result of identifying the constitutional ideology of 'centralised' African polities with the structural reality meant not analysing the intrinsic contradictions of power and material interest—a form of analysis which could be carried out only by starting from the basic reality of present colonial domination.

Even when later anthropologists began to refer to the colonial presence as part of the local structure they generally did so in such a way as to obscure the systematic character of colonial domination and to mask the fundamental contradictions of interest inherent in the system of Indirect Rule.[14] The role of new political-economic forces brought about by European colonialism (labelled "Social Change") were usually not thought to be directly relevant to an understanding of the dynamic of African political structures operating within the colonial system of Indirect Rule (labelled "Political Anthropology").

With regard to the orientalist's view of typical Islamic political rule there are several negative features I want to point to. The first is that no serious attempt was made until relatively recently[15] to

[13]M. Fortes and E. E. Evans-Pritchard, *op. cit.,* p. 1.
[14]For example L. A. Fallers in his well-known study of the Basoga of Uganda, *Bantu Bureaucracy,* (Cambridge, 1956) focuses on the way in which "co-existence in a society of corporate lineages with political institutions of the state type [introduced by the colonial government] makes for strain and instability" (p. 17)—an essentially Parsonian problem. He is not concerned with the colonial system as such, but with role conflicts inherent in the positions of African headman and civil-servant chief, and European District officers.
[15]An example is I. Lapidus's excellent monograph *Muslim Cities in the Later Middle Ages,* Cambridge, Mass., 1967.

explore in detail the process of mutual accommodation between
Islamic rulers and their subjects—as noted, surprisingly enough, by
Gibb, who has been so ready elsewhere to project the orientalist's
image of Islamic rule:

> We know, in fact, exceedingly little of the inner relations between
> the government and the people... It can scarcely be doubted
> that government, in its administrative aspect, was not merely
> a set of forms imposed upon the people by the will of the
> conqueror, but an organism intimately associated with the
> structure of society and the character and ideas of the
> governed, and that there was a constant interplay between
> governors and governed. It is necessary to clear the ground of
> the misconceptions engendered by the abuse of European terms
> such as despotism and autocracy, and to submit all the
> traditional organs and usages of government to re-examination,
> in order to bring out the underlying ideas and relations, and the
> principles which guided their working.[16]

But something that we do know a little about is the populist tradition in Muslim societies as expressed in the repeated popular revolts[17] deriving their legitimation from Islamic ideology, as well as
in the popular distrust of aristocratic institutions[18] (which is by no
means the same thing as "oriental cynicism in relation to political
life"). Most orientalists have tended to see these revolts as evidence
of disorder and decay rather than as the re-affirmation of a populist
tradition in Islamic politics.[19] Why, instead of emphasising disorder
and repression and explaining this by reference to an intrinsic flaw
in Islamic political theory (usually invidiously contrasted with
Greek and Christian political theory) did orientalists not attempt
to account for the continuing vitality of a populist tradition within
changing socio-economic circumstances? More important, why,

---

[16]H. A. R. Gibb and H. Bowen, *Islamic Society and the West*, Vol. I, Part
I, London, 1950, p. 9.
[17]Arab historiography from Tabari to Jabarti is full of information on these
revolts. Useful summaries of revolts in the early period of Islam are available in W. Montgomery Watt, *Islam and the Integration of Society*, London, 1961. For a work on working-class organisation and rebellion in
medieval urban Islamic society, see C. Cahen, *Mouvement Populaires et
Autonomisme Urbain dans l'Asie Musulmane du Moyen Age*, Leiden, 1961.
But in both works there is little discussion of the dialectical relationship
between political-economic experience and ideological response—although
Montgomery Watt makes some attempt in that direction.
[18]This point is interestingly made by M. G. S. Hodgson, "Islam and Image",
in *History of Religions*, Vol. II, Winter, 1964.
[19]See E. Abrahamian, "The Crowd in Iranian Politics 1905-1953" (*Past and
Present*, no. 41, 1968) for an attempt at describing the active rationality of

when generalising about the essence of Islamic political rule, did orientalists not recognise that their textual sources represented the particular moral stance of a mobile class of religious literati-cum-merchants with a need for political orderliness in particular periods of great social upheaval? Finally, why did orientalists make no attempt to analyse the way in which developing class relations within late medieval Islam were affected by its changing commercial position vis-a-vis Europe and Asia (especially under the impact of European mercantilism) and the significance of such developments for relations between Islamic rulers and their subjects?[20]

**IV**

Despite the great differences in the images I have been talking about, one pre-disposition that both disciplines appear to have shared is the reluctance to talk explicitly and systematically about the implications of European development for the political systems of non-European societies. There are other parallels also, in the orientation of the two disciplines, to which I now turn.

The functional anthropologist stressed consent and legitimacy as important elements in the political systems of relatively small homogeneous ethnic groups in Africa whose history was assumed in most cases to be inaccessible, and which were seen and represented as integrated systems. In general he equated empirical work with fieldwork, and therefore tended to define the theoretical boundaries of the system under investigation in terms of practical fieldwork. His interest in a-historical, 'traditional' systems (set within an imperial framework which was taken for granted) led him to emphasise the unifying function of common religious values and symbols, and of 'age-old' custom and obligations in the relationship between tribal rulers and ruled. Where the anthropologist was faced with available

political crowds in the modern Islamic world. (I am indebted to Peter Worsley for this reference.) "While European journalists have invariably portrayed oriental crowds as 'xenophobic mobs' hurling insults and bricks at Western embassies," observes Abrahamian, "local conservatives have frequently denounced them as 'social scum' in the pay of the foreign hand, and radicals have often stereotyped them as 'the people' in action. For all, the crowd has been an abstraction, whether worthy of abuse, fear, praise, or even of humour, but not a subject of study." (p. 184). It seems that sometimes there is little to distinguish the attitudes of European journalists from that of orientalists.
[20]Social and economic history of the Islamic world is in its infancy (see M. A. Cook (ed.), *Studies in the Economic History of the Middle East*, London, 1970)—an indication of the extent to which idealist explanations in terms of "the religious essence of Islam" have been in vogue among orientalists. This is not unrelated to the fact that orientalists have typically worked on composed literary texts and not in archives. See also R. Owen's

historical evidence relating to conquest—as among the Zulu and Ngoni of southern Africa, or among the Fulani-Hausa of Northern Nigeria—he was of course aware of the importance of force and repression in African political history. But the functionalist perspective made it difficult for him to absorb the full significance of such events into his analysis and so they were generally seen as preludes to the establishment of integrated on-going African political systems which constituted his principal object of enquiry. It is common knowledge that this mode of analysis in social anthropology derives from Durkheimian sociology, which never really developed an adequate framework for understanding historical political processes. The interesting thing is that for a long time the social anthropologist writing about African political systems felt no need to overcome these theoretical limitations. The role of force in the maintenance of African systems of political domination (or of the colonial system of which they were a part) received virtually no systematic attention. The primary focus was usually on the juridical definition of rights and duties between the chief and his subjects.[21]

At this point it should be noted that the orientalist's image of political rule in Islamic society covers a historical span of several hundred years, from the middle ages (the so-called formative period of Islam) until the eighteenth century—a period of economic development and decline, of conquests and dynastic wars, and rule by successive military elites, notably Mamluke and Ottoman. The orientalist, concerned to present a relatively coherent picture of typical rule for such an epoch, could scarcely leave the element of force unmentioned. But the interesting point is that the element of force is not only mentioned, it is made the defining feature of the total political picture, which is then sometimes contrasted with the

critical review of *The Cambridge History of Islam* in *The Journal of Interdisciplinary History* (in press).

[21]This is also true of Gluckman, who is usually cited as being one of the first anthropologists to have dealt directly with problems of force and conflict in traditional African societies. Gluckman's view of conflict has typically been a juristic, legalistic one, whence his particular interest in "discrepant and conflicting rules of succession" which he sees as the primary focus of traditional African rebellions" (See his Introduction to *Order and Rebellion in Tribal Africa*, London, 1963). For this reason he fails to make an analytic distinction between *'popular'* armed uprisings and *dynastic rivalries*. The question as to whether a particular internal military challenge against the state's authority is rooted in (actual or potential) class consciousness is more basic than the task of labelling it 'rebellion' or 'revolution'. His failure to appreciate this helps to explain why Gluckman paid no attention to the question of African popular rebellions against European colonial rule.

allegedly different character of political rule in Medieval Christendom. (The suggestion being that since Islamic society lacked a true conception of *political authority*, i.e., of political domination based on general consent, it was inevitable that force should play such a central role in the Islamic political order).[22]

The orientalist concerned to generalise was here faced with a theoretical problem with which the functional anthropologist has not been much troubled. For the anthropologist reared on a-historical Durkheimian sociology, society and polity were usually coterminous. The horizontal links of 'tribal society' were conveniently definable in terms of the vertical links (whether hierarchical or segmentary) of 'tribal political organisation'. But for the orientalist concerned with Islam there was hardly ever such a convergence after the de facto break up of the Abbasid Empire. So in his desire to characterise a distinctive 'Islamic society', on the basis of a considerable body of textual material relating to many eventful centuries, he is led to adopt a partly functionalist perspective: for the emphasis on the integrative role of Islam as a religion is reminiscent of the social anthropologist's treatment of the integrative function of 'tribal' religious values in many African political systems. Islamic history thus collapses into an essentialist synchrony, for much the same reasons as African history does in the hands of the functional anthropologist.

Since the orientalist is concerned by definition with 'a society' of much complexity, he must stress what may be called a form of horizontal integration: the fact that Muslims seemed bound together, despite their subjection to different secular rulers, by their common loyalty to Islam as a religious system—an Islam which was interpreted by, and indeed embodied in, an 'international' community of learned men—the ulama, the sufi shaikhs and so forth. This horizontal religious consensus is then opposed by the orientalist to a vertical political dissensus, in which "everything else is merely temporary and more or less forced accommodation to the whims of a changing constellation of political overlords". This contrast between an integrated Islamic society and a fragmented Islamic polity has encouraged orientalists to oppose the supposedly universal authority of the *sharia* (Islamic law) to the changing constellation of political regimes and practices, often accompanied by

---

[22] See Gibb in Proctor (ed.), *op. cit.*

violence—an opposition with which the medieval Muslim writers were themselves much preoccupied. In fact it may be argued that insofar as the modern orientalists can be said to have an explicit interpretive theory, this is largely quarried from the historically conditioned writings of the great medieval Muslim theorists—ibn Khaldun, Mawardi, ibn Taymiyya. The result is a remarkable blurring between historical object and interpreting subject.

My suggestion here is that ultimately the functional anthropologist and the orientalist were concerned with the same theoretical question: what holds society together? How is order achieved or destroyed? The former, viewing 'tribal' society as *defined* by (normative) polity, focussed on the consensual relations between African rulers and ruled. The latter, viewing sharia-defined society as *fragmented* by (secular) polity, focused on the repressive relations between Islamic rulers and ruled.

## V

I have been trying to argue that both functional anthropology and orientalism, by selecting certain phenomena, by not asking certain questions, by approaching history in a certain way, by taking the problem of social order as their basic theoretical concern, tended to project characteristic images of the political structure of the non-European societies they studied. I am now going to suggest that the historical formation of these European disciplines helps us understand better why the selection and omission occured as they did.

What I want to emphasise here is this: that in contrast to the modern discipline of Islamic orientalism, functional anthropology was born *after* the advent of European colonialism in the societies studied—after, that is, the First World War when the *Pax Britannica* had made intensive and long-term fieldwork a practicable proposition.

Tribal rulers could be viewed as representative partly because the anthropologist in the field coming from a crisis-ridden Europe, experienced them as conforming to 'traditional' political norms (as these had come to be underwritten by a paternalist colonial administration). Colonial ideology generally stressed the essential continuity, and therefore the integrity, of African political cultures under colonial rule. The anthropologist, it may be argued, was prepared to accept the total colonial system (while quarrelling with particular colonial policies in relation to 'his tribe') because he was impressed by its obvious success in maintaining itself and in securing an apparently benign form of local order within the ethnic

group he observed so intimately. He was concerned, as the European administrators for their own reasons were equally concerned,
with protecting subordinate African cultures, and was therefore
prepared to accept the colonial definition of African polities, and to
restate that definition in terms of consent. (Consider to what extent
this image has begun to break down with decolonisation in the '60s.)
   The point is that unlike nineteenth century anthropology, the
objectification of functional anthropologists occured within the
context of *routine colonialism*, of an imperial structure of power
already established rather than one in process of vigorous expansion
in which political force and contradiction are only too obvious.
   Orientalism belongs to a different historical moment, and its
methods, assumptions and pre-occupations are rooted in the European experience of Islam prior to the advent of Western colonialism
in the Middle East. Among the cultural forebears of the modern
orientalists were the medieval Christian polemicists who sought to
defend the values of Christendom against the threat of Islam.[23]
Although modern orientalists rarely engage in overt propaganda,
and have adopted a more secular and detached tone, they have still
been concerned to contrast Islamic society and civilisation with their
own, and to show in what the former has been lacking. In particular,
they have been concerned to emphasise the absence of 'liberty',
'progress' and 'humanism' in classic Islamic societies, and in general
to relate the reasons for this alleged absence to the religious essence
of Islam.[24] Thus in contrast to the social anthropologist whose intention has often been to show that the rationality of African cultures is comprehensible to (and therefore capable of being accommodated by) the West, the orientalist has been far more occupied
with emphasising the basic irrationality of Islamic history.
   Norman Daniel, in his valuable study *Islam, Europe and Empire*,

[23]See N. Daniel, *Islam and the West, The Making of an Image*, Edinburgh,
1960; and R. W. Southern, *Western Views of Islam in the Middle Ages*,
Cambridge, Mass., 1962.
[24]Thus the influential orientalist von Grunebaum: "It is essential to realise
that Muslim civilisation is a cultural entity that does not share our primary
aspirations. It is not vitally interested in analytical self-understanding, and
it is even less interested in the structural study of other cultures, either as
an end in itself or as a means toward clearer understanding of its own
character and history. If this observation were to be valid merely for contemporary Islam, one might be inclined to connect it with the profoundly
disturbed state of Islam, which does not permit it to look beyond itself
unless forced to do so. But as it is valid for the past as well, one may
perhaps seek to connect it with the basic antihumanism of this civilisation,
that is, the determined refusal to accept man to any extent whatever as
the arbiter or the measure of things, and the tendency to be satisfied with

(Edinburgh, 1966) has traced the European experience of Islam—
and especially of the aggressive Ottoman Empire of the sixteenth
and seventeenth centuries—which helped to fashion its image of the
tyrannical Islamic polity in the nineteenth century. He suggests that
the three most important elements in this experience were fear of
Turkish power, the absence of a Muslim gentry and the subordinate
position of Muslim women. "To the mind of aristocratic Europe",
Daniel writes, "tyranny was common to all three—to the external
threat, to a polity internally servile and to an enslavement of
women. As time passed,. there was increasing communication with
eastern countries and gradually, as the centres of power in the
world shifted, fear gave way to patronage". (p. 11). But the image
of a tyrannical Ottoman structure, as Daniel goes on to show,
remained unquestioned throughout the nineteenth century, and became reinforced through the special notion of Islamic misrule—in
the double sense of inefficient government and fiscal oppression
(both, he might have added, grave sins in the eyes of a self-con-
sciously progressive capitalist Europe).

It was towards the end of the nineteenth century on the eve of
massive imperial expansion, that the foundations of modern orientalism were laid.[25] The literary, philological method of his study
(based on chronicles and treatises acquired from Islamic countries
and deposited in European libraries) meant that the orientalist had
little need for direct contact with the people whose historical culture
he objectified, and no necessary interest in its continuity. In so far
as he addressed himself to the contemporary condition of Islamic
peoples, he saw in it a reflection of his idealist vision of Islamic
history—repression, corruption and political decay.

Most members of the European middle classes before the First
World War viewed the imperialist ambitions of their governments
as natural and desirable.[26] In keeping with these attitudes the opinions that prevailed among them regarding prospective or recent
victims of colonial conquest were usually highly unflattering. This

truth as the description of mental structures, or, in other words, with
psychological truth." *Modern Islam,* Berkeley and Los Angeles, 1962, p. 40.
For an extremely interesting response by a Muslim intellectual see Moham-
med Arkoun, "L'Islam moderne vu par le professeur G. E. von Grunebaum" in *Arabica,* vol. xl, 1964.
[25]Cf. C. J. Adams, "Islamic Religion" (Part I), in *Middle East Studies Association Bulletin,* vol. 4, no. 3, October 15, 1970, p. 3.
[26]Cf. H. Gollwitzer, *Europe in the Age of Imperialism: 1880-1914,* London,
1969. For a study of British public opinion in relation to events preceding
the British occupation of Egypt in 1882, see H. S. Deighton's excellent
article, "The Impact on Egypt on Britain", in P. M. Holt, (ed.), *Political*

was as true of Asia as it was of Africa in the latter half of the nineteenth century.[27] In this period, influential writers such as Ranke
and Burkehardt, Count Gobineau and Renan, although in disagreement on important matters, were significantly united in their con-
temptuous views of Islam.[28] In this respect, their perspective was
not profoundly different from that of the founders of modern orientalism—e.g. Wellhausen and Nöldeke,[29] Becker and Snouck Hurgronje.[30] It would have been surprising had it been otherwise.
Leone Caetani, an Italian aristocrat, was exceptional among orientalists in condemning European colonial expansion into Islamic
countries.[31] In his commitment to empire and the White Man's
Burden, Snouck Hurgronje was far more typical.[32]

The orientalist's image of repressive relations between Islamic
rulers and their subjects is thus rooted not only in the historic
Christian experience of aggressive Islam (an experience the West
had never had in relation to Africa),[33] but more importantly in the
bourgeois European evaluation of 'unprogressive' and 'fanatical'
Islam that required to be directly controlled for reasons of empire.

As recent rulers of vast Muslim populations, the imperialist rulers
could attempt to legitimise their own governing position with arguments supplied by the orientalists: that Islamic rule has historically
been oppressive rule (colonial rule is by contrast humane), that
Islamic political theory recognises the legitimacy of the effective
*de facto* ruler (colonial rule is manifestly better than the corruption,
inefficiency and disorder of pre-colonial rule), that political domination in Muslim lands is typically external to the essential articulation of Islamic social and religious life (therefore no radical damage
has been done to Islam by conquering it as its central political
tradition remains unbroken).[34]

It is therefore at this ideological level, I would suggest, that the

and *Social Change in Modern Egypt*, London, 1968.
[27]Cf. V. G. Kiernan, *The Lords of Human Kind*, London, 1969, and the
documentary collection edited by P. D. Curtin, *op. cit.*
[28]Cf. J. W. Fück, "Islam as an Historical Problem in European Historiography Since 1800" in B. Lewis and P. M. Holt, (eds.), *Historians of the
Middle East*, London, 1962.
[29]J. W. Fück, *op. cit.*
[30]Cf. J.—J. Waardenburg, *L'Islam dans le miroir de l'occident*, The Hague,
1962.
[31]J. W. Fück, *op. cit.* For further details on Prince Caetani, see A. Bausani,
"Islamic Studies in Italy in the XIX-XX cc." in *East and West*, vol. VIII,
1957.
[32]With respect to Holland's colonial role in Indonesia, Snouck Hurgronje
wrote: "Il ne s'agit que d'eveiller une prise de conscience...considerant que
l'independance de la vie spirituelle et la libération de son développment de

two objectifications of political rule again converge. For the orientalist's construct, by focusing on a particular image of the Islamic tradition, and the anthropologist's, by focusing on a particular image of the African tradition, both helped to justify colonial domination at particular moments in the power encounter between the West and the Third World. No doubt, this ideological role was performed by orientalism and by functional anthropology largely unwittingly. But the fact remains that by refusing to discuss the way in which bourgeois Europe had imposed its power and its own conception of the just political order on African and Islamic peoples, both disciplines were basically reassuring to the colonial ruling classes.

de toute pression matérielle est l'une des plus grandes bénédictions de notre civilisation. Nous nous sentons pousses par un zèle missionaire de la meilleure sorte afin de faire participer le monde musulman à cette satisfaction." This was what ultimately justified colonialism: "Notre domination doit se justifier par l'accession des indigènes a une civilisation plus élevée. Ils doivent acquérir parmi les peuples sous notre direction la place que méritent leurs qualités naturelles." Quoted in J.—J. Waardenburg, op. cit., pp. 101 and 102. See also W. F. Wertheim, "Counter-insurgency research at the turn of the century—Snouck Hurgronje and the Acheh War", in Sociologische Gids, vol. XIX, September/December 1972. (I am grateful to Ludowik Brunt for this last reference.)

[33]For a discussion about the various elements that went into the making of European views about Africa at the end of the eighteenth century and the first half of the nineteenth, see P. D. Curtin, The Image of Africa, London, 1965. According to Curtin this earlier image was on the whole far more favourable than the one prevalent in the latter part of the nineteenth century—i.e. on the eve of the Partition of Africa.

[34]The orientalist's image is still very much alive and still rooted in a structure of sentiments remarkably akin to that displayed by the founders. ("Although there are exceptions," observes C. J. Adams in his survey article, "in the cases of individuals or particular fields of study (Sufism, for example, or Islamic Art and Architecture), to be sure, on the whole one is struck with the negative tone—or if negative be too strong a word, with the tone of personal disenchantment—that runs through the majority of [orientalist] writing about Muslim faith." Op. cit., p. 3). I attribute this persistence to the fact that despite profound changes in the world since the late nineteenth century, the power encounter between the West and the Muslim countries continues to express itself typically in the form of hostile confrontations (for reasons too involved to discuss here) and the methods and techniques of orientalism as a discipline, with its basic reliance on philological analysis, remain unaffected. These facts and not mere 'excellence' account for the continuity noted by Adams: "In fact, basic nineteenth-century Islamic scholarship was so competent and exhaustive that it has intimidated many later scholars from attempting re-examinations of fundamental issues. Much of what the pioneers of Islamology wrote has scarcely been improved upon, not to say superseded; it has merely been transmitted and continues to be the most authoritative scholarship we possess in many fields." (loc. cit.). Of how many other historical or social science disciplines can such a statement be made?

# Part 2: Case Studies

# SOCIAL ANTHROPOLOGY AND INDIRECT RULE. THE COLONIAL ADMINISTRATION AND ANTHROPOLOGY IN EASTERN NIGERIA: 1920-1940.

## Helen Lackner

Any attempt to look at the role anthropologists could play at present and in coming years should, it seems to me, start by analysing the history and development of anthropology since its origin as a separate discipline. Going back to the records of the 1930s and 1940s, it becomes clear that the concern of anthropology was then to be of use, directly or indirectly, to the colonial administration; that, therefore, anthropologists then saw their work as relevant to the world they lived in. When we now read these books, many of which are classics, we should be aware of the context in which they were written and read them in this light.

I cannot pretend to cover this vast field, or to analyse the history and the theory of anthropology; I merely wish to look in some detail at a few problems and to suggest some directions towards which further research could be directed. This is a very tentative and fragmentary attempt at examining the development of social anthropology in Eastern Nigeria during a period of considerable political agitation, which was also a time when British social anthropology was expanding vastly in cooperation with the policies of the colonial administration; anthropology was being accepted by colonialism and anthropologists were being employed by the administration.

Within the theoretical and historical framework that is here broadly outlined, this study may contribute a further element towards explaining the emergence of Biafran Nationalism, by showing

[1]A first draft of this paper was presented as a dissertation to London University in 1971.

how the administrative system during the colonial period systematically exacerbated all possible contradictions between the pre-colonial structure of the South East and the forms of administration imported from the North whose pre-colonial political system was in contrast with that of the south; the hierarchical authoritarian structure of the North was the model for indirect rule in the Ibo area which was acephalous and fragmented. These contradictions were systematically made worse throughout the Colonial period and continued under the neo-colonialist administration that took over after "Independence" in 1960. It would be interesting to do more research on this point. This might show how artificial "borders" created  by imperialism and the forms of administration within them have affected pre-colonial nations, either by "integrating" them into wider frameworks (Biafra in Nigeria) or by splitting them between many states, (Manding in West Africa); such problems raised by colonial policies bring up the National question. It is worth finding out what role, if any, was played by anthropological studies in the determination of these policies.

**The Creation of "Nigeria".**
The end of the legitimate slave trade (1807) in Nigeria meant very radical changes in the trading pattern. The British continued to trade with the same people, but the commodities were now palm-oil and ivory. After 1886, the trade was monopolised by the Royal Niger Company, which, after the 1885 Berlin Conference had acknowledged Britain's claim to the area, was given power by Britain "to administer, make treaties, levy customs and trade in all territories in the basin of the Niger and its affluents".[2] At that time, the Delta was declared "The Oil Rivers Protectorate" (1885). Over the next few years, Britain extended her control over the area through traders and the establishment of consuls; when, in 1893, the Protectorate was extended to the hinterland, the whole area was renamed the Niger Coast Protectorate and in 1900 it became the Protectorate of Southern Nigeria. Meanwhile Lagos had been annexed as a colony in 1861 and in 1906 was amalgamated with the South to become the Colony and Protectorate of Southern Nigeria. The North had in 1900 become the Protectorate of Northern Nigeria when the British Government took over from the Royal Niger Company. In 1914 Lugard amalgamated the two areas to form the Colony and Protectorate of Nigeria.
The way in which this country was formed was due far more to

[2]J. S. Coleman: *Nigeria, Background to Nationalism*, p. 41.

external than to internal pressures. By the time of amalgamation
"Nigeria" was an artificial entity with no internal cohesion on which
to base a unified state: the North was composed of centralised
Islamic Emirates whose organisation had given rise to Lugard's
Indirect Rule and the South East was made up of the remnants of
the former decentralised trading States whose very structures had
been destroyed by the British[3]. The areas had previously been administered in different ways because British interests in the North
and the South were divergent. Most of the country had been taken
over during the Scramble: pressure on Britain's trade from France
and Germany tilted the balance in favour of those forces in Britain
who supported full-scale colonisation; this indicated the defeat of
those who believed that trade was possible without necessarily
being accompanied by occupation and administration of territory.

Despite amalgamation the North and the South remained separate entities and were administered as distinct provinces; the unification of administration was a slow and unthought process:

Although the broad principles of the native administration
system were slowly extended from the north to the south, the
different policies and conceptions of colonial administration
which had evolved in each of the two Protectorates during the
fourteen years of their separate existence continued to dominate
official thought and action[4].

Previous to amalgamation more thought had been given to the
administration of the North than to that of the South. This meant that
later, the higher ranks of the administration in the united Nigeria
were dominated by officers whose main experience and allegiance
was to the North and who were unaware of the fundamental differences between the North and the South. Such men decided on policies for the South and, not surprisingly they made some decisions
which had unsatisfactory results.

What were the main events in British Nigeria between amalgamation and the Second World War?

The first Governor was Sir Frederick Lugard (1914-19) who introduced to the South a version of Indirect Rule modelled on that
operating in the North: Native Courts and Native Authorities were
introduced in the South in 1914 and 1916 respectively. Lugard
wanted to unify the administration of the country by creating the

[3]For an excellent account of the history of the Niger Delta in the pre-
British period, see K. O. Dike: *Trade and Politics in the Niger Delta
1830-1885.*
[4]J. S. Coleman, *ibid.,* p. 46.

same institutions everywhere. Apart from the two just mentioned, he immediately proceeded to investigate the possibilities for the introduction of direct taxation in the South. This proved feasible in some parts, but seemed inadvisable in the East, because of what the Administration termed the "backwardness" of the Ibo.

The next Governor, Sir Hugh Clifford (1919-25) had a different interpretation of "Indirect Rule" from Lugard's and spent his time consolidating institutions rather than introducing new ones. During his term of office, the situation in the East was investigated, because, at that time already, it seemed clearly unsatisfactory[5]. The report made many recommendations which at that time were not implemented but were returned to ten years later after the Women's War. In 1925 Sir Graeme Thomson succeeded Clifford and without much consultation, decided to extend direct taxation in the East in the form of a poll tax to be levied on adult males. Assessment of the population for tax was begun in 1927 and caused fewer disturbances than had been expected. However many precautions were taken in 1928 when the tax was to be collected for the first time. The Government had concentrations of troops and police everywhere in case of need. In fact that year the tax was collected with little difficulty. But before the Government had found time to congratulate itself on such a success, things went wrong.

In 1929, which was a bad year in many ways, the slump started affecting the palm-oil prices, and thus the general standard of living in the East. It was also becoming apparent to the people that the introduction of taxation had brought few if any benefits, despite the claims made by the Administration in their pre-taxation propaganda. A rumour developed in the East that women were also to be taxed and this was confirmed when one particular Warrant Chief Okugo counted women and children when assessing his area. This incident started off what came to be known as the "Women's War" or the "Aba Riots", in which thousands of women in the East fought the Administration[6]. They were primarily concerned with the destruction of the Native Courts and the Warrant Chief system,

---

[5]See the Reports by Grier and Tomlinson in 1922 and 1923 on Policy in the Eastern Region.
[6]The most detailed published account of the Women's War is in M. Perham, *Native Administration in Nigeria*, pp. 206-220. The Report of the Second Commission of Enquiry gives enormous amounts of detailed information on what happened, how and why; it is by far the most comprehensive document on the subject. "Report of the Commission of Enquiry appointed to inquire into the disturbances in the Calabar and Owerri provinces, December 1929", *Sessional Paper no. 28 of 1930*, Government of Nigeria.

totally foreign institutions which had been imposed on the area regardless of local traditions. The women protested against taxation and the fall in palm-oil prices. The war lasted almost three weeks and the Government had to call in troops to bring it to an end. They shot and killed large numbers of women. This event considerably affected the Colonial Administration and its officials were thoroughly shocked by it. First, it was an indication of the total failure of the policies they had adopted to administer the area and thus demanded radical changes in outlook. Second, a long-lasting revolt by thousands of WOMEN (anywhere) who moreover were neither accompanied nor led by men was a totally unheard of and outrageous phenomenon for a colonial Government, a male chauvinist institution *par excellence*; it therefore called for urgent investigation to ensure that such an outrage be not repeated. Two Commissions of Enquiry were set up to discover the causes of the war and to make recommendations, the second of which went thoroughly into the background of these events. The contradictions which were brought to light by the Women's War are directly relevant to the theme of this study:—the dogmatic introduction of Indirect Rule from the North into the area without any previous attempt at either estimating its suitability or adapting it to the specific conditions of the South-East;—the total ignorance of the Ibo's social, political and economic structures. The discovery of all these failures induced the government to develop its interest in anthropological studies. We shall first look at the problematic of Indirect Rule and its development in Nigeria.

**Indirect Rule**
Indirect Rule as a form of colonial administration arose as an answer to a combination of factors. The British were faced with the problem of administering vast expanses of conquered territories throughout the planet with little money (because London's colonial policy at that period refused to spend much on administration) and few men. Added to this, their previous experience in India had been in centralised societies, ruled more or less autocratically by princes.

Northern Nigeria fitted easily into the pattern since it was composed of Islamic Emirates, with Emirs who had considerable authority and a clear hierarchy: on the surface therefore local social organisation seemed quite suited to Indirect Rule. Having conquered the Emirates, Lugard was well aware of this and it allowed him to introduce Indirect Rule in Africa. He determined a policy described as follows by Lord Hailey:

On the one hand, the Emirs were given Letters of Appointment which made it clear that they were not regarded as possessing sovereign powers, and that they were to obey the laws of Nigeria. 'The policy of Government was that these Chiefs should govern their people not as independent but dependent rulers.' In the terms subsequently used, their status was to be that of Wakils or Governors, exercising only such jurisdiction as might be conferred on them by law. On the other hand, when in 1903 the territory was divided into 14 Provinces, the Residents in charge of them were told that their duty was to act as advisers to the Emirs, not to usurp their functions.[7]

Lugard is regarded as the initiator of Indirect Rule or Native Administration, and after Amalgamation in 1914 he imported it lock stock and barrel to the South. This had disastrous effects to which we will return. But let us now look at the controversy about Lugard's concept of Native Administration.

One of his most virulent critics says "one can see that Lugard's idea of rule was simple autocratic rule from himself downwards"[8]; in his book Nicolson portrays a dictatorial ambitious man primarily concerned with his own political advancement, with little interest in the welfare of those whom he administered. He gives the impression that what we know as Lugard's Indirect Rule system, was nothing more than a channel for his own decisions to be transmitted to the people and implemented by them. Whatever the case may be, Lugard's ideas were not followed precisely by his successors, and while he saw Indirect Rule as a way to transmit orders through the people's traditional rulers, his successors saw it as the government of colonial subjects through their own institutions. Lugard saw it as a form of Local Government that would be a medium for the introduction of radical changes in the society:

> However, many of Lugard's successors followed a policy of minimal interference in the process of local government, preferring to let the traditional political institutions develop along their own lines rather than along lines laid down or suggested by the European administrator. In its extreme forms such a policy came close to a Protectorate or 'Native States' policy, whilst that of Lugard, in its extreme forms, came close to Paternalism.

Lugard's policy can be characterised as *Interventionist* Indirect

[7]Lord Hailey, *Native Administration in the British African Territories*, Part III, West Africa, Nigeria, London, H.M.S.O. p. 48.
[8]I. F. Nicholson, *The Administration of Nigeria 1900-1960*, O.U.P. 1969, p. 137

Rule, that of his successors, *Non-Interventionist* Rule.[9]
In fact what came to be known as Indirect Rule in Africa was the system of Colonial Administration first applied by the British in Nigeria. There was no elaborated set of principles to guide administrators, no "Guide to Indirect Rule"; Indirect Rule usually developed as a policy from decisions taken empirically. Its practice demanded that it be "theorized" and we are now looking at the ideology of this form of administration as it was developed by its practitioners, mainly servants of the Colonial Administration at all levels of the hierarchy.

As seen by Lugard's successors, Indirect Rule meant that:
the European colonial powers should govern their African subjects through their own political institutions. Here it is very necessary to emphasise that Indirect Rule, at least in theory, did not mean government of African peoples through their chiefs. In practice, Indirect Rule laid heavy emphasis on the role of the chief in the government of African peoples, even for those peoples who traditionally did not have political as distinct from religious leaders.[10]

As it was first introduced in the North of Nigeria, Indirect Rule was a very successful system of administration. This was due mainly to the already very hierarchised organisation of the Emirates which were autocratic and were thus good vehicles for the administration, as it thought it could add a new level at the top of the hierarchy and the system would continue to operate. However the notion that Indirect Rule allowed the traditional system to develop along its own lines is obviously a mystification. It was clearly impossible for the colonial administration to use the native system without distorting it, since any system operates to bring about certain ends, and the aims of the British were clearly different from those of the previous system; therefore the dynamic had been changed. Administrators seemed to be unaware that the "changes" they demanded would induce a thorough disruption of the original political system and destroy its base. As Crowder put it:
The use of indigenous political institutions for the purposes of local government was contingent on certain modifications to these institutions. These modifications fell into two categories: modifications of aspects of traditional Government that were repugnant to European ideas of what constituted good government;

[9]M. Crowder, *West Africa Under Colonial Rule*, London 1968, p. 169.
[10]*Ibid.*, p. 169.

and modifications that were designed to ensure the achievement
of the main purpose of colonial rule, the exploitation of the colonised country. Examples of the former would be the abolition of
human sacrifice or the abandonment of certain methods of treating criminals. Examples of the latter would be the introduction
of taxes, designed to stimulate production of cash crops for
export.[11]
It is precisely because the British Government's aims and interests
were different from those of the traditional systems that they found
it necessary to impose basic changes in the traditional system. Different economic and political interests could not fail to change the
ideology of the ruling structure. This is very clear in cases like that
of land tenure (in the traditional system there is no private ownership of land, because ultimate ownership is the prerogative of the
ancestors, gods or whatever, whereas after British occupation, land
became just another object of investment). The ideological basis of
the traditional system has been destroyed. This has been put very
well by Rattray:

> In introducing indirect rule into this country, we would therefore
> appear to be encouraging on the one hand an institution which
> draws its inspiration and validity from the indigenous religious
> beliefs, while on the other hand we are destroying the very foun-
> dation upon which the structure we are striving to perpetuate
> stands. Its shell and outward form might remain, but it would
> seem too much to expect that its vital energy could survive such
> a process.[12]

Indirect rule was, within its own limits, quite successful in the
Northern Emirates, because of the hierarchical nature of the tradi-
tional system. But what happened in the South? As far as the
South-West is concerned, success was limited, due to the fact that:

> Although fairly strong traditional authorities were in power in
> that area, the kings (obas) were ultimately accountable to, if not
> the mouthpieces for, councils of hereditary title holders and rep-
> resentatives of societies. The idea of direct taxation was only
> slowly and reluctantly accepted.[13]

The real problems however appeared in the South-East. Unlike
the North, which previous to colonisation had been hierarchised and
centralised, the political organisation of the South-Eastern Ibo area

[11]*Ibid.*, p. 169.
[12]R. S. Rattray, *Ashanti Law and Constitution,* London 1929, p. ix.
[13]J. S. Coleman, *ibid.*, p. 51.

had been decentralised and small scale. The village had been the political unit, and political "authority" articulated through mass meetings; chiefs and council elders occupied merely presidential functions and were invested with no executive power. Other forms of organisation such as age-grades, secret societies, and women's organisations could if necessary act to counter any decision.

The first steps towards the introduction of indirect rule in the South-East had been the setting up of Native Courts in 1914 and Native Authorities in 1916, these measures had been taken to put Lugard's principles into application. These institutions bore no relation to the traditional political system. Very early on, this form of administration was seen to be an abysmal failure. Clifford, in 1919 immediately suggested that it be investigated. This investigation produced the reports by Grier and Tomlinson in 1922 and 1923, summarised thus by Crowder:

> Indirect Rule had been an almost total failure. Despite superficial trappings, the area was in fact administered directly. The warrant chiefs were exceedingly unpopular with the people and were backed up by little, if any, traditional authority. They were generally corrupt. Worse still, the native courts, the main agencies for British Administration, were deeply resented. The court clerks and court messengers abused their positions of power so blatantly that they were described in the report as 'licensed libertines'.[14]

Despite the very early awareness of the failure of this system, and the recommendations made by Grier and Tomlinson no steps were taken. Among their recommendations were some relating to investigation of traditional institutions but no changes were made and the system was maintained. When in 1926, Governor Thomson decided to introduce direct taxation into the area, those were the channels used. Direct taxation was seen by Thomson in Lugardian terms:

> 'without a tax there can be no treasury and without a treasury no real eventual measure of self rule' (Lugard: The Dual Mandate) . . . it must be clearly understood that the present proposals are not primarily inspired by financial considerations.[15]

In the same document Ruxton, the Lieutenant Governor of the Southern Provinces says that the:

> chief reason for introducing taxation is an administrative one: there can be no true advance without direct taxation and no pro-

[14]M. Crowder, The Story of Nigeria, 1962, p. 231.
[15]Colonial Office, Correspondence, November 1926, file X811-.

gress in self-government without experience in controlling at least a part of the revenue locally raised. Moreover, to tax 18 provinces and to leave 6 untaxed for no avowable reason must have an ill-effect on both the taxed and the untaxed.[16] Thus the introduction of direct taxation was seen to be an essential concomitant of indirect rule, and in this case, it demonstrated the bankruptcy of the system. This was revealed by the Women's War, which was directed as much against the Native Courts and the Warrant Chiefs as against taxation as such.

It was only after 1930, that the problems of Indirect Rule in the South were seriously faced by the colonial administration. The Report of the Commission of Enquiry into the Aba Riots emphasised the importance for government to be familiar with native institutions. This was given official sanction when Lord Passfield, then Secretary of State for the Colonies, wrote:

> The need for further enquiry into the social organisation of the inhabitants of the South-Eastern Provinces naturally suggests the question to what extent the services of investigators trained in anthropological science has been, and may still be profitably employed . . . I propose to take steps to improve and increase the amount of instruction in anthropology imparted to newly-appointed administrative officers who are busily engaged in the work of administration to carry out anthropological research of great value.[17]

It is now becoming clear how, in the understanding of top-level administrators, the failure of Indirect Rule in South-Eastern Nigeria was seen to be directly related to lack of knowledge of local conditions and Ibo social Organisation. Lord Passfield's recognition of the use of anthropologists seems to be a good starting point for a more careful look at the colonial government's attitude towards anthropologists. We will later attempt to examine the dynamics of the relationship between indirect rule and British School social anthropology.

**The Colonial Office's View of Anthropology**
Throughout the colonial period, the Colonial Office had a most am-

[16]*Ibid.*
[17]Despatch from the Secretary of State for the Colonies to the officer administering the Government of Nigeria regarding the Report of the Commission of Inquiry into the Disturbances at Aba and other places in South-Eastern Nigeria in November and December 1929, *Cmd 3784, of 1931.*

biguous attitude towards anthropologists, at times wanting to hire them and at other times maintaining that the work could be done just as well by political officers. They wavered in a similar manner over the value of anthropological work as such.

In the correspondence arising out of the Aba Commission Report[18] the whole issue of the employment of anthropologists was thoroughly debated in the Colonial Office. The survey goes back to the employment of Northcote Thomas and also discusses contemporary issues.

The memorandum on the employment of Northcote Thomas, compared to the letters discussing the problem in 1930, shows that the terms of the debate had not changed, even though the outcome had. In the first decade of the century the Lugardian anti-anthropologist faction won and the anthropologist was dismissed; in the late 1920s at the time of post-Lugardian Indirect Rule, under the influence of Clifford and more emphatically after the Aba Riots Report and Lord Passfield's despatch, anthropology was in high regard.

Let us look at Northcote Thomas's career: he was the first government anthropologist ever to be appointed, first in Nigeria in 1906 then in Sierra Leone where he was transferred in 1913. He wrote a six-volume "Report on the Ibo-speaking Peoples of Nigeria" published in 1913. The first and fourth volumes deal with "Law" in two Ibo areas, and the other volumes are concerned with languages and proverbs.

In 1930 a memorandum on the employment of Northcote Thomas was circulated in the Colonial Office by a Mr. Fiddian[19] who tells us that Northcote Thomas was appointed Government anthropologist in 1906 because it was felt that the information collected in a questionnaire sent to District officers was insufficient and it was necessary to have it studied and elaborated by an expert. Northcote Thomas spent three tours of service in the Ibo and Edo areas. In 1912, when the termination of his appointment was considered Mr. James, who opposed this suggestion, sent a report saying:

> there was no question of the ultimate value of anthropological
> work in connection with the problem of administering a country

---

[18]Colonial Office, *Correspondence arising out of the Aba Report, 1930-31*, file no. 1003.
[19]Colonial Office, *Ibid.*, Document E, Memorandum entitled "Appointment of an Anthropologist to West Africa" by Mr. Fiddian, dated 16 December, 1930.

like this, but he feared it was sometimes difficult to avoid over-
looking the ultimate benefits in view of the apparently small results achieved in actual practice in the early years of such work.[20]
The appointment was renewed, but when the question next came
up, it was handled by Lugard[21] who says in his report:

> I am, generally speaking, inclined to think that researches into
> native law and custom are best conducted by Political Officers
> and I have found that in Northern Rhodesia there is no lack of
> qualified officers who are deeply interested and quite capable of
> reproducing their work in book form . . . [22]

Lugard then recommends the termination of Thomas's appointment, and he is transferred to Sierra Leone. In the same memorandum Fiddian writes about the next developments in the administration concerning anthropology.

Governor Clifford had initially shown more interest in the workings of native institutions and had asked Grier and Tomlinson to
report on the state of Indirect Rule in the East from the point of
view of Native affairs. In 1923, Governor Clifford thought of:

> forming an anthropology department on the grounds that con-
> ditions in Nigeria were 'changing so rapidly that many things of
> great scientific value' were vanishing. It was not, apparently, pri-
> marily in Sir H. Clifford's view, a matter of direct interest to the
> administrative side. The Lieutenant-Governor, Southern Pro-
> vinces, and the Acting Lieutenant-Governor, Northern Provinces,
> expressed themselves strongly in favour of encouraging ethno-
> logical and anthropological research . . . (they were of the opin-
> ion . . . that scientific study of tribal origins and institutions is
> vital to successful administration, and that much valuable infor-
> mation was being lost for the want of collating and sifting by an
> expert hand.[23]

The plan for such a department was never implemented. There
were only however, reports such as Grier and Tomlinson's on the
administration of the East and local Residents' reports over the
period when the introduction of direct taxation was being planned.
These reports often emphasised the problem of the administration's

[20] Ibid.
[21] G. Leclerc, Anthropologie et Colonialisme (1972). His interpretation is that
Lugard supports the employment of anthropologists (see pp. 48-52). This
book will be discussed further in the conclusion. It is to be noted however,
that Leclerc, who uses Nigeria as his most precise and frequent illustration,
appears to interpret many points differently from me.
[22] Colonial Office, Ibid. Document E.
[23] Ibid.

ignorance of native affairs, as can be seen from the following report of 1928:
> I find no record of any attempt having been made to enquire into the native institutions and turn them to good account ... The first step to take ... is to make a thorough enquiry into the clan and town organisation throughout the province.[24]

The accumulation of problems in the East, combined with many reports similar to the one quoted above and the willingness of the upper ranks of the administration led in 1927 to the appointment of an anthropological officer in the South.[25] Despite this the debate went on in the Colonial Office about the value of anthropology. Commenting on the Fiddian memorandum another Colonial office administrator wrote in his minutes:
> With regard to the anthropologist, I am inclined to sit upon the fence ... The anthropologist is presumably a man with a scientific turn of mind. If he has not got the scientific turn of mind he is no use as an investigator. It does not always follow that a man of this kind will either fit in well with the administration or that he will render immediate assistance to them.[26]

His attitude is brought out quite clearly in his references to Northcote Thomas who, says Flood:
> was a recognised maniac in many ways. He wore sandals, even in this country, lived on vegetables, and was generally a rum person.[27]

Flood goes on to explain that clearly residents did not want:
> to have an object like that going about ... partly because he was calculated to bring a certain amount of discredit upon the white man's prestige.[28]

Commenting on this issue, Tomlinson writes:
> The need for further investigation makes me all the more inclined to agree with Mr. Fiddian about the importance of anthropologi-

[24]Colonial Office, *Correspondence, 1928,* file no. 183, para. 9. Report by W. E. Hunt, then Resident of Warri Province, dated 10.1.28.
[25]At this time also, local residents and all local administrative officers were first asked to write "Intelligence Reports" on the traditional institutions in their areas. These reports were regularly produced and finally, by the middle 1930s, they numbered in hundreds—199 in 1934 (see the *Annual Report* of the Government of Nigeria for 1934, p. 8). These reports were used in deciding on policies for the reorganisation of Native administration in the Eastern Province.
[26]Colonial Office, *Correspondence arising out of the Aba Commission Report, file no. 1003,* Document F by Flood, dated 19.12.30.
[27]*Ibid.*
[28]*Ibid.*

cal research. This does not necessarily mean that trained anthropologists should be brought in from the outside. There are plenty of officers already in the service who have received adequate anthropological training. The great thing is that their enquiries should not be conducted in the spirit of antiquarian research, but should be directed to those problems, i.e. to the problems presented by native society as a living and changing organism, which are of immediate practical importance to the Administrative Officer. What is meant is that they should be followers of the school of which such men as Professor Malinowski are the chief exponents.[29]

Governor Cameron was appointed in Nigeria at the height of the debate, when the Recommendations of the Commission of Enquiry were being discussed. Taking up the point made by Lord Passfield, in his Despatch, Cameron writes:

The work of tracing out native institutions has been done in the past, in both Nigeria and Tanganyika, very competently by administrative officers without any special anthropological training. The best use to which the anthropologist can be put in this connexion, in my judgment, is to place him at headquarters where he can study the reports rendered by officers engaged in the field on this class of investigation and direct them and guide them as to further avenues to be explored. For the most part the Anthropologist attached to the Southern Provinces is being utilized in this manner . . . [30]

This debate appears to be the most thorough one that took place in the Colonial office about anthropology. What emerges from it is that in the post-Lugardian period there was general agreement that knowledge of the native institutions was necessary for good administration. Disagreements were due to a split between those who thought that local political officers with a minimum of anthropological training could do the work just as well and those who believed in employing professional anthropologists. Finally a compromise was reached by increasing the anthropological training of all staff and by the appointment of anthropological offiers in the North and in the South.

Aside from the discussions in the Colonial Office itself, many discussions took place in milieus interested in colonial administra-

[29] *Ibid.* Document T Minute by Tomlinson, dated 3.1.31.
[30] Colonial Office, *Correspondence File no. 1056*, 1931; letter from Governor Cameron to Lord Passfield, dated 17.8.31.

tion. In 1934 Miss M. Perham gave a talk to the Royal Society of Arts on Indirect Rule in Africa.[31] In the discussion following the talk the problem of anthropologists was raised and similar points to those we have seen were put forward by academics as well as by administrators. Similarly in the pages of the J.RAI and *Man* the problem was discussed from the beginning of the century. We shall return to this later, but would just mention that *Man* saw fit to print in its pages Lord Lugard's "Address at the Reception to Dominions Premiers and Delegates to the Imperial Conference" (10 October, 1930) entitled "Anthropology and Administration"[32].

Lord Hailey's "African Survey", first published in 1938, which was intended as a guide on African affairs to all those concerned with the administration of colonies and with trade, has a whole section on "Studies in African Social life"[33]. This is a survey of the activities of anthropologists in Africa of the necessity for such studies, and of the possibilities of anthropological training. Lord Hailey maintains that professional anthropologists are necessary because they are best qualified to make full-time lengthy and detailed studies and he regrets the absence of direct support from Governments.

The administrative officer as an anthropological enquirer works under certain disadvantages. His relations with Africans are apt to be coloured by the fact that he represents the government . . . When . . . inquiries on specific subjects have to be undertaken . . . the government officer with a training in anthropological methods is likely to prove a successful investigator only provided that he is allowed to devote sufficient time to the purpose. The professional anthropologist should, however, be able to provide a more complete picture of native society, and, in areas where native institutions are least understood, he is likely to be of great assistance in providing the government with the knowledge which must form the basis of administrative policy. In general, it may be said that governments are likely to derive the greatest advantage from inquiries undertaken by anthropologists in association with their own technical or administrative officers.[34]

These ambiguities in the official section of opinion appear to have carried on throughout the Colonial period. Anthropologists on the

[31]*Journal of the Royal Society of Arts,* vol. LXXXII, 1934.
[32]*Man,* vol. 30, 1930.
[33]Lord Hailey, *An African Survey,* London 1938, pp. 40-67.
[34]*Ibid.,* pp. 47-8.

other hand had a much firmer line on their relationship with the
Administration; it is their position which we will examine in the
next section.

### Anthropologists from Administration to Academia

From the creation of the Royal Anthropological Institute until the
Second World War, anthropologists were interested in developing a
closer relationship with Colonial Administrations. This we will see
in the records mentioned in the J.RAI and *Man*. After 1945 a
definite shift towards academic distance and away from involvement
in politico-administrative affairs took place[35]; this can be seen by
the absence of any articles on the connection with administration
and in a much more academic tone in book-reviews and other
articles.

We will now look in more detail at the evolution of attitude as it
is reflected in the J.RAI and in *Man*. In 1896 the British Association passed the following resolution:

> that it is of urgent importance to press upon the government the
> necessity of establishing a Bureau of Ethnology for Great Britain,
> which by collecting information with regard to the native races
> within and on the borders of the Empire, will prove of immense
> value to science and to the Government itself.[36]

This project failed for lack of financial support, but a few years
later (in 1908) it was taken up again with the collaboration of the
RAI and got as far as a deputation to the Prime Minister, Asquith.
A memorial was presented to the Prime Minister[37] stressing that
administrators should have anthropological training, that anthropology is of direct relevance to administration and all matters concerning natives. In the discussion with the Prime Minister, great
emphasis was laid on the fact that anthropology is of great importance to traders who might, for lack of knowledge of local customs,
ruin their position, by behaving unsuitably or attempting to sell the
wrong things. The deputation quoted in this respect the example of
the Prussian Government who made a point of giving anthropological education to its traders, at great expense.[38] The main point was
to demonstrate the benefits to Government of using anthropologists:

---

[35]Leclerc thinks that after the war, anthropologists were very vocal about
their relationship to administration. I have found no evidence for this.
[36]Proceedings of the British Association, 1896, quoted in *J.RAI* vol. 59,
1929, p. 38.
[37]*J.RAI* vol. 38, 1908, pp. 489-92.
[38]*Man*, vol. IX 1909, p. 857.

It has long been felt by anthropologists that the study of anthropology possesses not merely a scientific interest but has also great
practical utility for the nation . . . From mere ignorance of local
habits and customs, travellers, missionaries and others not infrequently have provoked the natives instead of gaining their sympathy, and thus not only have nullified the results of costly expeditions, but also have caused political difficulties and compli-
cations.[39]

Indeed, from the beginning of the century onwards, the RAI was
emphasising at every opportunity the need for a closer relationship
with the government. The pages of its journal continuously reflect
this interest. In 1914 Sir R. Temple[40] gave a lecture to probationers
of the Indian Civil Service, entitled "The value of training in Anthropology for the administrator"; it is general and not particularly
enlightening in terms of anthropology but was printed in *Man*.[41]
Temple was in fact very active in trying to develop Anthropology
as an aid to administration. He was constantly encouraging the development of teaching departments and of Institutes; he chaired a
committee aimed at "devising practical measures for the organisation of anthropological teaching at the Universities . . . "[42]. At that
time there was already a move in favour of setting up an "Imperial
School of Applied Anthropology". This was formulated at a conference chaired by Lord Selborne and attended by representatives
of Government, University and Museum circles, at which the following resolution was passed :

That this Conference . . . is of the opinion that, in the highest
interests of the Empire, it is necessary so to extend and complete
the organisation of the teaching of Anthropology at the Universities of Great Britain, that those who are about to spend their
lives in the East or in parts of the Empire inhabited by non-
European races, shall at the outset of their careers possess, or
have the opportunity of acquiring a sound and accurate
knowledge of the habits, customs, social and religious ideas and
ideals of the Eastern and non-European races subject to His
Majesty the King-Emperor"[43].

[39]*J.RAI* vol. 38, 1908, pp. 489-90.
[40]Sir R. Temple was very active over a period of years; some of his talks
and activities are related in the J.RAI e.g. *Man,* vol. 14, 1914; vol. XXI,
1921.
[41]*Man,* vol. 14, 1914, item no. 19.
[42]*Man,* vol. 21, 1921, p. 151.
[43]*Ibid.,* p. 152.

This project was dropped in 1914 because of the War but taken up again after the War by Temple who in 1921 outlined in detail what should be done to set up this school.

Throughout the 1920s and the 1930s, the yearly presidential Addresses to the RAI reflect the concern on the part of Anthropologists to develop their subject of study to fit the demands of the administration of colonies. Many of these addresses refer precisely to the problems involved in the relationship between Anthropologists and administrators. In 1929 Professor J. Myres spoke on "The science of Man in the Service of the State"[44] in which he discusses the relationship of anthropology and the government, the attempts at setting up various anthropological institutions and the development of the teaching of anthropology to Colonial Office staff. In 1934, the Rev. E. W. Smith spoke on "Anthropology and the Practical Man"[45]; in 1944, Lord Hailey spoke of 'The Role of Anthropology in Colonial Development"[46] at the meeting celebrating the centenary of the RAI.

All the articles for the period up to 1945, including reviews, stress in a very precise way a direct link between anthropological work and administration of the Colonies. The question asked is "How useful is this kind of work to Administration?" even when dealing with academic topics or works; book reviews are written relating books to the administrative context: for example the review by Lucy Mair of Meek's "Law and Authority in a Nigerian Tribe" (1937)[47] first gives a historical sketch of indirect rule in the East, and then looks at the value of the book in terms of how the administration can use the village traditional system for the nomination of chiefs. The review by Meek of S. Leith-Ross's "African Women" in 1939[48] first examines the importance of studying women in the Eastern Nigerian context, in terms of the War, and picks out for attention in the book items relating to westernisation, problems of education and the church. The book is looked at in a purely practical way from the point of view of administration and judged useful as such. Nothing is said of its formal academic qualities which are in fact remarkable by their absence. Similarly in 1943 Margaret Read's review of Margaret Green's 'Land tenure in an Ibo village'[49] considers the

[44]*J.RAI*, vol. LIX, 1929, pp. 19-52.
[45]*J.RAI*, vol. LXIV, 1934.
[46]*Man*, vol. 44, 1944.
[47]*Man*, vol. 37, 1937, item no. 226.
[48]*Man*, vol. 39, 1939, item no. 100.
[49]*Man*, vol. 43, item no. 29.

book from the point of view of its contribution to solving problems of social and economic change.

After the war on the other hand the whole tone of discussion changes. Articles are concerned with anthropology as an academic subject, there is a great interest in developing theory and reviews are written in terms of academic merit. For example P. Bohannan's review of M. Green's "Ibo village Affairs"[50] stresses the book's value as an academic study, the quality of its anthropological analysis when in fact this study was written in the same spirit as S. Leith-Ross's, that is as an aid to administration, a study of women because there was concern in the Administration about Women in Eastern Nigeria after the Women's War.

A long article in 1949 'Anthropology and Colonial Affairs'[51] is a summary of the contributions by Evans-Pritchard and Firth to a meeting at the RAI. The article gives an account of the Colonial Social Science Research Council and how useful it can be to anthropologists. Despite statements like:

Anthropology is benefitting a great deal in some ways by its new reactions to colonial affairs[52]

the general tone is one that is revealed more by this statement:

in some academic circles, there is a fear lest the colonial tail wag the anthropological dog—lest basic scientific problems be overlooked in favour of those of more pressing practical interest[53].

The concern is no longer so much about anthropology helping colonial administration, instead the emphasis is on developing theory and becoming a full-scale academic subject. Another view on the value of the CSSRC is given by Lucy Mair in 1950 who says of the then Colonial Development and Welfare Fund created in 1940:

Some of the investigations that this fund has made possible have been dictated by the personal interests of the workers, but others have been carried out at the request of governments who believe that they can utilize the results.[54]

After this date, the problems of colonial administration hardly appear in the RAI's publications and there are more and more articles on theory; there is a feeling of wanting to forget the sordid past of involvement in concrete problems. This has been done so successfully that today, people tend to assume that anthropology is totally

[50]*Man*, vol. 49, 1949, item no. 85.
[51]*Man*, vol. 49, 1949, item no. 179.
[52]*Ibid.*, p. 138.
[53]*Ibid.*, p. 138.
[54]L. Mair, *Anthropology and Social Change*, London 1969, p. 41.

unconnected with any concrete political activities.

Clearly this change of emphasis in Anthropology as well as the present theoretical and other problems of the subject are related to the historical changes that have taken place in the Colonial World since the end of the Second World War.

## Anthropological Work

Let us now see what anthropological work got done in Eastern Nigeria, particularly as a consequence of Lord Passfield's recommendation that such work should be undertaken. Before 1930 there had been only a very limited anthropological interest in Eastern Nigeria; Basden, a missionary, had written a book "Niger Ibos" (1938) after spending 40 years in Iboland. The first Government anthropologist Northcote Thomas in the first decade of the century had written a long report on the Ibo. The bankruptcy of Indirect Rule in the East, the Women's War in 1929, and the recommendations of the Commission of Inquiry supported by the Secretary of State for the Colonies, all combined to encourage a great development of anthropological studies in Eastern Nigeria; some of these studies were by professional anthropologists, but most were by administrators. These works none of which are by major anthropologists, are all functionalist studies of specific problems. The choice of problems dealt with can also be looked at in terms of the specific difficulties faced by the colonial administration in that area at that time. There are for example a large number of studies of land tenure[55] over a period of 10 years. Of these four, three are by administrative officers who have followed the advice of the Colonial Office and developed a more profound interest in anthropology. The main concern of these studies is to give a clear and complete picture of land tenure systems, which would be of use in determining policy.

The other topic which is uncommonly emphasised is that of women. Two women anthropologists (M. Green and S. Leith-Ross) went to Iboland in the early 1930s to study the local women. This was due to the interest in women taken by the administration following the Women's War, when there was seen to be an urgent need to analyse both Ibo women and Ibo society as seen by women.

The two volumes devoted by Northcote Thomas to topics other than language are entitled *'Law and Custom of the Ibo of the Asaba*

[55]See: M. Green, *Land Tenure in an Ibo Village*, 1941; J. D. Field Sale of Land in an Ibo Community, Nigeria, in *Man*, vol. 45, 1945. L. T. Chubb, *Ibo Land Tenure*, 1947, a Report made for a committee chaired by Lord Hailey; G. I. Jones, Ibo Land Tenure, *Africa*, 1949.

*Districts, S. Nigeria"* and *"Law and Custom of the Ibo of the Awka Neighbourhood, S. Nigeria"*. These are Thomas's books on anthropology, both of which have long sections on religion and on rituals for all moments of life. These books are descriptive rather than analytic. They do however describe the main moments of life in the area referred to and give an idea of the rules and regulations that are applied to religion, marriage, dispute-settlements and various other matters. One point of interest is that Northcote Thomas does mention some people as being "chiefs" or "kings" in his areas, and suggests that they have positions of authority. This is relevant since it poses the question whether his statements were taken into account when the Warrant chief system was introduced in the area at about the same time as his studies.

In a more general way his works are still in the tradition of prefunctionalist evolutionist anthropology. The emphasis is on laws, inheritance, land ownership, religion, rituals, etc., but he does not consider kinship to be the basis of social organisation, as functionalists do. His remarks on kinship are brief and he is clearly less interested in that than in any other aspects of his studies. He also looks at his work in terms of western administrative concepts, and there is evidence that he has paid great attention to collecting material on matters that would be relevant to the administration.

Of the work in the 1930s which followed the Women's War, the outstanding authors are C. K. Meek, M. Green and S. Leith-Ross. We shall examine their books in turn, emphasising only their main concern.

C. K. Meek was an administrative officer who was transferred to the South as anthropological officer in 1929. His book was published in 1937 and its preoccupations are made quite clear merely by its title: "Law and Authority in a Nigerian Tribe". His introduction starts with a description of the Women's War and its rôle in shaking the administration out of apathy. He explains the failure of Indirect Rule through the absence of chiefs. His job as government anthropologist was to assist in the investigations being carried out by local administrators into:

> the indigenous social and political organisation of the peoples of South-Eastern Nigeria, with a view to setting up native Administrations which would be more in accordance with the institutions and wishes of the people.[56]

Meek had to leave Nigeria in 1932 for health reasons and wrote this

[56]C. K. Meek, *Law and Authority in a Nigerian Tribe*, 1937, p. xi.

book feeling that his material:
> might be of value to students of anthropology and sociology, as
> well as to Administrative, Judicial and Educational Officers of the
> Colonial Service.[57]

His study is directed:
> towards ascertaining the general principles by which the Ibo
> community governed themselves.[58]

His understanding of anthropology is very much that of an administrator and he says that the Government's attitude towards anthropological research has always been:
> that it should serve as the handmaiden to administration by
> throwing light on the history, relationships, organisation, and
> thoughts of the people, and so providing data which would help
> the Government to make the fullest use of Native institutions as
> instruments of local administration.[59]

His book does not reflect these interests. His first chapters are on
religion, and this because:
> religion is . . . the handmaiden of the law . . . Among the Ibo,
> religion and law are so closely interwoven that many of the most
> powerful legal sanctions are derived directly from the gods[60]

He finds the social and political structure "closely interwoven" with
law and authority:
> the necessity of studying the social structure is proportionately
> greater among peoples lacking a central form of government, as
> their modes of regulating conduct are highly complex and by no
> means obvious to a European observer.[61]

In fact, in the chapters devoted to political and social structure his
description does centre on leadership, he is more interested in finding out who dominates the operation of the system than in examining the system itself. His later chapters are about the kinds of
groupings that can be found among the Ibo, like title associations,
age-grade societies; in these also he is primarily concerned with their
development under European rule, and in the case of the title system
tells us that it is collapsing because of the new priorities that are
emerging. In the chapters on law, and the final ones, he merely
describes procedure.

His concluding chapter is called "Practical Conclusions" and by

[57]*Ibid.*, p. xii.
[58]*Ibid.*, p. xii.
[59]*Ibid.*, p. xv.
[60]*Ibid.*, p. 20.
[61]*Ibid.*, p. 88.

this he means concrete advice to Government. He first redefines
Indirect Rule and says that it should be possible to apply it to decentralised societies such as the Ibo, but that it is more difficult
because there are no rulers.

This book can be regarded as very useful both for the anthropologist, who is given all the information he needs presented in a
functional framework, and for the administrator for whom this
emphasis is intended and who can then see how he can use the
traditional social system in reorganising the administration.

The second book is S. Leith-Ross's "African Women" (1939). This
is a study specifically of women, when as a consequence of the
Women's War, she and M. Green were given Leverhulme scholar-
ships to go and study Ibo women. S. Leith-Ross is more general and
less anthropological, surveying the position of women from an isolated rural area to Port Harcourt. It is more a travel diary and a
collection of observations than an anthropological analysis. In this
sense it is quite interesting insofar as she reports some of the reactions to the Women's War that were mentioned to her. She also
describes some of the main *rites de passage* in life in the four areas
she has picked out, how the organisation of institutions like bride-
wealth, for example, change from being more "primitive" to being
more "westernised" depending on the area studied. She defines her
four types of women as—primitive in the absolutely non-westernised
area,—sophisticated and primitive women in the villages with minimal regular contact with the administration,—women in transition
in the smaller towns, and sophisticated women in the large towns
(this categorisation is reminiscent of Redfield's Folk-urban con-
tinuum). She also examines the problem of westernisation in towns,
of urbanisation, of the relationships between blacks and whites, the
rôle of missions, education, new crafts etc. On the whole it is an
interesting narrative; the main reproach one can make is the total
absence of analysis in the academic anthropological sense. The approach to the problems of Nigeria of that time are useful in the
sense that they reveal very clearly the attitude of an "enlightened
administrator", paternalistic and extremely ethnocentric which most
likely reflected the author's background and outlook as the widow
of an officer in Nigeria and the sister of another.

Margaret Green's book on the other hand is a very typical anthropological monograph. Though she did her fieldwork in the 1930s at
the same time as S. Leith-Ross, her book was only published in
1947. It is not specifically about women, but it does put considerable
emphasis on the rôle of women, and on women's organisations. The

main point of the book is to provide an anthropological analysis of
a small village. She describes most of the institutions of the village
and fits them into a structure, locates her small village within the
village group, and analyses her material mainly in terms of local
kinship groups (unlike Meek); she sees the divisions within the
village in terms of kinship, and looks closely at the social structure
in terms of exogamy. Exogamy helps to explain how women can be
so well organised over a large area producing women's organisations relating both to the village of marriage and to the natal village.

Throughout her book we also find that she is looking for people
who have special authority, to see how much authority they have
and how it is determined and distributed. She is a functionalist in
her approach and believes that "in any society institutions arise in
answer to needs"[62]. Therefore to establish indirect rule in the area:

> it is necessary not only to discover indigenous institutions but also
> to understand the part they play in the society which has evolved
> them.[63]

There is considerable stress on law and on dispute settlement with
detailed examples of cases and why they were not brought to the
Native Court but kept within the traditional system:

> The Court was there but in point of fact the people of Umueke did
> not use it. In all the time that I was in the village I only heard of
> one case taken to it.[64]

This is an excellent ethnography of the Ibo and it is highly regarded
by structural-functionalists. It does throw light on the situation of
women and in its general clarity makes it a book that would be
appreciated by administrators in its emphasis of very topical questions: the type of authority structure, and the marked independence
and self-mindedness of women.

In the 1940s and 1950s many other anthropological works on the
Ibo were published, either studies of specific problems by administrators, or anthropologists, or general ethnographies like that of D.
Forde and G. I. Jones. Jones also wrote studies on the choice and
rôle of chiefs in East Nigeria.

## Colonialism and the Development of Anthropological Theory

It is clear from the way anthropology was introduced and later used
in South-Eastern Nigeria by the Colonial Administration that there

[62]M. Green, *Ibo Village Affairs*, pp. 77 note 1.
[63]*Ibid.*, p. 77.
[64]*Ibid.*, p. 104.

is a close relationship between anthropology and administration. It also seems clear that the need for anthropologists arose from the introduction of Indirect Rule as a form of government.

We have seen how the theory of the nature of Indirect Rule evolved from Lugard's position to one that defined it as self-administration by the people according to their traditional system, within the limits permitted by the Colonial Government, that is, as long as it did not come into any kind of conflict with the interests of the colonial government. Let us look at some of the characteristics of Indirect Rule to see how its theory rather than its practice necessitated an interest in anthropology.

Those who supported indirect rule can be identified as paternalistic, europocentric "humanitarian imperialists". These feelings combined to make a defence of Indirect Rule since it was supposed to be a form of government that protected the natives by maintaining their traditional, pre-colonial institutions. These institutions were supported and encouraged as long as they were "good" (i.e. by Christian moral standards), and promoted the economic interests of the colonisers. Indirect Rule was good because it was an opportunity to teach the "natives" how to govern, to show them what "proper" (i.e. European style) governing methods were like; it also helped to promote higher standards of civilisation, by preventing barbarous practices (these were defined as practices unacceptable to Europeans). But the basic point about Indirect Rule is that the colonisers must be familiar with the "native's" traditional political system. And such knowledge is best acquired by anthropological methods. The knowledge wanted is mainly about political organisation, ideology and religion, all of which are necessary in an attempt to use the traditional system. The fact that the type of administration to be studied is local administration (because at higher echelons, the British operated the system themselves) explains the interest in the social organisation of small groups, villages, or clans. . . ; the studies wanted are empirical, descriptions of how things operated and how are problems solved.

The kind of questions posed about native systems by apologists of Indirect Rule relate to very small-scale social organisation, to beliefs in supernatural powers and to problems of authority. But it is accepted by these writers that such questions cannot be answered with any degree of reliability without knowledge of the principles behind them. This emphasis on the mode of operation of traditional institutions is very close to functionalism. The great enthusiasm for Malinowski shown by people concerned with administration arises

from his type of functionalism and his methodology i.e. his concept
of concentrated long-term and detailed fieldwork.

Functionalist theory in social anthropology is the type of analysis
of colonial communities that answers best the questions asked by the
ideologues of Indirect Rule. The studies of Ibo social structure,
helped the administration by providing it with valuable information
about institutions that it needed to understand; what chiefs were
there and how much and what kind of power did they have? How
institutionalised and how close-knit were the women's organisations?

In the case of Nigeria it is possible that the problems created by
Indirect Rule in the North and in the South-East may have contributed to the crisis of the 1960s of the Biafran secession. Biafra
could be seen as a continuation of the claim to self-determination of
a nation that was thwarted in its development since the arrival of the
British. Britain tried to integrate the East with the rest of Nigeria
when it had always been different and this integrationist policy continued under the neo-colonialist government which took over on the
"independence" of Nigeria. Further research would be essential to
turn this last remark into more than mere speculation.

It seems that the development of British social anthropology and
particularly of the functionalist theories that have characterised it
throughout the colonial period, are responses to British imperialism
and its particular form of colonial administration, Indirect Rule. To
demonstrate this, it would be necessary to compare British social
anthropology in the context of Indirect Rule with the French system
of direct rule of its colonies and the fact that French social science
developed a very different form of anthropology, (including structuralism) which have to be explained in terms of French colonial history and ideology. Functionalism should also be compared with
American cultural anthropology and Dutch anthropology, in terms
of their infra-structures and the particular colonial formations that
they may be concerned to justify and support.

There has recently been some attempt to do this, unfortunately not
by a Marxist. Gerard Leclerc in *Anthropologie et Colonialisme*
(1972) surveys social anthropology since its origins and relates it to
colonial history and suggests that functionalism arose because of the
demands of Indirect Rule for knowledge of this type, and that a
similar development did not take place in France because anthropologists were independent of government which did not require
their services: therefore they had the opportunity of developing an
independent theory. He also surveys American cultural anthropology and suggests that it differs from functionalism in its support

for cultural independence and its opposition to the imposition of western values on colonised societies.

Despite the fact that it furthers most of the ideas I have suggested here, Leclerc's book is disappointing. It has an interesting analysis of the problems of ethnocentrism which he traces back into the 18th century; he also attempts to connect his work with present trends in the anti-imperialist movement. Unfortunately his comparison between the developments of British/French anthropology with British/French colonialism is more a series of successive statements than a historical and dialectical analysis of these phenomena, and he therefore fails to prove his point. It is also distressing to notice that despite his interests his frame of reference and his methodology remain bourgeois; in discussing anti-colonial movements, he does not refer to the more radical of them, nor does he discuss their actual politics; similarly his analysis throughout remains at the level of culture, and even that is discussed without reference to infrastructure or to the reality of imperialism in the contemporary world. It is however, worth reading because he does attempt to widen the subject and include it within a more comprehensive framework.

The present crisis in social anthropology lends further support to my hypothesis. The crisis has become worse at a time when colonies have become "independent" and there is no more need for colonial administration, Indirect Rule and the anthropology that they brought about. Structural functionalism is now redundant and neocolonialism is a form of imperialism which requires different information and approaches. It is not clear whether the work of traditional anthropologists is relevant. The United States has replaced Britain and France as the main imperialist nation, their own cultural relativism (their leading anthropological theory previously) has developed into evolutionism, a theory which provides a good basis for a high level of interventionism under the guise of "civilising the natives"..

In Europe on the other hand anthropology is in a state of deep crisis and has not yet found a new rôle for itself. In Britain the theories that have followed structural functionalism are many and inconclusive, none of them are as comprehensive, nor has any of them been able to dominate the anthropological scene. In France, there has been a diversification in anthropology, some branches getting more sociological, while others tend towards philosophy.

Meanwhile the tendency remains for anthropologists to work for and support the current form of imperialism, while at the same time attempting a liberal concern for the welfare of the natives. To counter this we require a Marxist analysis of pre-capitalist societies, following the lead of the French Marxist anthropologists, to study the changes that these societies have gone through during the colonial period, and the nature of their present transitional stage. This should be followed by a careful study of the debate between Marxists on the conflicting theories of the nature of development (i.e. perhaps most importantly must a state go through the stage of capitalism or not?). At the practical level, these efforts should be combined with a clear alignment on the side of anti-imperialist and anti-capitalist revolutionary struggles everywhere.

BIBLIOGRAPHY
A. E. Afigbo: Herbert Richmond Palmer and Indirect Rule in Eastern Nigeria, 1915-1928, in the *Journal of the Historical Society of Nigeria*, vol. 3, no. 2, December 1965.
N. Akpan, *Epitaph to Indirect Rule*, 1956.
J. C. Anene: *Southern Nigeria in Transition*, 1966.
W. Bascom and M. Herskovits: *Continuity and Change in African Cultures*, 1959.
G. T. Basden: *Among the Ibos of Nigeria*, 1921; also *Niger Ibos*, 1938.
G. Gordon Brown and Bruce Hutt: *Anthropology in Action*, 1935.
R. L. Buell: *The Native Problem in Africa*, 1928.
A. C. Burns: *History of Nigeria*, 1929.
D. Cameron: *Principles of Native Administration and their application*, 1935; also *Native Administration in Nigeria and Tanganyika*, 1937.
L. T. Chubb: *Ibo Land Tenure*, 2nd edition, 1961.
A. Cohen (Sir): *British Policy in Changing Africa*, 1959.
J. S. Coleman: *Nigeria, Background to Nationalism*, 1958.
Colonial Office: *Correspondence files* for years 1925-1940; *Administrative Reports* for years 1929-1940; *Sessional Papers* and *Minutes of the Legislative and Executive Councils* 1929-1940.
W. Crocker: *Nigeria, a critique of British Colonial Administration*, 1936.
M. Crowder: *The story of Nigeria*, 1962; also *West Africa under Colonial Rule*, 1968.
K. O. Dike: *Trade and Politics in the Niger Delta, 1830-1885*, 1956; also *100 Years of British Rule in Nigeria, 1851-1951*, 1956.
K. Ezera: *Constitutional Developments in Nigeria*, 1964.
D. Forde and G. I. Jones: *The Ibo and Ibibio speaking peoples of South-Eastern Nigeria*, 1950.
W. N. M. Geary: *Nigeria Under British Rule*, 1927.
W. G. A. O. Gore (Lord Harlech): *African Politics in the High Commission Territories*, 1944; also *British Policy and Administration in Tropical Africa*, 1941.
M. M. Green: *Land Tenure in an Ibo Village*; also *Ibo Village Affairs*, 1941 and 1947 respectively.
A. H. M. Kirk-Greene ed.: *The Principles of Native Administration in Nigeria*, 1965.
Lord Hailey: *An African Survey*, 1938; also *Native Administration in the British African Territories, Part III: West Africa*, H.M.S.O. 1951.
P. Harris: *Local Government in Southern Nigeria*, 1957.
G. I. Jones: Ibo Land Tenure in *Africa*, 1949; also Dual Organisation in Ibo social structure, in *Africa*, 1949; also *Report on the Position and Status*

and *Influence of chiefs and Natural rulers in the Eastern Region of Nigeria*, Enugu, 1956; also *Trading States of the Oil Rivers*, 1963.
A. L. Kroeber ed.: *Anthropology today*, 1953.
G. Leclerc: *Anthropologie et Colonialisme*, Paris, 1972.
F. Lugard: *The Dual Mandate in British Tropical Africa*, 1922.
L. P. Mair: *Studies in Applied Anthropology*, 1957.
B. Malinowski: Practical Anthropology, in *Africa*, 1929.
C. M. K. Meek: *Law and Authority in a Nigerian Tribe*, 1937; also *Changing Cultures of West Africa*, 1948; also *Land, Law and Customs in the Colonies*, 1946; also his work on Northern Nigeria.
W. R. Miller: *Have we Failed in Nigeria?* 1947; also *Success in Nigeria?* 1948.
I. F. Nicolson: *The Administration of Nigeria, 1900-1940*, 1969.
S. Ottenberg: Improvement Associations among the Afikpo Ibo, in *Africa*, 1955; also Comments on Local Government in Afikpo division, in *Journal of African Administration*, 1956.
M. Perham: Some Problems of Indirect Rule in Africa, in the *Journal of the Royal Society of Arts*, 1934; also *Native Administration in Nigeria*, 1937.
S. Leith-Ross: *African Women*; also *Beyond the Niger*, 1951.
Royal Anthropological Institute: *Journal of the Royal Anthropological Institute* for the years 1900-1950, and *Man* 1900-1950.
P. A. Talbot: Some Foreign influences in Nigeria, in *Journal of the African Society*, 1924; *The Peoples of Southern Nigeria*, 4 volumes, 1926; also *Tribes of the Niger Delta*, 1932.
W. Northcote-Thomas: *Report on the Ibo-speaking Peoples of Nigeria*, 6 volumes, 1913.
E. R. Wolf and J. G. Jorgensen: Anthropology on the Warpath in Thailand in *The New York Review of Books*, 19 November, 1970.

# PAX BRITANNICA AND THE SUDAN: S. F. NADEL
## James C. Faris,

It should not be necessary, in 1972, to restate the contingent as well
as logical relationships of science to society—in both content and in
form, our science has served society.[1] This is generally the way it
always has been, always will be, and always should be. What we are
attempting to do here is to continue to re-examine the exact nature
of this functional relationship between science and society to see
precisely what the relationship between anthropology and imperialism is, and to see why it appears the way it does.[2] My task consists
of detailing this in the theory and practice of S. F. Nadel—perhaps
one of the most clear examples from the previous generation of
social anthropology.

Let me make some introductory remarks, however, about an
enterprise of this sort. It seems that there are two major pitfalls in

[1] Cf. J. Stauder, "The Functions of Functionalism", Paper delivered to the
Symposium *Marx II: Anthropology and Imperialism*, American Anthro-
pological Association Annual Meeting, New York, November 1971. B.
Magubane, "A Critical Look at the Indices Used in the Study of Social
Change in Modern Africa" in *Current Anthropology*, 12, 1971; J. Moore,
"Perspectives for a Partisan Anthropology", in *Liberation*, 16, 1971; P.
Newcomer, "Social Process: Critical Notes for a Method of Study", Un-
published Ph.D. Thesis, 1972, University of Connecticut.
[2] We now have the beginning of some histories (cf. M. Harris, *The Rise of
Anthropological Theory*, New York, 1968; J. Moore, op. cit.) and some
explicit epistemological statements (cf. D. Goddard, "Limits of British
Anthropology" in *New Left Review*, 58, 1969; J. Banaji, "The Crisis of
British Anthropology", in *New Left Review*, 64, 1970; G. Berthoud, "Social
Anthropology and Marxian Thought", Paper delivered to the American
Anthropological Association Annual Meeting, San Diego, California, Nov-

these types of analyses. One may be seen in the argument that anthropological scholarship is, by and large, scientifically adequate, but it has just unwittingly (to be generous) served the wrong interests.[3] I think this view is altogether wrong.

Our science as well as our politics must change if we are to understand our past, transcend our present, and plan for the future. Heretofore, the fact that some anthropologists may have been politically liberal, or even left-leaning, is simply irrelevant. They may have even attempted to aid local oppressed peoples in various ways—but without an analysis of the generation of such oppression, very little could come of their efforts. In fact, they probably acted to inhibit oppressed peoples from overtly attacking the colonial regime. It is of course wrong to attribute insidious motives to the vast majority of anthropologists, but functionalism had its functions[4] quite apart from any conscious intentions of its proponents. If our science doesn't change with our politics, we can hardly be of much intellectual help in struggles against various manifestations of imperialism. Not only must the content and application of our science change, but also our theory and methodology.[5]

The other pitfall I think rests in the possibility of a theoretical renaissance without the benefit of practical politics—dialectical materialism is a fascinating explanatory foundation in itself. But it is a rational philosophy based in real life and life processes, and thus it can hardly be worthwhile without first establishing the social relations which enable it to fully function. *Talking* about things rather than *doing* things will ultimately have a stultifying effect on theory. With these two warnings in mind, let me return to Nadel— a man whose efforts in anthropology hardly span twenty years, but who left a vast legacy in field monographs, theoretical study, and methodological comment.

### I. The Task (or, what it was in aid of)
Nadel, perhaps more clearly than most others of his generation, well

ember 1970; P. Newcomer, op. cit.)

[3]Cf. K. Gough, "New Proposals for Anthropologists" in *Current Anthropology*, 9, 1968; G. Berreman, "Is Anthropology Alive? Responsibility in Social Anthropology", ibid. I am assuming that *no one* would today still argue that anthropology is simply irrelevant (cf. G. Berreman, "Anemic and Emetic Analyses in Social Anthropology" in *American Anthropologist*, 68, 1966.)

[4]Cf. J. Stauder, op. cit.

[5]There were, of course some anthropologists whose sympathies were quite in accord with the political structure they served. In the files of the old colonial research institutes are to be found examples of the most blatant racism.

understood the unity of theory and practice. He constantly regarded himself as a practical, even applied, anthropologist, and all his field work was at explicit government request. In his first book Nadel remarks:

It has been said that modern anthropology is destined to be of great assistance to colonial governments in providing the knowledge of the social structure of native groups upon which a sound and harmonious Native Administration, as envisaged in Indirect Rule, should be built. Let me say that I for one firmly believe in the possibility of such cooperation betewen anthropologist and administrator.[6]

He urged anthropological knowledge be put to use and chided those anthropologists who kept aloof from doing so:

While certain anthropologists would remain aloof from these practical questions, others consider it their right and duty to 'apply' anthropology in practice. I count myself among the latter...'pure', value-free anthropology is an illusion.[7]

In every one of S. F. Nadel's major works he stresses the unity of theory and application. He was much more explicit about this than many of his colleagues: "I do not mean merely than the anthropologist should 'diagnose and predict' ",[8] for he was convinced of the merits—and loyal to—the policy as well as the ideological mission set the discipline:

...the right and duty of anthropologists to judge, criticise, and add constructively to social development and political planning of all kinds. I said 'of all kinds'; for the application of anthropology to problems of colonial policy is only one special aspect of a wider issue.[9]

Nadel felt, as his employers already knew (after all, this is why they hired him) that very likely "the blunders of the anthropologists will be 'better' blunders".[10]

Both of his field monographs were explicitly planned to be of practical value to colonial governments—*A Black Byzantium* (1942) was introduced by Lugard, and *The Nuba* (1947) had a forward by Maj. Gen. Sir Hubert Huddleston, Governor-General of the Sudan —and both emphasised the value of close cooperation. Nadel was

[6]S. Nadel, *A Black Byzantium*, London, 1942, p. vi.
[7]S. Nadel, *The Foundations of Social Anthropology*, London, 1951, pp. 52-3. See also page 3 of the same work.
[8]Ibid., p. 55.
[9]Ibid., p. 54.
[10]Ibid., p. 55.

not just an anthropologist with a choice about cooperation, he was hired to do specific jobs. Rockefeller money enabled the International African Institute to send Nadel to Nigeria in 1932—where his excellent work for them led to his being recommended to the Government of the Sudan to help them with their "pressing problems"[11] amongst the Nuba. Nadel arrived in the Sudan in 1938.

After the Nuba research, Nadel's political biography continues in 1941 with an appointment to the British Military Administration in Eritrea as Secretary for Native Affairs—a job he apparently executed with efficiency, for he was commended by the Commander-in-Chief of the Middle-Eastern Forces for outstanding services:

...applying anthropology to the administration of peoples of various origin and tradition, with all the *understanding of primitive mentality* and *appreciation of administrative problems* which he showed during his two years in the Nuba Mountains[12]

With such excellent credentials, he later progressed through a Senior Lectureship at the London School of Economics, a Readership at Durham, and finally to Canberra, where apart from the Chair in Anthropology at the Australian National University, he also became Dean of the School of Pacific Research. In this post, Nadel died in 1956.

I would like to look in more detail at his actual field research— the situation in which it was conducted, just how it was conducted, and just how his work was concretely applied. I am personally most familiar with his Nuba researches in what was the Anglo-Egyptian Sudan, and shall focus on this principally.[13]

Nadel was asked to work amongst the Nuba for several reasons. The first of these stems from the direct grief they caused the Government. With no political hierarchy into which the Government could easily plug Indirect Rule, how to effectively control some 300,000 people was a paramount problem. Military patrols were the *modus operandi* until just two years before Nadel arrived.[14] As

[11]S. Nadel, *The Nuba,* London, 1947, p. xi.
[12]Ibid., p. xii, emphasis mine. While in Eritrea, Nadel investigated land tenure, among other things (S. Nadel, "Land Tenure on the Eritrean Plateau", in *Africa,* 16, 1946.) Research in the administrative archives and military records relating to the area might reveal just why this knowledge was needed.
[13]The 'Nuba' is the label given to the entire group (some one-third million people) of relatively small autonomous distinct agricultural societies that occupy the hills and mountains of central Kordofan Province, Sudan. While culturally similar, these societies have no traditional political structures beyond the village or village group level.
[14]*The Nuba,* p. 494.

Huddleston casually expresses the contact between the Government and the Nuba in his introduction to Nadel's book, "contact...frequently culminated in a small military patrol directed now against one hill and now against another"[15] and punitive patrols were common—later to be, at least in one case, the result of Nadel's own applied anthropology.[16]

Nadel's principal guide line, in fact, for field work amongst certain of the Nuba societies (and not amongst others), was politicomilitary expediency. He states that "tribes whose administration presented imperative problems were considered before others".[17]

Nadel's assignment was quite specific, and the book "was primarily planned to be of practical value to administrators and others".[18] The Government felt the Nuba were:

...being powerfully affected by the authority of the Government, the forces of economics and the influence of science... Their lives were still largely conditioned by superstitions and customs imperfectly known to the administration...was the constructive effect of the administration outweighing the destructive? Keen officials, especially technical officials, were apt to override native customs rather than make use of them.[19]

A new policy phase had indeed opened in British imperialism, and in the Sudan, Nadel was one of its local agents. He provided the information necessary for the Administration to 'make use of' local customs (this will be examined in more detail below). Overriding indigenous societies had become too dangerous and uneconomical —controlling people with sociology was easier than controlling them with troops, and 'making use of' their customs not only facilitated Administration and kept them controlled, but under the policy of Indirect Rule, it had the additional and very critical effect of *keeping them Nuba.*

This latter factor is particularly important, for the Nuba are the furthermost North of any of the pagan societies of the Sudan, and were viewed by the British as an important buffer against the progressive move South of Islam. Missionary activity amongst the

---

[15]Ibid., p. xi.
[16]Ibid., p. 355 n. This happened in the hill group of Jebel Tullishi where Nadel was instrumental in setting up a Native Court and anchoring Government-sponsored Chiefships. This court led to difficulties, and the Government, only two years later, sent a military force to drive the Tullushi out of their mountain homes and settle them on the plain.
[17]*The Nuba*, p. 7.
[18]Ibid., p. xi.
[19]loc. cit.

Nuba had lagged behind that of other parts of the non-Muslim
Sudan, however—undoubtedly because of the difficulty in pacifying
the Nuba—but the area and its people were of primary importance
to the Government in its policy of containing Islam and Arab influence.[20] Sections of the Nuba Mountains were official 'Closed Districts'—which meant that no Arabs could enter without explicit
permission. With the marked lack of success in missionary activity,
this essentially meant *any* change was inhibited, making it, in the
overall, a far less costly and ultimately less dangerous operation.[21]
The most conspicuous effect of this policy (and one must therefore
speculate about the real reasons for the policy) was then to *inhibit
any development at all*. Portions of the eastern and southern Nuba
Mountains are essentially today as they were at the turn of the century. The Government policy failed, however, and did not, in fact,
successfully inhibit the spread of Islam and Arabisation. But it
became the excuse for the *lack of* education and development. We
can better understand, then, why Nadel's instructions were "that he
would study the economic and political organisation, their religious
beliefs and their psychological and social background".[22] He states,
in fact, that his conclusions "are intended to summarise the results
from the viewpoints of a common political administration, and the
common future of Nuba culture under the impact of Arab civilisation".[23]

Although Nadel was supposed to aid the effort to curb Islam, he
regarded uncompromising Christian missionaries with as much suspicion as Muslim zealots. He could well see that missionaries of the
fundamentalist sort were no asset to the task ahead, for they, as well
as the Arab *faki* "clash as much with the life as we, in the enlightened West, know it, and with the fruits of our long evolution which
we now desire to share with the backward races of the world".[24]
However more insidious Nadel found the threat of Islam, he clearly
saw its inevitability, and says,

    True, we also insist on Nuba village schools [as opposed to the

[20]S. Hurreiz, *Linguistic Diversity and Language Planning in the Sudan*,
African Studies Seminar Paper No. 5, 1968, Sudan Research Unit, University of Khartoum.
[21]M. Abdel-Rahim, *The Development of British Policy in the Southern
Sudan 1899-1947*, School of Extra-Mural Studies Publication, University of
Khartoum.
[22]*The Nuba*, p. xii.
[23]Ibid., p. 10.
[24]Ibid., p. 512. This is not the only example of Nadel as moralist—as will be
seen below, it was also at the base of his functionalism.

*kuttab* and *khalwa*—rural Koranic schools; it should also be mentioned here that very few of these village schools were actually established] meant to keep aloof from Arab influence, or occasionally design romantically savage garbs for tribal police: but these efforts can hardly count for more than an odd detour in an otherwise straight road.[25] rival of Christianity, but the steadily encroaching Islam".[26] We find a similar statement about Islam amongst the Nupe of west Africa, and "here it is not the pagan religion which is the greatest Yet Nadel did not appear to understand much of the syncretism characterising Islam in the Nuba Mountains. In a discussion about the adoption of Islam, he states "often the motives behind this conversion are stated naively"[27] and quotes a discussion he had with a Nuba man about rain magic:

[He] said to me once, during a discussion of rain magic, that he, of course, did not believe in rain makers and rain sacrifices: he knew that 'rain came from Allah.' As there is a mission working in this tribe, I asked if he meant the Mohammedan or Christian God? He replied: 'I mean the Allah of the *Hakuma* [Government] and the police in Talodi'.[28]

It seems to me this is a more poignant statement about the link of symbols to social relations than Nadel realised. It is anything *but* naïve.

## II. The Techniques (or how it was accomplished)

The general impression the casual reader gets from Nadel's book is that the Nuba are not very pleasant: "from our description a Tullishi society emerged fraught with tension and conflict".[29] We find out elsewhere, however, that the Tullishi had been repeatedly the focus of military attracks and punitive patrols (and would be again, thanks to Nadel; see above, note [16]). And he speaks of the "dour, reserved, and suspicious attitude of the Mesakin" and of their "pessimistic, neurotic mentality",[31] particularly in contrast to nearby

[25]Ibid., p. 487.
[26]S. Nadel, *Nupe Religion*, Glencoe, 1954, p. 231. This book, curiously enough, deals only with pre-Islamic practices and rituals. Although my paper concentrates on Nadel's research in the Sudan and on some of his general theoretical contributions, similar analyses are needed of his fieldwork in West Africa.
[27]*The Nuba*, p. 485.
[28]Loc. cit.
[29]Ibid., p. 356.
[30]Ibid., p. 321n, p. 323n.
[31]Ibid., p. 317.

Korongo, whom Nadel found friendlier. Here again, we must study the book carefully to learn that:

If the reserve and suspicion of the Mesakin were restricted to their interaction with us, this might be explained by the fact that the Mesakin, unlike the Korongo, had to suffer punitive police action.[32]

In contrasting the Tira and Moro societies, Nadel states, "Moro culture, compared with Tira, is also one in which individual violence appears more unrestrained; obsession with magic fears greater; and the emotional balance under stress more precarious".[33] Only elsewhere do we find that Islam had permiated Tira culture to a far greater degree[34] and that the Moro have always been troublesome to the Government.

The principal reason the Nuba were thus so unpleasant to Nadel is because he represented a hostile agency—in short, an enemy. He was serving an administration that not only physically attacked local societies, driving them from their homes, forcing migrations, imprisoning (and very frequently hanging) their men and women, and he was an apologist and defender of that system. Nadel's unsympathetic comment on this oppression is revealing:

*They may not have taken kindly to their enforced migration...* occasionally an *unfortunate misunderstanding* aggravated the situation, as when the Tira were made to move down to a low hillock of which their traditions spoke of as an unhealthy disease-ridden site, which had once already been abandoned by their ancestors.[35]

If we turn to Nadel's fieldwork techniques, we find another reason why the Nuba appeared so hostile. As a fieldworker, Nadel has left a considerable legacy of method and technique that can help us more clearly understand his role.[36]

In an essay on the use of interviews, we find the basis of Nadel's

[32]Ibid., p. 317n.
[33]Ibid., p. 265.
[34]Ibid., p. 238.
[35]Ibid., p. 6, emphasis mine.
[36]Among other things, Nadel was a pioneer in intelligence testing in British social anthropology. He saw the goal of this to be able to arrange groups on some type of scale that might measure relative superiority and inferiority (S. Nadel, "The Application of Intelligence Tests in the Anthropological Field" in F. C. Bartlett, et. al. (eds.), *The Study of Society*, London, 1939). This was not just to be quantitative measures along a single existing scale, but comparison on a new basis. The most recent statement of this in Britain is to be found in the blatant racism of H. J. Eysenck (*The I.Q. Argument* London, 1971).

relationship with indigenous peoples. It is clear he prefers 'raw savages'—he cautions against using educated informants,[37] or educated people locally as researchers. Nothing suffices like the rigorous inductive methodology of the European scientist—and the sophistication of local people only "blurs their view" and "distorts valuable information".[38] Nadel prefers instead, his own "bullying" technique:

> As a rule the most successful approach lies in stimulating the informant emotionally and thus overcoming his indolence or his reluctance to discuss certain points... I have found it most profitable to stimulate the emotionality of a few chief informants to the extent of arousing almost violent disputes and controversies...a 'bullying' technique of this type amounts to the deliberate introduction of leading questions, a practice against which fieldworkers are frequently warned. But the leading question has its legitimate place in the anthropological, as in other interviews, provided that it is handled carefully and, above all, with full knowledge of its dangerous nature. The risks which this technique involves are not negligible; wrongly applied, it may lead to complete misinformation.[39]

Of course Nadel only worried about the danger of misinformation—he had access (at least in the Nuba Mountains) to a police squad[40] and appears to have been able to summon informants at will.[41] However motivated, then, informants could only *appear* hostile, and could not constitute a physical danger to Nadel. It is small wonder, however, why they appeared so insolent.

In discussing field participation, Nadel suggests that some anthropologists may involve themselves more fully, but stresses that it is really not necessary to get too involved: 'he may be admitted to secret rites, yet disregard with impunity important ritual rules, such as food taboos and submission to severe flogging in an initiation ceremony".[42] With this kind of contempt for local custom, it is not surprising that Nadel urges that anthropologists "capitalise...on their 'stranger value' ".[43] Nowhere in this essay on interviews, nor indeed in his entire Nuba monograph, does Nadel mention the anthropolo-

[37]S. Nadel, "The Interview Technique in Social Anthropology" ibid., p. 322.
[38]Loc. cit.
[39]Ibid., pp. 322-23.
[40]*The Nuba*, .p. 347.
[41]*The Nuba, p.* 335.
[42]"The Interview Technique", p. 326.
[43]Loc. cit.

gist as friend, much less an ally in local struggles against colonial oppression.

## III. The Theory (or how it was justified)

As I stressed in the introductory remarks, theory and practice cannot, should not, and never have been separated. And as mentioned, functionalism has its functions; far from just a legacy which effectively blinded us from fully understanding and explaining social relations (which it did), it was more importantly a necessary intellectual tradition answering to the central questions facing imperialism—*control*. And it did its job. Of course, as Asad[44] has suggested, most anthropologists were not conscious of the job they were doing, and only operated as they had been taught—functionalism was the guiding paradigm and the appropriate strategy for 'normal science'.[45] Some, however, understood its implications more clearly than others, and their ruling class allegiance was more explicit. S. F. Nadel, I'm afraid, belongs to this latter group.

As mentioned above, the unity of theory and practice in Nadel is remarkable—and had it served different interests, we might even call it enviable. In the Nuba monograph, Nadel tells us:

> This book fall to some extent in the category of 'applied anthropology': its primary purpose is to provide an anthropological study which should prove helpful in the practical tasks of government...But this is in now way a handbook: it aims at much more than mere description—at analysis and causal explanation; it deals with the different tribes and their changing institutions, not as so many disconnected topics, but as steps in a gradual, often comparative investigation.[46]

It is, in fact, in his commitment to application that Nadel's theory becomes comprehensible. A poignant summary of Nadel's ultimate resolution of theory and practice may be seen in what is perhaps the last thing he ever wrote—the final paragraph of *The Theory of Social Structure*.

> ...in employing the criteria of command over persons and benefits I have introduced concepts connoting, if only implicitly, purpose and utility, since command always means command for some purpose. Earlier on, I justified this step by saying that these criteria help to retain a degree of relevance in structural

[44]T. Asad, *The Kababish Arabs*, London, 1970, p. 10.
[45]T. Kuhn, *The Structure of Scientific Revolutions*, Chicago, 1962.
[46]*The Nuba*, p. 8.

analysis, I would now say that they help to retain, or provide, the necessary linkage between the theory of social structure and the social universe of purpose. You may call this an insurance against a heuristic isolation which can be driven too far, or a reminder that we live in societies where there are jobs to be done.[47]

From Nadel's perspective, of course, the overriding job was control. His functionalism focused exactly where his application focused—on control and regulation. For those of you that have had to suffer through *The Theory of Social Structure* as graduate students as I had to, you may remember that items from his symbolic calculus became part of the everyday lexicon—*c a* [control over actions] and *c r b* [control over rights and benefits], Nadel's critical elements in social structure, were a part of the heritage. And how could one dispute it? It made such obviously good sense inasmuch as it appeared to describe well the situation in which we found ourselves. But good sense for *whom*? This was not the sort of question that was tolerated (or even considered) in my graduate student years. Nadel's theoretical model for the analysis of other societies was derived from the task required by imperial nations. Control was paramount in their concern with colonised peoples, and Nadel thus argued that this was the natural state of affairs everywhere—the paramount concern of all societies.

However appropriate and useful Nadel's theory may have been for regulating people, one of the reasons for this conference is because the theory fails to tell us why societies are the way they are, how they came to be that way (and not any other way), and in what direction social evolution will go in the future. These are theoretical as well as applied questions. I think it is first necessary to see why functionalism, particularly as manifested in Nadel, is inadequate as explanation. Its status epistomologically has been reviewed in several places, but I would like to look in more detail at the implications of its logic.

Functionalism, with its rigorous commitment to empiricism, can never be more than a description that does not transcend the facts on which it is based. Defenders of the faith frequently state something like: "But you can't deny that societies function and that it is of paramount importance to their survival." Of course, but this is precisely why it is useless as explanation—it is as trivial as it is true. To explain all behaviour as functional (or dysfunctional) be-

[47]*The Theory of Social Structure*, London, 1957, pp. 158-9.

cause it must ultimately ensure survival is to turn effect and consequence into cause.[48] And since we have no test (i.e., we don't know very much about how societies functioned that *didn't* survive), it is spurious cause at best.

Without knowing something about why things come to be the way they are, to argue that they are functional explains nothing. Functionalism has no way of sorting out which 'things' are relevant and which are not—everything must have a function—and so we get weak discussions of core functions and primary functions,[49] or ultimate cause in psychology, morality, or species-specific predispositions. Of course 'things' do something (or did something), otherwise they would not be here—but the questions of scientific relevance (i.e., explanatory relevance) is why do they do it, and why do they do it in this manner. Functionalism simply cannot cope with any 'why' questions.

Functionalism usually 'explains' one institution or thing as being causal to another, but when functionalists attempt to *trace* causal chains and nexes, we either get the reduction to individual psychology or pan-human predispositions, as mentioned above (i.e., all men seek power;[50] or humans must self-regulate[51]). Or we get the familiar tautologies—the function of something is to do what it does; or the somewhat more complex circularity—witchcraft exists to channel anxieties, produced by structural disharmonies, brought about by anxieties, produced by witchcraft.[52] Where Nadel is not circular, psychological, or moralistic (see below), he is presented with problems of relativity.

For Nadel, functionalism is predicated on "certain absolute requirements—the integration of societies and the survival of populations",[53] for "without it, we could not legitimately speak of adjustment of maladjustment, that is, invoke a criterion of adequacy."

[48]"Historically speaking, functional analysis is a modification of teleological explanation, i.e., of explanation not by reference to causes which 'bring about' the event in question but by reference to ends which determine its course." C. Hempel, *Aspects of Scientific Explanation*, New York, 1965, p. 303.
[49]S. Nadel, "Social Control and Self Regulation" in *Social Forces*, 31, 1953.
[50]Cf. E. Leach, *Political System of Highland Burma, London*, 1954.
[51]S. Nadel, op. cit. (1953).
[52]S. Nadel, "Witchcraft in Four African Societies: An Essay in Comparison" in *American Anthropologist*, 54, 1952. (Reprinted in S. Ottenberg (ed.), *Cultures and Societies of Africa*, New York, 1960. Pagination in references from this edition.)
[53]S. Nadel, The *Foundations of Social Anthropology*, London, 1951, p. 375.

As we have seen, Nadel's relativism—his ideas about "adjustment" —are based on assumptions of the *pax Britannica*, for why is it that a raid on a D.C. post, a refusal to be recruited into forced public works projects, or refusal to obey a Government chief, or to pay taxes, is considered maladjustment? Whose survival are we talking about? The criteria of adequacy which allows one to interpret a strike or revolt against colonial rule as maladjustment seems rather specific to one's class allegiance.

Returning to the problem of cause, I've noted above that if you examine carefully a functionalist, you will likely discover a moralist or a psychologist. Thus Nadel focuses heavily on 'self-regulation' in his writings, and while in the Nuba Mountains gathered an inordinate amount of data on witchcraft, suicide, individual aggression, and shamanism. This material was necessary to the mystification that his job required—for illustrating that frustrations and alienation have their origins in people's heads. In his widely read paper "Witchcraft in Four African Societies",[54] Nadel begins with the assumption that "witchcraft beliefs are causally related to frustrations, anxieties or other *mental* stresses precisely as psychopathological symptoms are related to mental disturbances of this nature"[55]

There is another very practical aspect to the mystification in psychological causes—for if people under drastic change and new forms of oppression expressed their frustrations *socially*, it was dangerous; but if they expressed them in neurotic tendencies, repression, or suicide,[56] it was much healthier for Europeans. It is small wonder, then, that so much is made of these manifestations of alienation, and the ways of dealing with them studied so carefully. Witchcraft could not harm Europeans, but only local people, so far better that the reaction to Europeans take this channel than a more effective social form.

In spite of two 'theoretical' books and several related essays, a major problem with Nadel is the incredible confusion about process and explanation. Certainly the job of science is to explicate processes. In so doing, however, we must assume that the world changes in discoverable ways, and that the relationships and pro-

[54]The two Nuba societies discussed in this essay are the Mesakin and the Korongo (see above). In this essay, however, we find no reference to the differential treatment of the two societies at the hands of the Government troops. For this see S. Nadel *The Nuba*, p. 317 u.
[55]S. Nadel (1952), op. cit., p. 408.
[56]*The Nuba*, p. xiii.

cesses in it are not random, capricious, or unique. What is of interest, then, is in fact change. The fundamentally reactionary character of functionalism is exposed since it focuses on why things do not change, rather than why they do. Since to accept a world that is always in change, constitutes a political challenge to the society supporting and sanctioning functionalism, so too does it become an intellectual challenge to functionalism as explanation. To accept industrial capitalism as the natural state into which all other societies would develop, and a natural state that would not fundamentally change—also demanded that the history of its own evolution be mystified (by positioning its origins in great men or great religions or unique events, etc.) and its persistence guaranteed (by the paradigms of functionalism).

Nadel's view of explanation was that it is but complete description.[57] Thus, to understand the world was to observe it and describe it. Theories were empirical and arrived at by inductive accumulation of facts. This is an amazingly naïve view for the times in which he worked. We *observe* things, but the processes by which these things came to be the way they are *must be the products of theory*.[58] Nadel's science was, however, committed to measuring rather than theorising—since in the allegiance to inductive empiricism, the only way in which he could reveal relationships was by correlating facts.[59]

Nadel's use of consequence as cause, effect as determinate, and his psychological reductionism sufficed as explanation. And this, he tells us, is simply complete description. Nadel's theory, inasmuch as it only generalises from the facts, is incapable of falsification. Facts for Nadel exist not to disprove theories, but to statistically verify them—a methodological mistake of a crippling kind in theory and explanation.[60]

[57]S. Nadel (1951), op. cit., p. 199.
[58]Cf. P. Newcomer, op. cit.
[59]As Marx reminds us, if the appearance of things coincided with their essence, there would be no need for science at all (*Capital*, New York, 1967, Vol. III, p. 817). Processes are seldom visible (cf. J. Faris, "Cognitive Studies and Materialism", Paper delivered to the Symposium *Marx 1: Science History and Materialism,* American Anthropological Association Annual Meeting, New York, November 1971). No one has ever seen biological evolution taking place—we see its consequences and products speciation and some of its mechanisms (differential reproduction and natural selection). But evolution is not a fact—it is a theory of how the facts came to be the way they are. It is not a law, and it cannot be proved; but it can easily be falsified—the hallmark of a well-constructed theory.
[60]Cf. J. Faris, "Concepts and Methodology in Social Process', paper presented to the Symposium *Marx III: Critiques of Theory,* American An-

The implications of this are far-reaching. Nadel's inductive empiricism forced him to view the world probabilistically—in quantitative terms with causal relationships established by correlations based on his ideas of their function. If all relationships can then be statistically defined and quantitatively determined, as in one of Nadel's matrices constructed about role systems, then any change must be treated as incremental, or quantitative. All qualitative distinctions can thus be reduced to their quantitative specifications. Thus, for Nadel, class is simply a type of stratification, law is simply one type of control custom, underdevelopment is simply quantitatively less than development, and local society is but a nation in microcosm. Let me look at these examples (all from Nadel) more closely.

Taking for example law: Nadel regards law as the codification of custom—which is in turn the inculcation of self-regulation to inhibit "individual learnings" and to "canalise human drives".[61] Law is, for Nadel, in essence written-down order. The reality in history, as most of us know, however, is that law is opposed to order.[62] Law is the product of state systems; it arose with the breach of customary order—not by everyone, but by the exploiting group, by the rising elite. Thus, the customary order no longer applies to all persons—some have law instead (backed in every case by force). This is, by any standard, a qualitatively different situation. The codification of customary order (normally this operation involves ignoring some customary order and introducing non-customary rules as well) is a transformation—to 'legally' insure the status of one group vis-à-vis another. It is not just a matter of writing down customs.

Nadel seems well aware, however, that some customs cannot become laws. If law is to serve a ruling élite, then some traditional customs (which in totality served the entire society and thereby inhibited stratification) must be dropped and others invented: "the transformation of customs into laws...is of a more controversial nature...the danger is obvious: it lies in the premature codification of what is...a tentative adjustment".[63] Those customs Nadel particularly wished codified surround political structures—governing structures that could be used in the colonial policies of Indirect

thropological Association Annual Meeting, Toronto, December 1972.
[61]S. Nadel (1953), op. cit., pp. 265-5. Note thet psychologism here—a characteristic of most functionalists.
[62]Cf. S. Diamond, "The Rule of Law Versus the Order of Custom", in *Social Research*, 38, 1971.
[63]*The Nuba*, pp. 509-10.

Rule. The major problem was in finding these—and most frequently the Government chief (who may or may not have been recruited from one of the priesthoods of the traditional acephalous society) was the focus of 'codified custom': "chieftainship and law must then become reflections of each other, the chief the agent of a law that is greater and more necessary than he...*law and chieftainship will thus attain their ulterior validity together.*"[64] Nadel saw that the "government-sponsored" (government-enforced) chiefship required law—that the traditional authority figures were simply different (though his lack of general theory prohibited him from seeing that they were *qualitatively* different), and any attempt to simply directly 'make use of' them was not possible. In discussing one such failure, Nadel quotes an informant:

> ..."our young men would never obey clan or family heads in
> political matters; they obey only the *Meks* and *Sheikhs* which
> the *Hakuma* has appointed." Unhappily for the anthropologist,
> then, the scientifically sounder organisation may prove impracti-
> cable, and indeed, unnecessary.[65]

Nadel is lamenting here the fact that he couldn't efficiently make use of local custom. He simply did not, however, understand just what is implied by a social system that has chiefs and political structures —the qualitative distinction between such a society and one without chiefs and structures to enforce legal codes. He did not understand that traditional custom and law are not simple arithmetic expressions of one another.

Similarly, Nadel failed to understand that classless societies (the local society) and class-based societies (the 'nation') are not quantitative expressions of each other. Societies with forms such as law, money, and property (class-based societies) are systems with wholly different implications from societies that are classless—societies ordered by custom and producing for use-value. In a society where everyone can have a pair of shoes, or a bicycle, or a car, or a plane or a yacht, there is no reason to have to protect property with law. We know, of course that in societies with planes and yachts, law is critically necessary to their maintenance because only a privileged few can have them. But the functionalist 'explanation' (the explanation which counts and which measures all change and differentials in increments) for societies of this type would involve something

---

[64]*The Nuba*, p. 498 (emphasis mine). Here Nadel is much more poignantly revealing and correct than he possibly wished to be.
[65]*The Nuba*, pp. 498-9.

about the fact that even though yachts are limited, if everyone just
works hard (or saves more), he or she too may have a yacht. Thus
the differences between the yacht owners and others is presented as
merely quantitative. There is stratification, of course (usually regarded as necessitated by technology, or some other external factor, such
as the fact that some people are just not as hard-working). But such
an explanation doesn't need class—it can stick to the empirical facts,
never transcend them, and account for the situation with stratification.[66] Nadel did exactly that—he simply viewed the world as if
there were no disjunctions or qualitative differences between societies, epochs, or things. He was thus able to argue: "traditional
Nuba morality is bounded by the small community: we want it to
embrace the whole tribe, the whole country. Why not teach just
that?"[67]

But as argued above, Nadel knew full well that some morals of
classless society had to be junked if local people were to participate
in class-based social organisation. His recommendation was to drop
these (and add law and chiefs)—then the Nuba and the governing
elite would differ only in degree! He urged:

The education of the Nuba, as of all primitive groups, should be
guided thus: let moral education take the form of a teaching
of tribal history, *modified and weighed in accordance with
modern values.* The principal tenets of social morality as we
visualise them, and as they are embodied in tribal structure
and the tribal past, are often the same; only their terms of
reference, the social range to which they refer, need reinterpreta-
tion.[68]

Thus, any qualitative differences are obliterated, and everything is
more or less of everything else. Even Nadel, however, could not
find *some* features of his ideal class-based state in local society (and
here again we find Nadel the moralist), so these he attributes to
*"universal moral tenets*—the evilness of murder, *respect for property* or *marital rights".*[69]

The qualitative differences were simply too great for Nadel to
generate them from any simple quantitative accretion, and he had
thus to introduce into classless local societies a morality derived
from capitalism to complete his functional schema. With this, every

[66]Cf. P. Newcomer, "Social Class and Social Stratification", paper delivered
to the Symposium *Marx III: Critiques of Theory,* American Anthropological Association Annual Meeting, Toronto, December 1972.
[67]*The Nuba,* p. 512.
[68]Ibid., p. 512 (emphasis mine).
[69]Loc. cit.

difference between 'them' and 'us' is simply a quantitative expression: customary order is really law, society is really the state, underdevelopment is really development.

Very little of what I have said is unique to Nadel,[70] for his theory and methodology is the legacy of most of us. But perhaps this is changing. Certainly the people on whom this sort of theory was applied are rising up to change it. I am glad to be able to say that this even happened to Nadel at one point, for after a lecture in London, he tells us:

> At the end of the talk a number of West African students in the audience violently attacked me, all my fellow workers in that field, and indeed the whole of anthropology. They accused us of playing into the hands of reactionary administrators and of lending the sanction of science to a policy meant to 'keep the African down'.[71]

It is time that we lend "the sanction of science" to eliminating oppression, and one (but only one) way of doing this is to make clear and attack the role of anthropology in creating, preserving, and implementing ideologies of oppression.

---

[70]Cf. J. Faris, "Review: *The Dialectics of Social Life* (by Robert Murphy)" in *Science and Society*, 36, 1972.
[71]S. Nadel, *Anthropology & Modern Life*, Canberra, 1953, p. 13.

# ANTHROPOLOGY AND COLONIAL RULE: THE CASE OF GODFREY WILSON AND THE RHODES-LIVINGSTONE INSTITUTE, NORTHERN RHODESIA
## Richard Brown

The problem of knowledge and power is, and always has been, the problem of the relations of men of knowledge with men of power.[1]
The relationship of anthropological knowledge to colonial power has been the subject of much recent comment. Apart from two highly critical articles in the *New Left Review* by Goddard and by Banaji, Kathleen Gough and others have also been contributing to a distinctly unfavourable image of the colonial anthropologist.[2] This work seems to show that scholarly advance—or perhaps more accurately, the advancement of scholars—requires a form of intellectual parricide: each generation, it appears, must murder its immediate ancestors. In this case not just the ideas, but also the academic morality of the scholarly ancestors is assaulted when it is claimed that the colonial anthropologist was simply the handmaiden of imperialism. Van den Berghe writes of him as "strongly com-

[1]C. Wright Mills, *Power, Politics and People*, ed. I. L. Horowitz (New York, 1963), 606.
[2]D. Goddard "Limits of British Anthropology", *New Left Review*, 58 (November-December 1969); J. Banaji, "The Crisis of British Anthropology", *New Left Review*, 64 (November-December 1970); K. Gough, "World Revolution and the Science of Man", *The Dissenting Academy*, ed. T. Roszak (Harmondsworth, 1969), 135; K. Gough, "Anthropology: Child of Imperialism", *Monthly Review*, Vol. 19, No. 11 (April 1968); J. R. Hooker, "The Anthropologist's Frontier: the last phase of African exploitation", *Journal of Modern African Studies*, I (1963); P. Worsley, "The End of Anthropology?", paper for 6th World Congress of Sociology, 1966, mimeo. A specific if ineffective attack on the Northern Rhodesian sociolo-

mitted to the preservation of the *status quo,* regarding the continent
as a vast ethnographic Garden of Eden" and suggests that it is only
recently that anthropologists have become aware of change. Besides
also allegedly harmonising with colonial rule and stressing only harmony in the societies he studied, the colonial anthropologist stands
accused of having deliberately adopted narrow horizons: he is supposed to have studied only social units least touched by modern
influences and to have ignored the world-wide setting in which
modern influences nevertheless made themselves felt.[3]

However, it is to be doubted whether the contrast between the
dark colonial days and the enlightened present is so stark as these
writings imply. Nor, because "colonial administration had an inherent need of cogent, objective information on the peoples over
which it ruled,"[4] should it be too readily assumed that anthropologists merely carried out mental labour for colonial administrators
or that the interests of the two groups neatly coincided. Readiness
to be an "applied anthropologist" and to subscribe to a belief in
objective and value-neutral social research did not necessarily mean
tame submission to colonial aims as Gerald Berreman appears to
think,[5] but can also be seen as a method by which the colonial
anthropologist sought to disassociate himself from colonial aims
while preserving the freedom to carry out research in colonial conditions on subjects chosen by himself.[6] In any case, as the quotation
at the head of this paper suggests, the relationship between knowledge and power is an indirect one mediated by particular men and
particular institutions and is thus subject to some degree of in-
determinancy. It may therefore be of some interest to examine the
particularities of a single situation, not least since the extensive
literature on the subject of the attempt to apply anthropological
knowledge to colonial problems remains at a very general level and
has yet to be supported by case studies.

The case of Godfrey Wilson and the Rhodes-Livingstone Institute
is an interesting one since it illustrates the fundamental ambiguity
which lay at the heart of the relationship between anthropology and
colonial rule. Furthermore, the RLI was the first institute of its

gical tradition was launched in B. Magubane's "A Critical Look at Indices
used in the Study of Social Change in Colonial Africa", *Current Anthropology,* 12 (1971), pp. 419-430, being easily refuted by those attacked in the
following pages of the same issue.
[3]P. L. van den Berghe, *Africa: Social Problems of Change & Conflict* (San
Francisco, 1965), 2-5.
[4]P. Anderson, "Components of the National Culture", *Student Power,* eds.
A. Cockburn & R. Blackburn (Harmondsworth, 1969), 265.
[5]G. D. Berreman, "Is Anthropology Alive? Social Responsibility in Social

kind in the dependent empire and it served as a model in many respects for those that were later established after the second world war in east and west Africa and in the West Indies.[7] The academic influence of the RLI was also great. Wilson's three successors as director—Max Gluckman, Elizabeth Colson, and Clyde Mitchell— were not only greatly influenced by him and the work he began while at the institute, like him they achieved world-wide renown as scholars. The remarkably high number of senior appointments in anthropology and sociology held by former research officers of the RLI are further evidence of its academic influence.

The foundation of the RLI in 1937 was an isolated event, but it was not wholly divorced from the general tendencies of the time which were favouring attempts to relate scientific knowledge to social problems. After the First World War the focus of colonial interest moved from the acquisition to the maintenance of control, and the first stirrings about 'development' as a consciously-induced policy began. Embodied in Lord Lugard's *The Dual Mandate in British Tropical Africa* (1922) and the French colonial minister Albert Sarraut's *Mise en valeur des colonies françaises* (1923), these shifts in the nature of colonialism were accompanied by the growth of an anthropology which its practitioners claimed was of great practical value. Within the discipline the crucial changes—associated with Radcliffe-Brown and Malinowski (both of whose first major works were published in 1922)—were the substitution of functional for evolutionary social theory and the stress on intensive field-work. The new emphasis on the workings and maintenance of social systems closely parallels the way in which, at much the same time, L. B. Namier was revolutionising the study of 18th century politics by leaving aside the traditional questions of chronological development in favour of asking how the political system actually worked in 1760. It was useless, Namier believed, to study the political events of the period unless one first understood the structure in which they occured. In a similar way, Malinowski claimed that those concerned with developments in Africa must first understand the workings of the societies with which they were in contact.[8] Support for anthropology was thus sought on the basis of its utility,

Anthropology", *Current Anthropology* (1968), 391-8.
[6]This argument is developed at length in the chapter by Wendy James.
[7]E. Chilver, "The Institutes of Social and Economic Research in the African Colonies", *Journal of African Administration*, 3 (1951) provides a useful overview.
[8]L. B. Namier, *The Structure of Politics at the Accession of George III* (London ,1929); B. Malinowski, "Practical Anthropology", *Africa*, 2 (1929).

and this appeal found a response from within the specialised but
overlapping circles which concerned themselves with colonial affairs.
The formation of the International Institute of African Languages
and Cultures in 1926 was the result. The International African
Institute, as it was later to become, was established by representatives of scientific, missionary and official colonial bodies, with the
specific aim of "bringing about a closer association of scientific
knowledge and research with practical affairs."[9] Its first chairman
was Lord Lugard, who—with Lord Hailey—was to be a key intermediary between the men of knowledge and the men of power.

The utilitarian aims of the IAI were to receive still wider pub-
licity in Hailey's massive and influential *African Survey*, the idea
of which was first canvassed by Smuts in 1929, but which was not
published until 1938. The *Survey* is well-known for the support it
gave to research of all kinds, but there was a special advocacy of
anthropological research "because policies which do not take into
account the nature of native societies are apt to provoke unforeseen
and unwelcome reactions."[10] The importance of Hailey's support
is seen in the unusual distinction paid to him when he was acknowledged by name in the government white paper dealing with the
formation of a Colonial Research Advisory Committee as part of
the 1940 Colonial Development and Welfare Act, the first act to
make substantial government funds available for colonial research.[11]

Nevertheless, the Colonial Secretary, Malcolm MacDonald, was
evidently in some fear of anthropologists. Discussing the composition of the new research committee, of which Hailey had been
invited to be chairman, MacDonald wrote: "I feel that I shall be
pressed...to include an anthropologist, but I gather that it will be
rather hard to find one who has not his own personal axe to grind,
and I am told that in any case anthropologists, as a class, are rather
difficult folk to deal with."[12] In reply, Hailey stressed the need to
appoint one "since there are many people, not themselves professional anthropologists, who will constantly make it their business to
remind you, that it is useless to provide for enquiry into the physical
sciences, unless you consider also the human elements to which the
result of these enquiries must be applied." After stating that he

[9]F. D. Lugard, "The International Institute of African Languages and Cultures", *Africa*, 1 (1928), 1-12.
[10]Lord Hailey, *An African Survey* (London, 1938), 40.
[11]Cmd. 6175 (1940), 1.
[12]Malcolm MacDonald to Lord Hailey, personal, 18 April, 1940, Rhodes
House, MSS Brit. Emp. s.342.

believed some of the colonial governments would also be disappointed if anthropology was omitted, Hailey went on, "But we must
recognise the limits within which support should be given to anthropological studies...[the] aim is not primarily to encourage academic
study; it is limited to discovering those things which our administration must know, if it is to make the best use of its resources for the
development of the people in the Colonies."[13]

However, important though these metropolitan developments
were, the RLI was not their direct product. Although the important
post-war research plans of the institute were to be largely funded
from C.D. & W., its formation in 1937 not only preceded the act
by three years, but also cut across official thinking which at this
time tended to favour Hailey's view that colonial research ought to
be centrally organised and conducted from Britain rather than from
local institutes situated in Africa.[14] In these circumstances, while it
is true that the general climate favoured experiments in applied
research, it was also the case that it would be difficult to get the
principle accepted that an institute should be founded in Northern
Rhodesia and difficult, too, to raise the necessary funds. Thus, unlike the later institutes, which were part of a wide-ranging colonial
office policy to underpin its post-war development plans with social
research, the RLI struggled into existence as a result of a local
initiative, and more despite than because of colonial office wishes.

The first suggestion came from Sir Hubert Winthrop Young at
the outset of his governorship of Northern Rhodesia in 1934 when
he proposed to the colonial secretary that a Livingstone memorial
comprising a museum and a research institute should be established
to carry out research in "archaeology, geology, and particularly anthropology." Interestingly, since laymen still tended to think of
anthropology as the study of weird rites and obscene rituals, Young
continued, "Livingstone was himself so interested in the habits and
customs of the peoples of Central Africa that it was thought that
emphasis should be laid on the sociological side of anthropology."[15]

Something of a *poseur*, Young thought of himself as a scholar
and the institute scheme probably appealed to his vanity and self-
importance.[15a] The scheme was also seen to be an attempt to placate

[13]Hailey to MacDonald, [-] May 1940, Rhodes House, MSS Brit. Emp. s342.
[14]Hailey, *Survey*, 1624-29.
[15]Minute by F. A. Stockdale, 15 August 1934, reporting conversation with
Young, CO 795/72.
[15a]This point was made to me by Dr. A. I. Richards at a seminar at the
Institute of Commonwealth Studies, 30 November 1972.

the traders of Livingstone, where it was proposed to site the institute, for the loss of business on the impending removal of the territory's capital to Lusaka.[15b]

Up to 1930 anthropological knowledge about Northern Rhodesia
had accumulated in characteristically random fashion through the
activities of amateur enthusiasts who were either officials of the
British South Africa Company, who administered the territory, or
missionaries.[15c] Professional study began with Audrey Richards who
carried out field-work on the Bemba in 1930-31 and 1933-34. A
pupil of Malinowski's, she concentrated on problems of nutrition
while also revealing the general outlines of the social and political
structure of the Bemba peoples. Further enquiry may show that
interest in the value to the administration of her research played a
part both in encouraging Young to propose the institute and in
maintaining his government's interest during the lengthy and painful
gestation of the scheme.[15d]

The three year delay from 1934 to 1937 in launching the proposal was due to the obstruction of the colonial office. Both the
permanent officials and the colonial secretary (Sir Philip Cunliffe-
Lister, later Lord Swinton) were lukewarm about the proposal,
doubting its value and fearing that undue burdens would be placed
on the finances of the local colonial governments of central Africa
in spite of Young's own optimism about raising money from private
sources.[16] Asked to make the value of his suggestion more explicit,
Young explained he had consulted with experts such as Julian Hux-
ley, Audrey Richards, J. H. Oldham and others, and that he was
guaranteed the support of the International African Institute by
Oldham, its administrative secretary. The main object of the research would be "to assist towards the formulation of the correct
economic and administrative policy for the mixed African and non-

[15b]Ellis Robins to D. O. Malcolm, 29 May 1937, C.O. 795/88; Professor M.
Gluckman to author, 8 December 1972.
[15c]After Livingstone in the previous century, the first work in this field which
deserves notice is C. Gouldsbury and H. Sheane, *The Great Plateau of
Northern Rhodesia* (London, 1911): both authors were employees of the
BSA Company. E. W. Smith (a celebrated missionary) and A. Dale (a
company servant) co-operated to produce *The Ila-speaking Peoples of
Northern Rhodesia* (London, 1920), widely regarded as one of the finest non-
professional ethnographic studies of an African people. C. M. Doke's
*The Lambas of Northern Rhodesia* (London, 1931) is not of the same quality,
but the author, a Baptist missionary, later became a Professor of African
languages.
[15d]Her first work, *Hunger and Work in a Savage Tribe* (London), 1932) preceded Young's proposal. The main study based on the Bemba, *Land,
Labour and Diet in Northern Rhodesia* was not published until 1939, after
the institute was already in being, but she reports that her earlier "Tribal

African community"[17], and in another document. Young further
stressed its utilitarian object on the grounds that relations between
white and black in central and southern Africa were perhaps "the
greatest problem in the Empire today" and the institute "will help
me and my successors, and possibly other authorities, by providing
expert advice upon the potential economic and political future of
the two communities..."[18] This led to an alarmed minute by an
assistant under secretary of state suggesting that Young should
be cautioned "against any statement...which might indicate that the
conclusions of the Anthropologist would have material weight in
deciding large questions of policy."[19]

None of Young's arguments convinced the secretary of state who
continued to write scornful minutes on the subject and who, although clearly against the proposal in principle, did not refuse his
support outright, but instead adopted the typical civil service tactics of delay by insisting that no decision be taken before the results
of Hailey's unofficial survey, which was then about to start in
earnest, were known.[20] Young was bitterly disappointed at being
so refused "something that would help me to do this difficult job"[21]
and he would have been still more annoyed had he known that
Hailey protested at the excuse Young had been given, fearing it
"would tend to embarrass his relations with the administrators if
the Survey were to be used as a means by which their schemes
might be indefinitely held up."[22]

One reason for the scepticism with which Young's proposal had
been received in official quarters was that Northern Rhodesia was
still considered a colonial backwater.[23] Although acquired through
the agency of Rhodes's British South Africa Company, it had escaped the notoriety of the violent encounters which had accompanied the company's colonisation of Southern Rhodesia. Nor,

Government in Transition. The Babemba of North-Eastern Rhodesia",
supplement to the *Journal of the Royal African Society*, 34 (1935), was
used administratively: letter to author, 26 January 1973.
[16]Minute by F. A. Stockdale, 15 August 1934; minutes by Cunliffe-Lister,
16, 23 August, 24 September 1934; minute by J. A. Calder, 10 September
1934; minute by E. Boyd, 11 September 1934, CO 795/72.
[17]Young, "Livingstone Memorial Institute", encl. in Young to Cunliffe-Lister,
29 September 1934, CO 795/72.
[18]Young to Cunliffe-Lister, 29 September 1934, CO 795/72.
[19]Minute by W. C. B[ottomley], 7 November 1934, CO 795/72.
[20]Minute by Cunliffe-Lister, 7 November 1935; Cunliffe-Lister to Young,
13 November 1934, CO 795/72.
[21]Young to Sir J.Maffey, 21 November 1934, CO 795/75.
[22]Minute by S. E. V. Luke, 2 July 1935, reporting conversation with Hailey,
CO 795/72.
[23]I. Henderson, "The Origins of Nationalism in East and Central Africa:

when the territory came under direct colonial office rule in 1924 and the B.S.A. Company was relieved of administrative responsibility, were there sufficient settlers to provoke the attention then being given to policy problems in Kenya. The development of the copperbelt shortly after the coming of colonial office rule led to some privately expressed concern about the effects of the mines on African life as was shown by the publication of *Modern Industry and the African,* an enquiry into copperbelt life on behalf of the International Missionary Council which included recommendations about the value of anthropology to both missions and government,[24] but the colonial office seemed singularly unaware of the copperbelt's significance. The explosion of anger by African miners in the strike of May 1935, when six were killed by police action, led to Northern Rhodesia being given unaccustomed prominence in British newspapers, and it began to be realised that the copperbelt presented novel problems of industrialisation which were not to be found elsewhere in British Africa.[25] The 1935 riots, however, did little immediately to forward Young's plans.

Young used his review of the copperbelt situation following the riots to revive his scheme. He pointed out to the new colonial secretary, Malcolm MacDonald, that the growth of industrialisation was "beyond the experience of the local Administration" and that what was needed was an institute "for the express purpose of studying this important problem, which cannot be thoroughly understood nor handled by the Government without some such expert advice..."[26] The permanent under-secretary's minute merely noted, "The Governor is obstinate about his anthropological institute,"[27] and the matter was left to drop. What made the difference was the arrival at the colonial office of W. Ormsby-Gore (later Lord Harlech), who made it clear that he approved of Young's scheme and wished the appeal for funds to go ahead even though the permanent officials still counselled delay until the publication of Hailey's survey.[28] By now, Young had modified the original proposal to make use of "the coincidence of the Rhodes Jubilee [in 1940] with

the Zambian Case", *Journal of African History,* 11 (1970), 596.
[24]J. Merle Davis, *Modern Industry and the African* (London, 1933), 375, 391, 393.
[25]*The Times,* 28-31 May, 4 June 1935.
[26]Young to Malcolm MacDonald, 29 August 1935, CO 795/78.
[27]Minute by J. L. M[affey], 24 September 1935, CO 795/78.
[28]Minutes by Ormsby-Gore, 4 February, 5 April 1937; minute by J. A. Calder, 26 January 1937; minute by G. J. F. T[omlinson], 27 January 1937, CO 795/81.

the Livingstone centenary, and [it] is somewhat expanded to appeal
to admirers of Rhodes as well as of Livingstone."[29] Whether this
addition had any bearing on Ormsby-Gore's decision is not known.
The public appeal for funds was issued on 30 June 1937,[30] a few
days after an ordinance setting up the institute under a board of
trustees had been passed by the Northern Rhodesia legislative council.[31] Young had used the opportunity of his presence in London
for the coronation of George VI to build up an impressive list of
signatories. Besides the colonial secretary, the institute appeal was
signed by the archbishops of Canterbury and York and the modera-
tor of the Church of Scotland who headed the list; then followed
the president of the Royal Society and other prominent academics
concerned with Africa, representing the world of science; the three
central African governors and governor-general of Canada represented the dependent and independent parts of the Empire; while
the ubiquitous Lords Lugard and Hailey represented the unofficial
voice of the establishment on colonial matters. A discreet hint of
royal patronage was added to the appeal by the statement that the
Duke of Kent, who had recently visited Northern Rhodesia, "has
full sympathy with this appeal and wishes it every success." In
commemorating the fiftieth anniversary of the foundation of the
Rhodesias in 1890 and the centenary of the arrival of Livingstone
in Africa, the appeal balanced the widely different associations
evoked by the two names. The appeal stated that the institute was
intended:

as a contribution to the scientific efforts now being made in
various quarters to examine the effect upon native African
society of the impact of European civilisation, by the formation
in Africa itself of a centre where the problem of establishing
permanent and satisfactory relations between natives and non-
natives—a problem of urgent importance where, as in Northern
Rhodesia, mineral resources are being developed in the home
of a primitive community—may form the subject of special
study.[32]

If the reference to "permanent and satisfactory" relations between
black and white was intended to arouse the enthusiasm of the
settlers in Northern Rhodesia itself for the institute, it failed to do

[29]Young to Ormsby-Gore, 5 April 1937, CO 795/81.
[30]*The Times; The Livingstone Mail* et. al., 30 June 1937.
[31]Ordinance No. 1 of 1937, *Supplement to the Northern Rhodesia Gazette*,
29 June 1937.
[32]See note 30.

so. Throughout the 1930's and indeed later, they saw their security not in science, but in wresting political power from the colonial office, either directly through achieving minority self-government or indirectly through amalgamation with Southern Rhodesia. The settler representatives in the legislative council thus gave the formation of the institute a cool reception, seeing it as no more than an experiment which they had no reason to oppose outright. Doubts were expressed about the ability of the territory to continue making contributions to its funds and there was concern that the research officers should be properly supervised.[33] Leopold Moore, the senior elected member and proprietor of the *Livingstone Mail*, joined the board of trustees, but in an editorial objected to the "sacerdotal patronage" of the Institute, fearing the diversion of the enterprise into "a means of disseminating religious propaganda as witness the BBC."[34] Sir Stewart Gore-Browne, also a leading settler, emphatically favoured scientific research of all kinds and his wife directly assisted the research of Audrey Richards. Nevertheless, the exclamation reported to have been made at one of his meetings that "we will *not* be governed by anthropologists"[35] and the view that the institute was an example of government wastefulness at a time when the territory should be "improving hospitals for the benefit of the living"[36] were more characteristic responses. But although the support of the settlers was important, especially to Young whose governorship was distinctive for the extent to which he sought to win their confidence, the financial and research future for an institute depended much more upon the attitude of the governments and the big business interests since it was they who were the powerful elements in the Northern Rhodesian equation of knowledge and power. The territory's African voice was as yet muted, while the settlers, although vociferous, numbered only 15,000 by 1940.

In the early years of the institute non-governmental contributions approximately equalled those of governments other than that of Northern Rhodesia.[37] The contributions from other governments came, firstly, from the British east and central African territories, who presumably took their lead from the secretary of state, and, secondly, from Southern Rhodesia, free since 1923 to take an inde-

[33]Northern Rhodesia Legislative Council *Debates*, 28, cols. 16-38 (26 & 28 June 1937).
[34]*Livingstone Mail*, 30 June 1937, p. 4, col. 4.
[35]*Journal of the Royal African Society*, 34 (1935), 383.
[36]S. Gore-Browne, "The Relations of Black and White in Tropical Africa", *Livingstone Mail*, 1 September 1937, p. 5, cols. 4-5.

pendent line, but whom Young had carefully wooed on the grounds
that the institute could be "a concrete application" of the policy of
"closer co-operation" recently approved by the colonial secretary,
a point of view especially likely to appeal to a convinced amalgama-
tionist like Huggins, the Southern Rhodesian prime minister.[38]
There was virtually no response to the appeal from private interests or purely British ones, and the non-government contributors
were, predictably, the main capitalist concerns (and trusts associated
with them) with interests in Northern Rhodesia, such as the British
South Africa Company, the mining companies of Broken Hill and
the copperbelt, and the Rhodes and Beit trusts. Yet support for the
institute from these obvious sources was neither straight-forward
nor easily won—as an unkind minute in the colonial office put it:
"Sir H. Young is finding that it is easier to catch your white ele-
phant than to keep it."[39] The BSA Co., resident director in Salis-
bury had cabled to the company president in London: "very
doubtful as to necessity or practicability of project especially on
vague and expensive lines indicated."[40] In a following letter he also
indicated preferences for direct government-sponsored inquiry and
for natural rather than social science, as well as wondering why the
South African government and universities were left out of the
scheme.[41] The BSA Co. president, the formidable colonial office
lobbyist, Sir Dougal Malcolm, passed on these and his own doubts
about the institute in a letter to "My dear Billy" (Ormsby-Gore),
wishing to know whether the colonial secretary had "any strong
feelings in the matter" before taking a decision about a company
contribution.[42] In reply, Ormsby-Gore made it clear that he wished
Young's appeal to succeed and hoped that the BSA Co. would
back it publicly since "if one company starts, I feel sure the rest
will join in."[43] Malcolm took the hint and the company advanced

[37]For example, in 1939 recurrent income was as follows:

| | |
|---|---:|
| Northern Rhodesia | £1,000 |
| Tanganyika | 100 |
| Kenya | 50 |
| Uganda | 50 |
| Nyasaland | 50 |
| Southern Rhodesia | 200 |
| Roan Antelope Mine | 200 |
| Nkana Mine | 200 |
| Mufulira Mine | 200 |
| Broken Hill Mine | 50 |
| Zambesi Sawmills | 58-5 |
| C. S. Knight | 50 |
| | 2,208-5 |

*Director's Report* . . . . *1938-9-40*, p. 7.
[38]Young to Sir Herbert Stanley, Governor of S. Rhodesia, 30 August 1934

a £5,000 capital grant. Even so, the copper companies needed further wooing before they agreed to back the scheme by making annual contributions.[44]

Among the measures taken to arouse the interest of the copper companies was the circulation of a revealing letter from Hailey. The letter clearly attempted to dispel the scepticism felt by the companies about the value to government and business of anthropological inquiry. It noted the changes which had come over the subject and stressed the shift from antiquarian and physical concerns to social ones, while also subtly managing to combine an impression of scientific respectability with practical value. He argued that anthropological study "is necessary if we are to base on any sure foundation the improvement we are seeking to make in African conditions, whether it take the form of increase in agricultural production, or the betterment of diet and living conditions, or of health or of capacity to labour." To these pragmatic arguments designed to appeal to the business ethic he added a patriotic appeal by pointing out that, "None of the African governments have at the moment any post of anthropologist or the like. It is to my mind characteristic, I refrain from adding discreditable, that the main contribution to essential studies of this nature comes from America."[45] Hailey was obviously referring to the Rockefeller foundation's support of the IAI and of its "Five-Year Plan of Research" (1931) which trained many leading figures in the subject (including prominent Africans such as Jomo Kenyatta and Z. K. Matthews). Hailey's own work, the *African Survey* was being paid for by the Carnegie Corporation, also an American foundation.

The big capitalist interests of Northern Rhodesia were, it is clear, doubtful of the value of independently conducted social research and yet were willing, after an initial show of reluctance, to contri-

and telegraphic reply, 17 September 1934, CO 795/72. Telegram, Stanley to Young, 17 May 1937, CO 795/88.
[39]Minute by J. S. W. Flood, 28 September 1937, CO 795/88.
[40]Telegram, Ellis Robins to D. O. Malcolm, 27 May 1937, CO 795/88.
[41]Robins to Malcolm, 29 May 1937, CO 795/88.
[42]Malcolm to Ormsby-Gore, 8 June 1937, CO 795/88.
[43]Ormsby-Gore to Malcolm, 25 June 1937, CO 795/88.
[44]Record of conversation, Young with Mr. Storke, a copper mine executive, 28 July 1937, who agreed to do "his utmost, when he got back to induce the Copper Companies to come into line with the B.S.A. Company and Sir Robert Williams' Companies, at least to the extent of offering some financial assistance to the Institute for the next three years." ZNA P2/1/1.
[45]Hailey to Young, 17 June 1937, ZNA B1/4/MISC/6/1.

bute to it; and this remained the pattern throughout the colonial period. The reason for this perhaps lies in their wish to retain good relations with the political authorities in London and Lusaka. In paying for research they were not hiring handmaidens, but were paying a form of hidden taxation by falling in with the expressed wishes of the colonial secretary and the governor of the territory in which they operated. In this way, they may well have hoped to help prolong the extremely favourable conditions under which the BSA Co. and the copper companies existed in Northern Rhodesia. In the year ending 30 September 1937, merely by existing, the BSA Co. earned £300,000 (principally from copper royalties) in Northern Rhodesia,[46] while the freedom of action the mines themselves enjoyed made observers liken the copperbelt to a state within a state. This interpretation that business contributions were basically a form of voluntary taxation gains support from the extraordinary letter in which Malcolm informed Young of the BSA Co. donation only after making it clear that he had little faith in the institute project, adding "Your appeal, supported as it is by very weighty authority including that of the Secretary of State for the Colonies, is one to which the...Company, in view of its history and traditions, would be very reluctant to return a negative reply".[47] Nor is it perhaps without significance that at this time there was not only mounting public criticism of the royalties arrangement in Northern Rhodesia, but also their legal validity was being questioned—unsuccessfully—by Young himself in largely secret correspondence with the colonial office.[48]

Thus the institute came into being at a time when the underlying climate of opinion favoured the attempt to use the new type of anthropology for practical purposes. Nevertheless, those in positions of formal and informal power, whether in government or in business were at the least divided about the proposal for a specialised institute staffed by professional scientists who would not be civil servants. It required Young's persistence, a willing colonial secretary, and Hailey's strong advocacy to get the project going.

As a formally independent institution, the RLI was not controlled

[46]D. O. Malcolm, *The British South Africa Company, 1889-1939*, (London, n.d.; privately printed), 56.
[47]Malcolm to Young, 12 July 1937, "Early History of the Institute" file. IAS.
[48]*The British South Africa Company's Claims to Mineral Royalties in Northern Rhodesia* (Lusaka: Govt. Pr., 1964), 26-28; P. Slinn, "Commercial concessions and politics during the colonial period. The role of the British South Africa Company in Northern Rhodesia 1890-1964", *African Affairs*, 70 (1971), 375-377.

directly as a government department, but by a board of trustees. As might be expected in an essentially authoritarian colonial structure, the composition of the board gave the governor the predominant voice. He was *ex-officio* president of the board of seven, and nominated two further members. The remaining members were two civil servants—the financial secretary and the provincial commissioner, southern province; and two settlers—the mayor of Livingstone (where the RLI was situated until the move to Lusaka in 1952) and the legco member for the Livingstone and western electoral area. The governor possessed a veto over all appointments.

A striking feature of the board of trustees of what was intended to be a scientific institute was the complete absence of scientists from the ruling body unless the governor chose to fill either or both of the nominated positions with scientists. In fact, he did not do so, but it is of some interest that it was nearly always the governor who took the more 'scientific' view in conflicts within the board of trustees. In fact, the RLI was as a rule more favoured by government house than by the secretariat. Why this should have been so, is not immediately clear. Possibly governors enjoyed ruling in a territory which had at least some pretensions to learning or perhaps in the colonial situation, where the governor rules as well as reigns, potential alternative sources of information are comforting additions to the chief secretary's near-monopoly of information.

How far an institute devoted to social rather than natural science would be able to operate both harmoniously and independently in a colonial setting was something which would have to be worked out in practice. There were no real precedents and, unlike the later colonial institutes of social research, there was no local university to which it could be attached and from which it could derive some protection from colonial pressures. Much would clearly depend on the choice of the first director. Here again the specialised lobby which took an interest in colonial affairs played an important part. When the institute had first been mooted in 1934, J. H. Oldham had stressed the need for a first-rate appointment and mentioned Godfrey Wilson as a possible choice.[49] Three years later, both Lugard and Hailey strongly recommended Wilson as a "Functional Anthropologist,"[50] and after the colonial office had been unable to find out "anything to the discredit of Godfrey Wilson"[51]—who was

[49]Minute by G. J. F. T[omlinson], reporting conversation with Oldham, 6 November 1934, CO 795/72.
[50]Young to Ormsby-Gore 24 May, 17 August 1937, CO 795/88.
[51]Telegram W. C. B[ottomley] to Young, 26 May 1937, CO 795/88.

then in Tanganyika—the board of trustees at its first meeting, perhaps ominously only after "considerable discussion", agreed to his appointment.[52] He was interviewed at a special meeting of the board and accepted appointment from the beginning of May 1938.[53] On this occasion he apparently created the wrong impression by beating the governor at chess,[54] but more serious disagreements lay ahead and were to lead to a more or less enforced resignation within three years. The nature of the conflicts throws considerable light on the position of the social scientist in a colonial situation.

Godfrey Baldwin Wilson (1908-1944) was the son of the noted Shakespearean scholar, John Dover Wilson.[55] At Oxford he read classics and philosophy before developing an interest in anthropology through his friendship with Monica Hunter, whom he married in 1935. Together they studied in Malinowski's influential seminar at the LSE before doing fieldwork among the Nyakusa in what was then Tanganyika. Monica Hunter's *Reaction to Conquest* (1936), a study of the Pondo not only in their "tribal" setting, but also as labourers on European farms and in the towns of South Africa, has been singled out as a notable example of a diachronic or historically-dimensioned study at a time when ahistorical and static studies are said to have dominated the field.[56] In fact, the rejection of history by the functionalists was never as absolute as is often implied, their attack being mainly directed at the "conjectural history" of human institutions which offended against the most elementary rules of historical scholarship.

Nevertheless a wide outlook, often alleged to have been absent from colonial anthropology, was an outstanding characteristic of Godfrey Wilson and was to inform all that he wrote before his premature death. His refusal to see any significant differences between social anthropology, sociology, and history, and his determination to bring economic and administrative factors into his analysis of central African society owed a good deal to Marx.[57]

[52]Minutes, 1st meeting, 27 July 1937, IAS.
[53]Minutes, 2nd meeting, 3 September 1937; Wilson to Lane Poole (PC, southern province), 6 September 1937, IAS A/16.
[54]Information kindly given in discussion by Professor Monica Wilson, 18 March 1971.
[55]See J. D. Wilson, *Milestones on the Dover Road* (London, 1969) and the obituary notice by Max Gluckman in the first number of the *Rhodes-Livingstone Journal* (1944).
[56]This breadth of view also informs her chapters in the recent *Oxford History of South Africa*, 2 vols, eds. M. Wilson and L. Thompson (Oxford, 1969; 1971).
[57]He described social anthropology and sociology as "two words for the

Indeed, *The Analysis of Social Change*, written jointly with his wife, and published posthumously in 1945, must be one of the most ambitious brief attempts to explain the overall processes of change since the *Communist Manifesto*. However, although impressed by Marxism as an explanatory system, in particular in connection with the world slump, Wilson was a devout Christian and a pacifist. Moreover, he believed passionately in the possibility of an objective social science. This was to be attained, he believed, by excluding all judgements of a moral kind: "Balanced judgement and sober sentiment belong to politics and philosophy, they do not belong to science, whose sole task consists in accurate description of events together with dispassionate analysis of the actual forces that determine them." He was aware of the problem of bias and selectivity in the facts themselves, but believed the problem could be overcome by "practice and self-knowledge, and by the use of a properly systematic and comparative technique."[58] Thus so far as knowledge and power was concerned he believed, "The scientists must make it their boast that both governments and oppositions can trust them equally because they say nothing that they cannot prove, because they are always pedestrian and never leave the facts. The men of affairs must make it their boast that they allow the scientists perfect freedom in their researches and pay to their results when published the attention which proven fact deserves."[59]

These ideals were soon to come to grief amid the realities of Northern Rhodesia at that time. Wilson came to the RLI with high hopes of proving the beneficence of modern social anthropology, for which he forsaw an extensive public role. Among the first of the institute's publications was an attempt to popularise the methods of anthropology,[60] and an early suggestion to the trustees was a scheme for associate membership by which amateur social enquirers would be trained by the institute staff in "modern techniques of study which are at once simple in application and quickly illuminating,"[61] but official reaction was predictable alarm at the pros-

same thing" in a letter to A. A. Smith (M.L.C.), 28 December 1938, IAS "Plans for Urban Research File". History and sociology were identical, except for minor details, wrote Wilson to C. E. Fripp, 13 August 1938, IAS 1/45.
[58]G. Wilson, "The Rhodes-Livingstone Institute of Central African Studies", *The Cambridge Review*, 14 January 1938, 172.
[59]G. Wilson, "Anthropology as a Public Service", *Africa*, 13 (1940), 47.
[60]G. Wilson and M. Hunter, *The Study of African Society*, Rhodes-Livingstone Papers No. 2 (1939).
[61]Wilson to Young & encl., 22 June 1938, ZNA B1/4/MISC/6/1.

pect of amateur researchers coming into direct contact with Africans outside the master-servant relationship[62]—Northern Rhodesia at this time had been described by Young's predecessor as so racially stratified that the Litunga of Barotseland was the only African with whom a white man was supposed to shake hands.[63]

The more serious conflicts arose out of the form and methods of Wilson's social research. In conformity with his views on scientific independence, Wilson at once faced the trustees with the request that he rather than they should propose the research programme for the institute. This was reluctantly agreed to, although two of the five trustees present thought the board itself should make a list of problems from which the director should select, and there was a general feeling on the board that the subject "should be of some value to Government in assisting it to frame its native policy."[64]

Far from seeking out the most remote and uninfluenced African society to study, as the stereotype of the colonial anthropologist suggests, Wilson's proposals went to the heart of the evolving Northern Rhodesian social system. Admittedly, there was no suggestion that the settlers themselves required direct investigation, but he proposed that the institute should discover what was happening in three types of situation concerning Africans:

(a) "in the new African society of...permanent and semi-permanent residents in urban and industrial areas" (according to official policy at that time such urbanisation neither was nor would be allowed to occur).

(b) to the "group that alternates regularly between urban and rural areas."

(c) to African society in the rural and "especially the denuded areas."[65]

The urban research he proposed to tackle himself, while Max Gluckman went to the rural area of Barotseland when a second anthropologist was appointed in 1939. Wilson specified a wide range of topics for investigation in the urban areas, including the nature of African ambitions and aspirations in a white-dominated society.[66] This and other topics proposed were sensitive issues in the eyes of

[62]Minutes, 6th (wrongly typed as "5th") meeting, 29 June 1938, IAS.
[63]L. H. Gann, *A History of N. Rhodesia*, (London, 1964) 282, referring to remarks by Sir Ronald Storrs.
[64]Lane Poole, "Research Proposals by the Director", 28 June 1938, recalling discussion at Wilson's interview, 3 September 1937, ZNA B1/4/MISC/6/1.
[65]Wilson, "Preliminary Plan of Research", 30 May 1938, for consideration by trustees at 6th meeting (29 June), IAS 1/45.
[66]Ibid.

government, but they were also issues on which, especially since the riots of 1935, it might most have welcomed information. Part of the problem as the government saw it was that Wilson had made it plain that he intended to carry out the investigations in the urban areas by the same means as anthropologists had been taught to apply in village society, by participant observation, and not just by consulting official records and statistics. Such Malinowskian field-work methods raised the delicate question of relations with the mining companies, to whom more or less complete power over their own labour compounds had been granted, and to whom the Nor-thern Rhodesia government rarely felt itself strong enough to dic-tate. Nevertheless, the trustees brought themselves to approve Wil-son's research programme subject to the proviso that he first occupy himself with some rural inquiry and did not pay the pre-liminary visit to the copperbelt he had originally proposed "until this could be arranged conveniently".[67]

From the first, nervousness at the prospect of research outside a safe rural area was the prevailing view in the secretariat where opinion also clearly feared that Wilson's proposals would alarm the mine authorities "who will be apprehensive lest the questionings stir up discontent."[68] It was suggested to the governor that research which would indicate whether the "prospects of re-establishing Native Local Government are deteriorating or improving" would be more valuable. This diversionary tactic was scotched, however, apparently by the governor himself.[69]

Administrators on the copperbelt were equally uneasy about the suggested research, likewise arguing that though it was doubtless important, it would upset the mines or could be done better at a later date. The provincial commissioner suggested that Wilson should be directed to begin on some other line of rail town "in order that some report may be received of his personality, tact, and methods before he comes to the copper belt."[70] In fact Wilson had already made careful approaches to the mines,[71] and the provincial

[67]Minutes, 6th meeting, 29 June 1938, IAS.
[68]Secretariat minute, 13 June 1938, ZNA B1/4/MISC/6/1.
[69]Minute by R. H. Hudson, 18 June 1938, reporting conversation with the governor, ZNA B1/4/MISC/6/1.
[70]H. F. Cartmel-Robinson to Hudson, confidential, 30 June 1938. See also minutes by the DC's at Mufulira, Ndola, Kitwe, and Luanshya, enclosed in Cartmel-Robinson to Hudson, 8 August 1938, ZNA B1/4/MISC/6/1.
[71]Wilson to Hon. S. Gore-Browne, 23 July 1938, IAS "Notes from Provincial Commissioners" file; letter to general mine managers at Nkana Luanshya, Mufulira, Nchanga, and Broken Hill, 19 August 1938, IAS I. 30.

commissioner was clearly taken aback when two mine managers provisionally agreed to permit Wilson to work in their compounds. Not daunted, the PC now raised new objections, fearing, as he put it, that Wilson "might introduce technical criticism [of new local government provisions] from the anthropologist's view without consideration of practical difficulties or real knowledge of local conditions." The new arrangements had only come about "after prolonged discussion between people experienced in native affairs, both in rural and urban areas, and that any interference at the last minute even by a trained anthropologist might lead to tension or indefinite procrastination."[72] The most the PC felt able to recommend was that Wilson be allowed to pay a short visit to the copperbelt "to obtain a mental picture of industrial conditions without doing any fieldwork."[73] In other words, Wilson was to look *at*, but not talk *to* African miners!

It was in these circumstances that Wilson reluctantly agreed to begin his urban research not on the Copperbelt, but in the African locations of Broken Hill, Northern Rhodesia's oldest mining town, where lead and zinc had been mined since 1902. He still intended to work on the copperbelt too, but after the outbreak of war the two mines which had earlier given permission for research work on their premises withdrew it and the PC informed him that the administration would allow no copperbelt research for the duration of the war. According to Wilson, the Broken Hill mine general manager "laughed at the nervousness of the Copperbelt authorities" and allowed research to continue. However, 1940 saw strikes by first the white and then the black miners. Seventeen of the latter were killed by the military when violence broke out despite the generally sophisticated industrial tactics employed by the African strike leaders, and Wilson was asked to suspend his research for a fortnight. Shortly afterwards complaints that Wilson fraternised with Africans during fieldwork—surely an indispensable part of the method—led the Broken Hill authorities to withdraw all permission for research.[74]

Sir John Maybin, Young's successor as governor, intervened and met the mine authorities in Wilson's presence, but they refused to alter their decision because, it was said, his "methods...might cause

[72]Cartmel-Robinson to Chief Secretary, 8 November 1938, ZNA B1/4/ MISC/6/1.
[73]Cartmel-Robinson to Wilson, 15 November 1938, ZNA B1/4/MISC/6/1.
[74]Wilson, "Report on the position of the RLI", 6 May 1940, IAS A. 25/ A. 126.

discontent and unrest besides undermining the African respect for
the European mineworkers."[75] By this time the position of the
institute as a whole had been caught up in new controversies. Of its
three scientific staff (an archaeologist, J. Desmond Clark, had been
appointed curator of the associated museum as well as secretary
of the institute) two were conscientious objectors and the third, Max
Gluckman, was rumoured to be of doubtful political loyalty because
of left-wing views. A motion that the institute be closed was introduced in legco by the unofficial members, while the budget committee considered that the trustees should terminate the director's
appointment.[77] Although the trustees, at the governor's prompt-
ing,[78] agreed to keep the institute going on a reduced scale during
the war, it was made clear to Wilson at an emergency meeting of
the board "that his position as a conscientious objector made it
undesirable that he should be allowed access to large bodies of
natives where an expression of his views might have a weakening
influence on native morale and interfere with recruiting."[79] In the
light of this opinion and the impasse over his industrial research,
Wilson offered his resignation and left the institute at the end of
April 1941, just three years after taking up his appointment.

His experiences were not merely personal for they also illustrate
the underlying friction which tends to exist between men of power
and men of knowledge as well as highlighting the ambiguity of the
colonial anthropologist's position in the colonial situation. Friction
arises because where those in authority require new social knowledge, they are also inclined to fear its implications. Anxiety is
aroused that they will be exposed in some way or that their authority will be undermined by an expert claiming esoteric knowledge:
defensively, doubt may be cast on the superiority of expert knowledge over everyday experience—all features which underlay the

[75]Confidential minutes of 14th meeting, 27 October 1940. (The trustees
held confidential and emergency meetings to discuss the position of the
institute and staff on 12 July, 22 September, and 27 October 1940. The
minutes of these meetings were not placed in the minute book held by the
IAS, but copies of at least two of them survive: the 13th meeting (22
September) in B1/4/MISC/6/1 and the 14th (27 October) in B1/4/MISC/
6/3).
[76]Confidential minutes, 13th meeting, 22 September 1940 (see previous note).
Wilson to Governor (Sir John Maybin), 27 August 1940, B1/4/MISC/6/2.
[77]Chief Secretary to J. D. Clark, secretary-curator of the RLI and museum,
informing him of the legco motion, 25 September 1940; "Budget Committee
Progress Report", Item 25, 17 October 1940; Wilson to Maybin, 18, 27
July 1940. ZNA B1/4/MISC/6/1.
[78]Minute by C. G. S. Follows circulating the governor's views to trustees,

attitudes of the copperbelt PC extensively quoted above. Moreover, the authorities may fear the effect of the research activity itself on the human subjects over whom they rule. The more authoritarian the system, the more these fears are likely to operate, as they so clearly did in the case of Wilson's urban research. The 1935 disturbances pointed to the existence of serious social problems and helped to establish a case for promoting detached scientific research which would, it was thought, at the same time be useful. Yet the very existence of the social problems made those in authority nervous of having them independently investigated. The existence of a problem calls for study, but because there is a problem, study is considered dangerous and likely to exacerbate the problem. Thus on a later occasion, one administrator favoured an anthropological study of the Sala-Soli group in Northern Rhodesia "because they had proved too resistant to authority in the past," but another administrator doubted whether it would be expedient to send an anthropologist to study them because "they were a group who had proved so resistant to authority."[80]

Colonial situations (but not only colonial situations) are prone to produce "agitator" theories of discontent. Where discontent is recognised it is explained as the result of contamination of otherwise contented subjects by outsiders, be they members of the colonised group or fraternising anthropologists. Since it was the avowed aim of the latter to explain phenomena like discontent by other more structural regularities, and also to acquire their information by face to face contact with the subject population, both the conclusions and the methods were suspect in the eyes of colonial administrators. Furthermore, the colonial anthropologist in N. Rhodesia was invariably a member of the dominant colour group in a sharply stratified racial society, but his methods and inquiries inevitably took him outside the rigidly defined patterns of customary behaviour. By so-called fraternisation with the subject group, the anthropologist aroused the resentment of the dominant Europeans who saw their norms being flouted by men who as temporary rather than permanent residents were in any case distrusted.[81] Their in-

26 September 1939, ZNA B1/4/MISC/6/1.
[79]Confidential minutes, 14th meeting, 27 October 1940 (See not 75).
[80]Minutes, 65th meeting, 9 December 1954, IAS.
[81]This hostility was forcefully expressed in editorials in the *Central African Post*, 10 and 17 April 1953, which led to a series of bitter exchanges between anthropologists and the comparatively liberal editor, Dr. Alexander Scott. See also the satirical and anonymous song "The Battle Hymn of the Research Experts", *The Northern Rhodesia Journal*, 3 (1956-59),

volvement in the daily life of a subject people, the outlook of the
discipline, and the often venomous hostility with which they were
faced from white settlers, combined to help make the anthropologists on the whole identify with the Africans.[82] Thus Sir Roy
Welensky tells us—presumably using information from his government's special branch files—that anthropologists were in 1953 exceptions to Kenneth Kaunda's "general indictment of Europeans"
because they "advised the people against federation and served as
informers for Congress."[83]

Although Wilson could not escape the colonial conditions of
Northern Rhodesia and in particular the consequences of the outbreak of the Second World War, this did not prevent his three years
as director from being fruitful. Apart from an important intellectual legacy to his successors, his Broken Hill research, abruptly
terminated though it was, resulted in his *Essay on the Economics of
Detribalisation in Northern Rhodesia,* a pioneering study of urbanisation processes in colonial Africa.[84] Moreover, the work is marked
not only by good scholarship in the technical sense, but also by that
breadth of view and imaginative sympathy for the colonised to
which attention was drawn earlier. Ironically, it begins with a no
doubt sincere claim to be no more than a bare description of "the
actual social conditions and the inescapable tendencies which determine the possible limits of Government policy, as they determine
those of all other forms of human behaviour in this present situation."[85] In spite of this disclaimer, Wilson's strongly humanist values
are clearly evident throughout the work which, for all its apparent
neutrality, is implicitly a passionate indictment of the Northern
Rhodesia of his day.

In the context of the current radical critique of colonial anthropology, a most interesting feature of the work is the way that it
emphasises the essential inter-relationships both between the rural
and urban areas and between Northern Rhodesia and the world
economic system. Thus Wilson shows how a local circle of poverty
was kept in being by "cheap and unskilled labour, disproportion
in the rural and urban populations, and a semi-primitive and un-

---

472: Dr. Andrew Roberts kindly drew my attention to this item.
[82]Besides the debate in the *Central African Post,* see W. Watson's contribution, "The Social Background", to the anti-federation book edited by C.
Leys and C. Pratt, *A New Deal in Central Africa* (London, 1960) and M.
Gluckman's evidence to the Monckton Commission Report, Appendix VIII,
Cmnd. 1151-IV (1960), 127-136.
[83]R. Welensky, *Welensky's 4,000 Days* (London, 1964), 55.
[84]In two parts, Rhodes-Livingstone Papers, 5 & 6 (Livingstone, 1941, 1942).
[85]Part I, 4.

balanced peasant agriculture."[86] This situation is ascribed partly to the presence of European skilled workers and farmers with interests in preventing permanent urbanisation, African rural development, African technical training, and African wage increases, and partly by a world economy directed "rather to the production of producers' goods, high dividends—and guns, than to that of consumers' goods, high wages—and butter."[87] Furthermore the *Economics of Detribalisation* is no mere static survey, but is suffused throughout with a sense of historic process arising from the occurrence of a central African "industrial revolution." In fact, though he shared much of the functionalist emphasis on social cohesion and harmony as the product of equilibrium, another target of the radical critique, his interest in social change made him equally aware that disequilibrium, such as he identified in Northern Rhodesia, was not merely maladjustment—it was the motor of permanent change. The final words of his study are:

. . . in the structure of Northern Rhodesia (as of the world at large ) radical social contradictions are evident today; and that, in consequence, that structure must be changed, in one way or the other, so as to resolve them. This necessity is not a moral necessity; it is objective and material.[88]

In short, Wilson attempted, consciously or unconsciously, a marriage of Marx and Malinowski, by attempting to deal within the same frame of reference with both cohesion and change. These ideas were further developed in *The Analysis of Social Change* with its fruitful ideas about extensions of scale. Where he differed from Marx—though Marx himself was sometimes equivocal on the point —was in believing that a "moving equilibrium" of even change, which was also real change, was possible.

For bringing out the underlying nature of the social and economic conflicts inside Northern Rhodesia resulting from the penetration of a modern mining economy on a massive scale and, moreover, relating these local factors to the world economy, Wilson was criticised by some contemporaries.[89] No doubt they were equally disturbed by the fact that his findings were not confined to a small coterie of scholars, but were extensively used in an influentially critical and popular study of colonialism in Africa, Leonard Barnes's *Soviet Light on the Colonies* (1944).

[86]Ibid, 37.
[87]Ibid, 54.
[88]Ibid, Part II, 82.
[89]M. H. R., "Godfrey Wilson" (obituary), *Africa*, 14 (1944).

In Northern Rhodesia, Wilson's more permanent influence was felt within the RLI. Although Audrey Richards was designated as his successor, she never took up the appointment, in part at least because of the lack of scientific representation on the board of trustees,[90] and it was left to Max Gluckman, who had worked under and admired Wilson, to keep the institute in being alone for the remainder of the war. Besides continuing his research on the Lozi, Gluckman spent a good deal of time preparing the seven year research plan which got under way shortly after the war ended.[91] The plan was to do much for the institute's reputation in scientific circles. Although in detail it was Gluckman's, the plan owed a good deal to the general ideas set out by Wilson in 1940 for submission to the proposed colonial research advisory committee.[92] By emphasising the effects of industrialization and labour migration, the plan helped to prevent the large number of first-rate empirical studies which emerged in the nineteen-fifties from being too parochial, but the proposed co-operative volume on the central African industrial revolution which would have done much to pull them all together was unfortunately never written.

After Wilson's vain attempt to make the institute a centre of social engineering, it increasingly evolved as a scholarly outpost of academic social anthropology which at this time was beginning its expansion in British universities.[93] This evolution took place partly because Gluckman prevented the institute from remaining in the exposed and isolated situation of Wilson's day by most emphatically insisting—against the wishes of both the board of trustees and the colonial office—on the need for research officers to undertake their writing up as well as their preliminary training in universities in Britain.[94] His own move into British academic life in 1947 helped to strengthen these links still further. The role of the institute was also influenced by the fact that most of the research officers who were appointed came to Northern Rhodesia not to pursue a permanent career or settle there. They were much more

[90]Audrey Richards to Sir John Maybin, 3 January 1941 and Richards to D. O. Malcolm, 12 January 1941, ZNA B1/4/MISC/6/1.
[91]Max Gluckman, "The Seven Year Research Plan of the Rhodes-Livingstone Institute", Rhodes-Livingstone Journal, 4, (1945), 1-32.
[92]Wilson "Draft of Proposals...", 3 March 1940, ZNA B1/4/MISC/6/1.
[93]M. Banton, ed, The Relevance of Models for Social Anthropology, (London, 1965), Introduction by Max Gluckman and Fred Eggan on the growth of academic social anthropology in Britain.
[94]Minutes, 46th meeting, 10 June 1947; Agenda, Annexure A, for 47th meeting, 25 August 1947, IAS A1b(2)/A80a. The shortage of housing in post-war Livingstone was also a factor in the decision.

concerned with obtaining a British doctorate and in advancing the
study of social anthropology generally than in ministering to the
needs of the Northern Rhodesia government. For their part, government officers, if they did not ignore the institute altogether,
complained that what the anthropologists wrote and said was unin-
telligible or of little use in making day to day decisions.[95] The RLI
answer was not to abandon fundamental research or discourage the
idiosyncratic research interests of its officers, but to suggest that
the government should stop expecting help from the RLI and
appoint its own government anthropologists instead![96] This was
hardly the marriage of convenience between science and government for which Young had striven twenty years earlier, but it was
a logical development of Wilson's insistence on the need for scientific independence. The government, however, did not accept the
suggestion that it should appoint its own experts and instead in
1956 the trustees, for the first time, brought in an outsider as
director, a colonial civil servant who had been a government anthropologist in Tanganyika. The era which had begun with Wilson
was over. Far from being an institute of colonial apologists, it had
developed as a surprisingly independent centre of learning and as a
means of outdoor academic relief for a tightly-knit group of sociologically motivated men. Of the twelve anthropologists, apart from
Wilson, who held full appointments in the period up to 1956 no
less than eleven now hold professorial rank. The one exception is
a government anthropologist in Rhodesia, the only one of the group
not to obtain his doctorate on the basis of research carried out at
the institute (excluding Gluckman and Colson who already had this
qualification at the time of their appointment). Financed by colonial
governments and, more reluctantly, by the copper companies and
their associates, the institute was nevertheless the servant of neither.
Yet the Wilson episode and the later withdrawal of facilities for
research in a mine compound involving A. L. Epstein's copperbelt
inquiry[97] are a clear reminder that the pursuit of knowledge at the
RLI did not occur in a vacuum. The full effects of this on the kind
of work done by the institute as well as its detailed history after
Wilson's resignation must be worked out at greater length elsewhere.

[95]"Seventh Conference of Research Officers", October 1953, mimeo., p. 22.
IAS.
[96]J. C. Mitchell, "The Need for a Government Anthropologist", encl. in
Mitchell to Secretary for Native Affairs, 11 January 1954, with copies to
the SNA's in Nyasaland and Southern Rhodesia, IAS C2/A9a.
[97]A. L. Epstein, *Politics in an Urban African Community*, (Manchester,
1958), xvii-xviii.

# COLONIALISM AND THE PERCEPTION OF TRADITION IN FIJI
## John Clammer

The object of this paper is to examine some of the ways in which colonialism or to be precise a colonial administration has succeeded in interposing a 'conscious model' of its own creation between the social reality and the 'home-made' or 'conscious' model of that reality of a subject people.[1] The subject matter of this study is Fijian society in the late nineteenth and early twentieth centuries and some of the activities indulged in by the British colonial government during that period in their attempts to codify the customary practices of the Fijian people with a view to thereby more effectively governing the native polity.

The effects of colonialism are pervasive, and by no means all of them stem directly from the activities of the colonial administrations. Planters, traders, missionaries and the editors of local newspapers in the colonial tongue contribute equally to the formation of a picture of the subject society in the eyes of those who see themselves as its 'natural rulers'. The discrepancies between the colonial and native conceptions of the society in question may thus be not only great but varied. I propose to examine the one point

---

[1]The notion of 'conscious' and 'unconscious' models is of course derived from Lévi-Strauss. See C. Lévi-Strauss, 'Social Structure' in A. L. Kroeber, (ed.) *Anthropology Today*, Chicago, 1953 and in C. Lévi-Strauss, *Structural Anthropology*, London, 1969.

at which all these viewpoints converge, notably in the conceptualisation of the constituent units of Fijian social structure at the supra-family level, in the determination of the economic and other activities properly associated with each of these units and with the significance of the alternative conceptualisations that have been offered in terms both of the practical issue of the governing of Fiji and of the anthropological one of understanding Fijian social structure.

I will thus begin with an examination of the 'conscious model' of Fijian social structure created by the colonial government in the late nineteenth century, abetted by the missionary and planter communities. I will reconsider the reactions of Fijians to this feat of the colonial imagination and the subsequent effects of this upon their own perception of what constituted 'traditional' social organisation when the new model was brought into conflict with the old ones. I shall review some of the ways in which anthropologists have reacted to this situation whether by accepting or modifying the 'official' version of Fijian social structure. Finally, I will attempt to draw some picture of what may honestly be said to constitute traditional Fijian social organisations when all the imported and subsequently self-generated conscious models have been cast aside.

By social structure in this context I mean only the hierarchical sequence of agnatic kin groups in their ascending order of inclusiveness which compose traditional Fijian society. I also mean 'structure' to include what might otherwise be called 'organisation', i.e. the activities and attitudes associated with each level of or unit in the social hierarchy and which is therefore part of its definition.

The native culture discovered in the Fiji Islands in the early nineteenth century by sandalwood traders and, after 1835, by Wesleyan missionaries, was exceptionally diverse. The large number and geographical spread of the islands composing the group and the varied topography and geology of these habitats was in itself sufficient to guarantee heterogeneity in economy and culture. To this ecological basis must be added in particular the effect of long term contacts with Tonga to the south-east and quite possibly other island groups as well, including Samoa, the Ellices and Melanesia to the west. The cultural differences between the Lau or easternmost group of islands within Fiji and the western high-islands is still marked. Likewise there is still debate as to the number of dialects spoken across the group. Depending on the precise definition of dialects there may still be distinguished up to a hundred localised and often only locally intelligible speech forms. This situation was

no doubt aggravated by and largely stems from the fragmentary,
factionalised and constantly warring society found by early European settlers in the islands. While the situation was better on the
surface at the time of cession to the British Crown in 1874 the
underlying problems opposing cultural unification of the group
still existed and to a great extent still exist to this day. It was the
first self-appointed task of the Colonial governors to bring 'order'
to what appeared to them to be this intolerable chaos.

The motive however was not an anthropological one, but a practical one, or rather two closely related ones. The first was to understand Fijian society in order to govern it more effectively by the
method of local 'indirect rule'. The second was to resolve the difficulties over land tenure which, in causing friction between white
planters and Fijians on the one hand and between different groups
of Fijians on the other, was the chief obstacle to the peaceful imple-
mentation of indirect rule.

It was not until the appointment of David Wilkinson as director
of the Lands Commission that, after fifteen years of futile effort
directed towards codifying the native land tenure practices, and
recording the ownership of lands on this basis, that Wilkinson's
original suggestion to the first permanent governor of Fiji was
implemented. Wilkinson's suggestion, apparently forgotten by all
but himself, was that there was no point in simply registering
a piece of land as belonging to a member of a social unit identified
only by its geographical name if the nature of the units claiming
proprietary rights in land was not first established. The relationships between the chiefs, who claimed to have the right to alienate
land, and the social groups with which they were associated, and
which often claimed other or contrary rights would also be clarified
once this was done. While Wilkinson was quite correct in his general
methodology he was unable to fulfil his theory in practice, because
(and the reason for this I will return to) of his inability to unambiguously define, even on the basis of his investigations, the exact
nature of the social units having land tenure rights.

It was as a solution to this problem that in 1912 one G. V. Maxwell was appointed Native Lands Commissioner, with the brief of
resolving once and for all the 'inconsistencies' which his predecessors had inevitably found to characterise traditional Fijian social
structure and land tenure practices. In less than a year Maxwell
succeeded in producing an account of traditional social structure
which named the social units involved and defined their relationships. Maxwell's model was as follows:

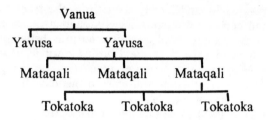

The system was thus characterised as a simple agnatic descent structure—the *Yavusa* being composed of direct descendants of a divine ancestor figure, whose sons founded the component *Mataqali* of each *Yavusa*. The *Tokatoka* are the minimal units having rights to land and were formed by sons of the founders of *Mataqali* when population growth dictated further subdivision. All these units are thus linked by kinship and by their subdivisional holding of tribal lands.[2] Upon its presentation to the Fijian Legislative Council this simple and hierarchical system was immediately enshrined as the 'official' doctrine of native social structure.

The Maxwell system is unambiguous, despite the severe difficulties of the same order as those which taxed his predecesors,[3] yet they were all resolved to Maxwell's satisfaction in less than six months of fieldwork. With the settlement of the nature of traditional social structure to the satisfaction of the administration the first step in the process we are examining was complete. The second is to observe the native reaction to this instant codification of their traditional polity.

This reaction began immediately. Indeed there is evidence that it began while the Commission was still collecting its evidence. It rapidly became apparent that the natives regarded the Commission as an impertinent inquisition which, while it could not legally be ignored, could at least be rendered relatively harmless by a number of means. One of these was to meet beforehand and for different landholders to agree between themselves an account of land rights which could be represented to the Commission as immemorially sanctioned by tradition.[4] An alternative was to invent social units which had never existed. This latter option was a favourite, for with a little forethought it was possible for the inhabitants of a district to organise themselves on the basis of the Commission's ideal struc-

[2]Council Paper 27 of 1914, p. 2. Fiji Legislative Council.
[3]*ibid.*, pp. 3-4.
[4]*ibid.*

ture of Fijian society, thereby preventing upsets in the local *status quo* and hurrying the Commission on its way without the crippling expenses of having to support the Commissioner, his aides, scribes, porters and the men from other villages in the district who had come to give evidence.

Maxwell was aware that evasions were constant and that 'evidence' presented to the Commission was often suspect, but he did not connect this with any inadequacy in his model.[5] In order to ensure the co-operation of the Chiefs in this project however, the Governor of Fiji in 1914, Sir Bickham Sweet-Escott, issued in the course of his address at the opening of the Council of Chiefs, a restatement and confirmation of the Maxwellian and now official administrative orthodoxy and a warning that failure to comply with it would be viewed with great disfavour by the Government.[6] The Government indeed possessed the ultimate threat—that it could register as landless any social units failing to comply with the Lands Commission's requirements and criteria and the land of such groups would automatically pass to the Crown if substantiated claim could not be laid to it. The Governor went on to *instruct* the Chiefs to see that preparatory meetings were held in all villages so that a uniform, officially acceptable and Fiji-wide register of all land titles and appropriate social groupings could rapidly be drawn up. This was seen to be doubly important when it was realised by Maxwell that 'the people are absolutely incapable of classifying themselves without assistance'[7] and that many villages were not certain of the groups to which they belonged and in some cases could not even identify their ancestor or *vu*.[8] Thus a policy that had begun with the first Governor of Fiji, Sir Arthur Gordon, was finally established in all its detail. The hallmark of Gordon's administration was his belief that:

> It is of the utmost importance to seize, if possible, the spirit in which native institutions have been framed, and endeavour so to work them as to develop to the utmost possible extent the latent capacities of the people for management of their own affairs without exciting their suspicion or destroying their self-respect.[9]

[5]*ibid.*
[6]Fijian Council of Chiefs. Opening Address by Sir B. Sweet-Escott, 20 May, 1914. Extract translated in P. France, *The Charter of the Land: Custom and Colonisation in Fiji*. London and Melbourne, 1969.
[7]Minute on C.S.O. 197/19. Central Archives of Fiji and the Western Pacific High Commission.
[8]R. R. Nayacakalou, 'Fijian Leadership in a situation of change', unpub-

The question to which we must shortly turn is how accurate the Colonial image of Fijian society was, what evidence there is for the 'Maxwellian Model' and what influence the official adoption of this system has had on the indigenous inhabitants.

But before doing this it is instructive to consider some of the ways in which the Colonial orthodoxy has been exploited by anthropologists and other commentators on Fijian society. I will initially draw my illustrations from the works of two writers—W. R. Geddes and G. K. Roth.[10] Thus Geddes argues that "Despite their exposure to alien influences the Fijians have retained their traditional social structure to a remarkable extent."[11] He goes on to state that rights to land "are vested in their patrilineal clans" and that many islanders "have been criticising the *traditional structure* and arguing for its abandonment on the grounds that it is hampering the economic advancement of the Fijians",[12] while others have taken a contrary view. Geddes's paper is not designed to take sides in this dispute, but to "describe the *traditional structure*, to analyse some of the more important changes which have influenced it, and to indicate what may be the effects upon it, and upon the cultural life of the Fijians which it sustains, of further possible changes."[13] Geddes's first assumption therefore is that Fijian social structure as observable in the field today is in fact that 'traditional' structure.

Geddes's second assumption is to argue that "Indeed, so neat and essentially simple was the system that we are tempted to speak of it as beautifully structured",[14] the operative words being 'neat', 'essentially simple' and 'the system'. The assumption, in other words, is of uniformity throughout the group and non-ambiguity and uniformity of the form of and relations between higher and lower order units of the structure within any one descent group. Indeed he goes on to argue that "The logical *consistency* of the

lished Ph.D. thesis, University of London, 1963, pp. 71-72.
[9]Sir A. H. Gordon, 'Paper on the System of Taxation in Force in Fiji, Read before the Colonial Institute', London, 1879, p. 178.
[10]W. R. Geddes, 'Fijian Social Structure in a Period of Transition', in *Anthropology in the South Seas*, ed. J. D. Freeman and W. R. Geddes, New Plymouth, 1959.
Also 'Deuba: A Study of a Fijian Village', Polynesian Soc. Memoir, 22, Wellington, 1945, and 'An Analysis of Culture Change in Fiji', unpublished Ph.D. thesis, University of London, 1948.
G. K. Roth, 'Native Administration in Fiji during the past 75 years', Occasional Paper, No. 10, Royal Anthropological Institute, London, 1951; and *Fijian Way of Life*, Melbourne, 1953.
[11]Geddes, 1959, p. 201.
[12]ibid., p. 201. My italics.
[13]ibid., p. 201. My italics.
[14]ibid., p. 202.

structure as a whole was an important feature of the system".[15] (Nowhere does Geddes rehearse his evidence for these categorical statements.) This consistency furthermore was alleged to be "conceptual, emotional and behavioural".[16]

Geddes goes on to describe Fijian social structure in terms of kin terminology, sex and seniority distinctions and behavioural norms governing relations between categories of kin. This leads logically into a characterisation of the group structure, i.e., the level of organisation with which I am concerned. Geddes's synopsis of the group structure, which may most instructively be compared with that of Maxwell, is as follows:

> By a corporate group we mean a group with a defined membership, all the members of which share in common rights, whether these be rights over property or rights to participate in group activities and share in the rewards thereof. Every Fijian belongs to a series of three such groups in addition to the elementary group of the family. As with the family these groups are patrilocal. The subsidiary groups within the larger have a hierarchical order in respect of one another based upon the principle of seniority of descent and persons belonging to them because their fathers belonged. They are therefore agnatic groups. In Fijian terminology they are called, in order of inclusiveness, the *Yavusa*, the *Mataqali* and the *Itokatoka*. We would describe them as the maximal, the major and the minor agnatic groups.
>
> Ideally, the series comprises a single descent line. In such case the mythology posits an original founder, who is known by name. The groups of the second order, the *Mataqali* are regarded as being founded by the sons of the founder of the maximal group. The third order groups, the *Itokatoka* may also in some instances be regarded as founded in the same way, namely by the sons of the founder of the *Mataqali*. . . . These third order groups are important in daily life but they are normally unimportant in the overall political and ceremonial structure.[17]

While Geddes concedes that only a few *Yavusa* in Fiji are of the 'ideal' type, in theory all *Yavusa* should possess its single ancestor god, place of origin, name, totem and *common ownership of land*,[18] although now many *Mataqali* have usurped these characteristics.

[15]*ibid.*, p. 202. My italics.
[16]*ibid.*, p. 202.
[17]*ibid.*, p. 205.
[18]*ibid.*, pp. 206-7.

War, population pressure, internal disputes, role differentiation as a result of the impingements of a cash economy and the removal of old sanctions and occupational categories with the introduction of Christianity have been the several causes of this. But on the other hand the necessity for survival of maintaining group cohesion in the face of these same pressures when applied from outside "explains why the phratry structure was so consistently maintained."[19]

Geddes continues by discussing the nature of Confederations (*Matanitu*) or groups of *Yavusa*, the descent versus the local principle in the kin composition of villages, and the traditional and changing functions of the units of the group structure. This latter, which is relevant to my argument, Geddes diagrammatically represents as follows:[20]

| Type of Grouping | Minor Agnatic Group or Patrilineage (*itokatoka*) | Major Agnatic Group or Clan (*mataqali*) | Maximal Agnatic Group or Phratry (*yavusa*) |
|---|---|---|---|
| Functions: | | | |
| A Numbers | Small co-operative tasks in farming, house repairs, etc. | Task requiring large numbers—fishing parties. | House Building, village site maintenance, track clearing, large fish drives, etc. |
| B Political | Leadership by senior agnate | Leadership by clan chief (*turaga ni mataqali*). Special political role in relation to *yavusa* chief. | Leadership by phratry chief (*turaga*). Division among clans of subsidiary political roles. |
| C Religious | | Guardianship by and worship of clan god. | Guardianship by and worship of phratry god. |
| D Ceremonial | Contributory unit in goods for ceremonial | Unit in Ceremonial | Validation and co-ordination of ceremonial by constituent clans. |
| E Proprietary Rights | | Land tenure | |
| F Obligations | Mutual aid circle of great intensity | Mutual aid circle of considerable intensity. | Mutual aid circle of less intensity. |

[19]*ibid.*, p. 207.
[20]*ibid.*, p. 214. Partial representation of Geddes's diagram.

While many of these functions, e.g., those of religion, have disappeared, the general format is held by Geddes to remain. One point however, stands out in particular—the ascription to the *mataqali* alone of proprietary rights over land. About this Geddes says:

> The chief factor at present giving stability to the descent grouping is the communal ownership of land, generally by the clan but sometimes by the phratry if it is a single patrilineal group. There is no individual ownership of the soil. Patrilineages may have use of particular sections of the clan land, but they cannot dispose of it either temporarily or permanently without clan approval. Clan ownership is embodied in the law of the Colony.[21]

Geddes goes on to claim that the communal system of work is traditional, and he contrasts this with individual enterprise,[22] and that the 'traditional' system of mutual aid and obligations has been one of the greatest restraints on economic progress. We thus have here a detailed exposition of the colonial dogma. We may divide this into a set of assumptions, vis: i) that the present social structure is the traditional one; ii) that social organisation is uniform geographically and structurally; iii) that the group structure is as determined by Maxwell; iv) that rights to land are or should be vested only in *mataqali;* and v) that the 'communal system' is the traditional form of economic (or at least labour) organisation.

Geddes is a social anthropologist. To underline my contention that he is not an isolated case in holding to these assumptions I will point briefly to some aspects of the work of my second example, G. K. Roth. I will take one principal example of his writings—his paper "Native Administration in Fiji During the past Seventy-Five Years: A Successful Experiment in Indirect Rule".[23] Roth notes that the chiefs who ceded Fiji to Queen Victoria did so on the condition that she "govern them righteously and in accordance with native usages and customs",[24] and he traces the failure of the immediately pre-cession Thakombau government, which was dominated by planting interests, to its incapacity on these very grounds.

The system of indirect government set up by the temporary governor, Sir Hercules Robinson, can be represented diagrammatically as follows:

[21]*ibid.,* p. 216.
[22]*ibid.,* p. 217.
[23]Roth, 1951.
[24]*ibid.,* p. 1 and 'Parliamentary Paper in Continuation of H.L. 120 and Cd. 3763, Colonial Office, October, 1908.

| | | |
|---|---|---|
| | Roko<br>(Provincial Chief) | Responsibility for Land,<br>records, births, deaths,<br>Native regulations. |
| (Council of<br>Chiefs (Non-<br>Legislative) | Mbuli<br>(*Tikina* or District Chief) | Detailed Administration:<br>Rates, dues, social<br>statistics. |
| | Turaga-Ni-Roko<br>(Village Headman) | Local Executive |

Scribes              Court officials           Police

This system, which was assumed to mirror the political structure of native society, was entrenched and extended by Sir Arthur Gordon with his policy of governing Fiji in accordance with native principles. So, says Roth:

> How precisely he wrought these principles into a practical policy acceptable to the Fijians is evident from a perusal of the code of Native Regulations made under the Native Affairs Ordinance which he enacted. This was the first code of Fijian custom set down in writing after discussion by representatives from all parts of the Colony and, generally speaking, the great body of custom that it contains has been understood for generations; and so it was not something new and therefore suspect to the Fijians to whom it was applied.[25]

Thus again we have the claim that, within the administrative structure on this occasion, "the basis of the Native Regulations is native custom."[26]

Central amongst the claims made for 'native custom' by Gordon was that "a system of government by councils of chiefs and elders [had] been in 'vigorous existence' before the time of cession". Roth continues:

> It has been customary for them to meet to consider matters relating to custom, alliances, and discipline, and the innumerable feuds attendant on their natural form of government in those days. In conformity with his policy of encouraging the use of native institutions whenever practicable the Governor gave statutory authority to three such types of council. Their members were thus enabled and required to take part in the system of Fijian local government."[27]

[25]Roth, p. 2.<br>[26]*ibid.*, p. 3.

Most important amongst these councils was the Council of Chiefs. Equally important was Gordon's land law of 1880 which recognised, according to Roth, "the force of custom which holds inseparably the Fijian social unit and the land that it owns-in-common. Such land is as much a part of a Fijian's entity as his name. ... [28] Roth goes on to repeat the orthodoxy relating to the names and proprietary rights of social units, and claims that the success, i.e. longevity, of Gordon's policy is proof enough of its correctness.[29] In going on to review the present day Native Administration Roth concludes that "the spirit of the undertakings given to the Fijians by Sir Hercules Robinson will be found in the principal measures that he initiated and in the Fijian Administration in its present form."[30] Roth was for many years Assistant Colonial Secretary in Fiji, and as such was in constant contact with the aspects of native life that he speaks about.

The question which has quite clearly lain behind all the preceding discussion is 'how much substance can be given to the claims of the colonial orthodoxy with respect to the aspects of Fijian society which I have particularly mentioned?' For the sake of clarity I will reduce the ideology of the colonial orthodoxy to a series of propositions which may be set out as follows:

1  Geographical and Structural Uniformity of Social Organisation.

2  Uniformity of Land Tenure practices, including rights over alienation of land.

2.1  Unambiguous nature and identification of the proprietary units in land matters.

3  The traditional nature of the Communal System.

4  The political structure of indirect rule equates to a close approximation of the indigenous political system.

4.1  The assumption that the traditional system of government was through a series of chiefly councils.

What evidence is there for these propositions?

I have already cast some doubt upon the possibility of even beginning to assume that social organisation was uniform throughout the Fiji group. 'Family *Resemblances*' certainly existed—for this must be the justification for calling Fiji by a single name imply-

[27]*ibid.*, p. 3. Also Sir A. Gordon, 'Native Councils in Fiji, 1875-1880', *Contemporary Review*, May, 1883.
[28]Roth, p. 4.
[29]*ibid.*, pp. 4-5.
[30]*ibid.*, p. 9.

ing that it was in some sense an entity—but not *uniformity*. To a
great extent this belief is less of an assumption than a prescription,
which has its origins not with the colonial administration, but with
its forerunners—the Wesleyan missionaries. From the outset the
missionaries had wavered between regarding Fijian as a 'general language' and as a collection of dialects.[31] The problem had more than
theoretical significance, for it became clear, once the work of Bible
translation was entered into, that either different versions would have
to be made in each major dialect, or a lingua franca had to be
selected from amongst tongues of the many speech communities.
The solution in part suggested itself, as Mbauan, the language of
the rising paramount Thakombau and his supporters, although very
localised geographically, was increasing in importance as a 'diplomatic' language in proportion to the waxing of Thakombau's for-
tunes. The first extensive grammar of Fijian—that of the Rev. D.
Hazelwood—was in fact a grammar (and dictionary) of Mbauan,
and the existence of this work clinched the matter. The first complete edition of the Bible in the vernacular also appeared in Mbauan
in 1847, and henceforth that dialect was considered the linguistic
vehicle for Christianity. The colonial administration thus inherited
a situation in which Mbauan was automatically accepted as the
language of government, a situation which equally obscured the
essential differences between localities and the difficulties of com-
municating with people within those localities. The importance of
this lies not only in the difficulties created by settling upon a
medium of official communication alien to the vast majority of the
population, but also in the anthropologically important consideration that kin group terminology varied widely from dialect to dialect. The Maxwellian System is Mbauan in its terminology, not
Fijian. Thus while the term *mataqali* has become used generally
to refer to the middle-range functionally defined communities, the
term *tokatoka* is exclusively Mbauan, sub-mataqali units being
called variously *kete* in Ba, *matani bure* in Macuata and Ra, *kausivi* in Bua, *bati ni lovo* in Cakaudrove and Lau, and by other
names elsewhere. The terminology has different implications in each
case.

But to return to the main argument. From the diversity of Fijian
culture at the time of the first missionary contacts—for example

---

[31]Davies, J., *A Grammar of the Tahitian Dialect of the Polynesian Language*,
Tahiti, 1823; and Cargill, D., Letter, 18th October, 1836. For discussion
and analysis, J. R. Clammer, *Literacy and Social Change in Fiji*, unpublished D.Phil. thesis, University of Oxford, 1972.

the marked differences between the Viti Levu hill peoples and the coastal peoples of Mbau and elsewhere over such fundamentals as the nature of their respective political systems which were still clear in the late nineteenth century—it is apparent that no one 'traditional' system of political, social or proprietary organisation existed. The inability of the various Lands Commissions to determine a land tenure system on any unified principle is therefore entirely understandable although it escaped the colonial administration. Enough has been said about the basic 'uniformity versus diversity' argument. We must turn now to some more detailed examples of the differences between the colonial 'conscious model' and reality. I will take two specific issues since the land tenure problem itself has been dealt with elsewhere.[32] These issues are that of 'Communalism' in Fiji, and that of the functions of the social units in the social structure.

## Communalism

Was 'Communalism' as conceived by the colonial administration 'traditional', or did it indeed exist at all? The colonial 'communal' thesis falls into parts: the belief that land was owned in common by a *mataqali* and the belief that labour was organised communally to work this land. There is no evidence for the former thesis; on the contrary, traditional practice appears to have been that *yavu* or house site land was owned by occupants of the house; that *qele* or cultivated land was vested in the extended families which cultivated it, subject (usually) to the payment of *sevu* or first fruits to the chief. *Veikau* or forest land, while regarded as being the property of the community (not necessarily a *mataqali*) which defended it, was *de facto* vested in the individuals who cultivated or exploited any parts of it, again usually subject to *sevu* prestations. Families or lineages disinherited by war or other misfortune could normally obtain these same rights in a new area by seeking the protection of its chief and presenting to him *tabua* (whales teeth).

Communal labour was equally never the normal organisation of manpower, but was only employed for specific and limited purposes, and always on a reciprocal basis. Communal labour on a house or in cultivation never dissolved the individual ownership over the property or its fruits.[33] Land could equally be granted, for example

[32] France, *op. cit.*
[33] As Dumont D'Urville recognised as early as 1827: J. S. C. Dumont D'Urville, *Voyage de la corvette l'Astrolabe pendant les années 1826-29, Histoire du Voyage*, IV, Paris, 1832. See also B. Thomson, 'General Report

on marriage or for services rendered in time of war, to individuals either by a chief, or by another commoner individual. There is also no evidence that there was a communal right to alienate land, a right which was often exercised by a chief on his or his community's behalf once the idea has been put to the Fijians. The Native Regulations nevertheless succeeded in enshrining the dogma of communalism as a traditional form of organisation. Subsequent debates on the evils of communalism, either relating to its crippling effects on attempts to foster economic progress by way of individualism[34] or in deploring its effects on the declining native population[35] were thus at a further remove from reality. The dogma was indeed reinforced by European inability to comprehend the customs of *lala* or tribute and service to chiefs, *kerekere* or mutual appropriation of property and *solevu* or feast giving, all of which were seen as aspects of the communal system, and therefore traditional, but also as severe brakes on economic and moral progress.[36]

## Social Units

Closely related to these questions is that of the nature of social units. The non-uniformity of terminology I have already indicated, but what of their functional uniformity? We must remember that the colonial government assumed both. We have just seen that propriety rights to land were never seen as being invested in the *mataqalis* as such since that land was not recognised as a communally exploitable commodity.

There is also clear evidence that even if agreement over the term *mataqali* could be reached, there was no accord amongst Fijians over what the term denoted.[37] The government nevertheless insisted that all land should be registered by *mataqalis*. This was despite the clear recording of individual ownership in Rewa by Thomson,[38] and the discovery by the Wilkinson commission that in the Yasawas land was held by individuals and for their immediate families, and that in this case no connection at all was claimed between the *mataqali* (or the *yavusa*) and the land.[39] Wilkinson's recommenda-

on the Rewa Province', Native Lands Commission.
[34]e.g. Sir Henry Jackson to the Colonial Office, 23 April, 1903.
[35]Report of the Commission Appointed to Inquire into the Decrease of the Native Population, Suva, 1896.
[36]*ibid.*, p. 6.
[37]'Notes on the Proceedings of a Native Council', Native Lands Commission, 22, 1876, pp. 50 and 53.
[38]Thomson, *op. cit.*
[39]'Final Report on Ba/Yasawa', para. 107, C. S. O. 2987/97.

tion that this method of recording land tenure was correct and traditional and should be adopted in lieu of *mataqali* registration was rejected on the grounds that it would be too expensive to expand the Commission staff and in any case too time consuming. Wilkinson's endeavours were not entirely wasted however, for although by modern anthropological standards his recording of social units and their associated terminology was crude, he nevertheless succeeded in breaking down the 'simple' model of Fijian social structure by identifying units (in Ba/Yasawa) which he called *kausivi*, *kete* and *lewe*, or 'septs',[40] and similarly in Bua land holding units which he described as Co-brotherhood, Family and Individual holdings which are subdivisions of *kausivi*.[41] Wilkinson's views were supported by Fijian opinion[42] which also supported the view that the very notion of 'tribe' was alien to many Fijians who could not identify the social unit to which they belonged at a structural level higher than their village (*koro*) or even house-site.[43] The whole situation was plunged into even greater confusion by Thomson's conclusion that the *yavusa* was a sub-division of a *mataqali* with a structural status similar to or the same as the *tokatoka*.[44] Fison, another 'authority' seems to have deduced that *mataqalis* were families comprising *koros* (villages),[45] of which the *yavusa* was again a minor division.[46]

The remaining problem is to determine how this 'colonial model' is reflected 'on the ground' in contemporary Fiji. Its first manifestation may be seen in the collective activities required of villagers by the Government and which include such tasks as house-building, the maintaining of paths and preservation of the village site. Modern communalism is entirely the child of the Colonial administration. It is organised through the Government headman, who receives his instructions where necessary from the *Tikina* administration. In addition to the activities mentioned, land-clearing for agricultural purposes, taro planting, and the maintenance of water sources and courses are common communal activities, the personnel of which

[40]*op. cit.*
[41]"Final Report on Bua', para. 3, C. S. O. 4903/02.
[42]"Ratu Sevenaca Senioli to the Governor, 20 July, 1904, C. S. O. 3824/04.
[43]"Notes on the Proceedings of a Native Council', Native Lands Commission, 1885.
[44]"Report of the Commission...into the Decrease of the Native Population, p. 92.
[45]L. Fison, *J.A.I.*, Vol. 10, p. 335. See discussion in R. W. Williamson, *The Social and Political Systems of Central Polynesia*, Cambridge, 1924, Vol. 2, pp. 50-55.
[46]L. Fison, *Land Tenure in Fiji*, London, 1881, p. 9.

in a larger village may be divided on a 'sectional' basis into work parties which are not based on kinship. The Government headman has legal sanctions which he can employ against individuals who refuse to co-operate in communal activities. In terms of the articulation of the social structure, Government 'communalism' has resulted in the increasing eclipse of the kin-principle *vis-a-vis* the local principle at the level of the village economy. This clearly runs contrary to the most commonly encountered form of the 'traditional' economy, which was based on autonomous family units. Thus as Sahlins says of Moala :

> The government-established political system, which tends to favour village organisation of communal production, is encroaching upon the native system, which allowed local kin groups (as well as families) greater autonomy. What is happening in Moala and Fiji is, of course, but one instance of a very general phenomenon, the integration of larger units of native structure at the expense of smaller by dominant, outside powers as a matter of convenience and effective administration.[47]

Sahlins traces the virtual collapse of the "self-integrated kin group economy" to this usurpation by the collectivity of the traditional tasks of the family based units.[48]

At the level of kin group terminology there has been a similar eclipse of the varied terminological distinctions throughout Fiji in favour of the officially sanctioned Maxwellian model, but only at the official level. The 'underground' languages of the non-Mbauan/official language groups continue to flourish amongst the different dialect groups in many instances. But this must be contrasted with the phenomenon also encountered where, especially in South-Eastern Vita Levu, the official dogma will be recounted to the investigator as traditional truth. Similarly land-tenure is often now seen as reflected truthfully by the colonial model, and rights over land will be claimed on the basis of *mataqali* membership, as when a person has a right to cultivate land of the *mataqali* into which he marries. This also contrasts with the principle often expressed that land is owned individually or by the extended family. Modern practice also clashes with the Maxwellian model over the unity of structure and functions of the *tokatoka*, which are still vague and diverse,[49] and

[47]M. D. Sahlins, *Moala: Nature and Culture on a Fijian Island*, Ann Arbor, 1962, p. 266.
[48]*ibid.*, p. 267.
[49]e.g. see *ibid.*, pp. 223-225 and pp. 237-240.

by no means always even fulfil the minimal criterion of being composed of members of a common stock. Much the same can be said of the *mataqali*.

Thus 'on the ground' common patrilineal descent is not insisted upon; there is often a failure to be able to name the founding ancestor; the *yavusa* is not regarded as a *group*; members of villages often have no idea of which *mataqali* they are supposed to belong to. The forcing of traditional organisation has led not only to the confusions I have mentioned which arise from the multitudinous discrepancies between the 'official' and 'practical' models of Fijian social structure, but also to such anomalies as *villages* being 'elevated' to the status of *yavusas* where one did not exist. Equally the combination of *tokatokas* into *mataqalis* often reflects Government policy and not actual (traditional) links between groups. Exceptions, which are practically the rule, have thus become subordinated to the concept of Fijian social organisation as a segmented lineage system which, via the mechanism of patrilineal descent, proliferates according to a symmetrical and logical pattern. Yet the 'lineages' are often merely 'stocks which do not originate from a common named ancestor, descent has many of the features of a cognatic system, arbitrary factors such as war or local residence patterns are often responsible for group formation which should be based (according to the model) on kin relations with the next higher order group, and asymmetry is the rule in the ordering of the (often in fact unattached) segments of a descent group. The unity of Fijian kingroup organisation is what Sahlins, in a slightly different context, calls a 'structural deception'. Fijian group organisation is in essence (and terminologically) not rigidly structured, but highly relativistic.[50]

In a more obviously practical context, i.e., in relation to present economic development and the connection between this and the racial situation in Fiji, the question of 'traditionalism' has more than a merely academic interest. This can be seen in two specific spheres—that of land ownership and/or leasing by members of the Indian community and in that of 'individualism', or the problem of whether or not and to what degree entrepreneurial activity in the rural areas by *galala* (persons exempted from communal obligations) should be encouraged. We can agree that much that passes for 'tradition' in matters of land tenure is not so, and yet it is the sanctions of 'tradition' which are used by the Fijian Council of

[50]For a discussion of Moalan organisation see *ibid.*, pp. 240 ff.

Chiefs and others to justify the status quo and to prevent Indians from acquiring freehold or very long lease land, although in fact most of the land owned by the Fijian community is never used by them.[51]

The long term economic results of the Colonial policy emanating from Gordon have become quite the opposite of the effect intended. The setting aside of a sacrosanct Fijians communal system has aggravated economic discrepancies between the ethnic groups. In fact the Fijians were forced into a dependency upon their colonial rulers and into a situation which while in ethos 'conservative', crystallised in practice into an inflexibility incapable of exploiting even the constructive aspects of the new communalism. The other side of this coin can be seen in the constant debate as to the desirability of 'individualism' in Fijian society in the colonial past and in the colonial heritage of today. It must be remembered that Gordon 'instituted' the communal system not only because he believed it to be traditional, but also to allow the Fijians free economic (and social) development within their own sector and specifically to prevent men being taken off the native lands and employed as wage labour on plantations. The chiefs supported Gordon in this, for they feared that the extension of the plantation economy would destroy the basis of Fijian social life and even prevent the Fijians from deploying enough labour in their own fields to maintain their self-sufficiency in food.[52] Yet the Commission of inquiry into the decrease in the native population, which published its findings in 1896 identified 'the communal system' as one of the leading causes of the decline of the Fijian population and the decay of cultural standards generally.[53] No action was ever taken to rectify the Gordonian illusion, largely because of Gordon's (by then Lord Stanmore) defence of his 'system' against subsequent attempts to tamper with it by succeeding Governors, and his opinion carried much weight in the Colonial Office and House of Lords.[54] The result has been the insulation of Fijian society against structural changes since the inception of the colonial era.

[51]For a discussion of this problem in a broader economic context, see E. K. Fisk, *The Political Economy of Independent Fiji*, Wellington, 1970, esp. pp. 38-39, and 72-73.
[52]Council of Chiefs, Account of discussion passed from Wilkinson to Gordon, January 8, 1872, in Lord Stanmore (Sir A. Gordon), *Fiji: Records of Private & Public Life*, 4 vols, privately printed, Edinburgh, 1897, vol. 3, p. 499.
[53]1896, 'Report', pp. 6 ff.
[54]France, 1969, esp. pp. 157 ff. Also Debates, 29 September, 1911.

The one half-hearted attempt to restore the balance in favour of 'individualism' has been the *galala* or exempted farmer system, but even so the right to deny exemption still lies with the local commune, and there are minimum conditions of income, standards of agricultural practice and land area worked which must also be fulfilled by a prospective *galala*. The conditions indeed are so strict that the bias is strongly against the individualist and in favour of the commune, and this is official administrative policy. There are thus contradictions at more than one level between the ideals of communalism and individualism. Such contradictions are heightened by the fact that in dichotomising the situation into Individual (progressive) v. Traditional (stagnation) the alternative basis for co-operative activities *outside* of the 'official' *mataqali* and *tokatoka* units have been overlooked. As I have already suggested in practice non-kin unit 'communalism' exists on the basis of *lala* (duties performed for a chief), need, friendship or simple economy. Yet such 'kin-alternative' organisation is not recognised in or by the 'system'. And such a state of affairs is likely to increase when it is remembered that generally although land is registered on a *mataqali* and *tokatoka* basis, the functions of those units which are alleged to correspond with this fact, no longer or never did, obtain. The result of colonial policy in economic terms has basically been to withdraw economic incentives by giving the community too great a share of the individual's time and produce and in then being unable to solve the problems that this has engendered within the context that colonial administration created for itself. The situation is seen to be even less fortunate when it is possible to show that in its origin it is partly merely semantic and arises basically from the failure to see that 'community' does not equal 'communalism' in an economic sense. It is certainly true that traditional Fijian society was communal, but economically it was based on largely autonomous households and not on 'collectivist' or 'communistic' *production*. Colonialism in Fiji created for itself a web of errors in which the entire society is now enmeshed.

It remains to conclude with some account of the way in which tradition and the new order are perceived and how the relationships between them are regarded. The willingness, in many cases, of the Fijian people to present to the Lands Commission a neat and tailor-made version of their land tenure system in accord with the preconceptions and desires of the commissioners, we have already discussed. The attitude of the Chiefs appeared in the early years to be equally flexible. Thus it was reported to Wilkinson, and through

him to Gordon, that the Council of Chiefs unanimously agreed that
all land was vested in the *mataqali* alone and that all land was in-
alienable.[55] As France quite rightly points out[56] this attitude was a
complete reversal of earlier native policy, and indeed of some later
outspoken native leaders, one of whom explicitly suggested that the
units recorded by the Europeans were figments of their colonial
imaginations.[57]

The units themselves were not the only things requiring double
vision on the part of the Fijians. Great difficulty was often experienced in discovering the name of the *vu* (ancestor) of a descent
group, but discovered it had to be, because the authorities had pro-
nounced that every group had one.[58] The shaky foundations of this
belief have been further weakened by recognition of the fact that
the general Fijian origin legend—the *Kaunitoni*—is itself a fabrica-
tion and was first recorded as a result of a competition held by the
newspaper *Na Mata* in 1892 and was published as the authentic
legend, without reference to the fact that Williams, Waterhouse,
Hunt, Pritchard and others denied the existence of any Fijian
origin legend at all.[59] Yet this legend has since been seen as authentic, by Fijians and foreigners alike. Of equal significance is the fact
that Fijian genealogies are generally shallow in depth, subject to
changes that new historical and political conditions dictate, and
often merge with mythical tales. The insistence on the discovery
and existence of ancestor figures was thus ill-conceived, yet because
it was required, passed into the orthodoxy.

Even today many Fijians are 'ignorant' of the *mataqali* and
*yavusa* units to which they are supposed to belong.[60] Yet "Whilst
in village life the system is ignored or evaded wherever possible, it
is, at the national level, lauded and defended as being at the very
foundation of Fijian social order."[61] The Council or Chiefs in particular has vigorously defended the system against proposed changes,[62] especially as it is regarded as the chief bastion against Indian
encroachment on Fijian lands and privileges. The aristocracy of the

[55]Regulation 27 of the Native Regulation Council. Also in 'Notes on the
    Proceedings of a Native Council', 1879, p. 77.
[56]France, 1969, p. 113.
[57]C. S. O. 3824/04, 1904, Ratu Seniloli to the Governor.
[58]R. R. Nayacakalou, 'Fijian Leadership in a situation of Change', p. 72.
[59]For details see France 1969, pp. 3-4; and France, P., 'The Kaunitoni
    Migration: notes on the genesis of a Fijian tradition', *J. Pacific History*,
    1, 1966. Also see Sahlins, 1962, p. 14.
[60]Council Paper No. 1 of 1958, p. 212.
[61]France, 1969, p. 174.
[62]Council Paper 29 of 1959.

native society have thus come to perceive the colonial system as immutable and immemorial tradition—so the commoner has little option but to do likewise. The concious use of this new tradition for political ends has been yet a further step. The eminent Fijian leader, Ratu Sir Lala Sukuna, thus often reiterated the Gordonian position as enlightened and forward looking thinking,[63] despite its obvious economic and (vis-a-vis the Indians) social shortcomings, quite apart from the fact that the newly lauded 'tradition' was, in the Sorelian sense, a myth.[64] The contradictions between the native and official systems have not been recognised (at least publicly) by those best placed to see them. The 'way of the land' has ceased to be what Fijians were told to regard as such, and has become that which the Fijians wish to regard as such, from the vital issues of their social structure, down to beliefs as trivial as the conviction that tobacco smoking is indigenous and not a habit introduced by Europeans.[65]

Colonialism has thus profoundly influenced the Fijians' perception of their own traditional polity and its sustaining beliefs. But from the initial imposition of a system based upon, but alien to, the original traditional system, the dogma of 'traditionalism' has become itself tradition, and as such is exploited by the present political leaders of the Fijian community. The recent de-colonisation of Fiji has been more apparent than real, for while the official demise of colonialism has meant the rejection of its overt influence and apparatus, its mental creations have not vanished with them. The colonial mentality has not disappeared from Fiji, but is now to be found amongst the Fijian ruling class, and not the British one. While this is, to say the least, unfortunate in Fiji's present precarious economic and racial position, it is to some extent understandable when the origins of the 'syndrome' are revealed. Fijian tradition has been transformed by the Colonial regime, and since the late nineteenth century Fijian society has been in the process of being transformed itself to fit this new image of 'traditionalism', and this process is not yet complete, and one hopes that it never will be. Colonialism in Fiji has succeeded not only in physically ruling an alien people, but in imposing its own ill though-out ideology or image of that society, and so dominating them mentally, and that many anthro-

[63]e.g. Council Papers 10, of 1945, and 5 of 1952. See also, for European Comment, Roth, 1951, esp. pp. 4 ff.
[64]G. Sorel, *Reflections on Violence*, London, 1970, speaks of political myth in terms of "warmly coloured images" which act as "springs to action".
[65]e.g. Sahlins, 1962, p. 4.

pologists have fallen into the trap of accepting the new image as the old, and confusing both with the authentic. Yet recent and well conceived fieldwork in Fiji and the publications resulting[66] have been (almost inadvertently, for they have not been intended as studies of colonial influence) analyses of facts which confront every Fijian with the lack of authenticity of his own social structure, but which few recognise as such. But this too is understandable, for the passage of colonialism has left not only the ruins of the old tradition, but also a shaky orthodoxy, the legitimacy of which is questioned only by those who are prepared to carry the dialogue between the competing demands of traditionalism and modernity into the post-colonial era.

[66]e.g. Sahlins, *ibid.*

# ANTHROPOLOGY AND IMPERIAL ADMINISTRATION: SIR ALFRED LYALL AND THE OFFICIAL USE OF THEORIES OF SOCIAL CHANGE DEVELOPED IN INDIA AFTER 1857
## Roger Owen

Sir Henry Maine's *Ancient Law* (1861) is often described as one of the most significant contributions to the early study of anthropology. It was also one of the first works to combine an investigation of the nature of Indian society with general comments about the pattern of all human social development. As Maine himself was to write in his *Village Communities in the East and the West* (1871), India was of enormous interest as "the great repository of verifiable phenomena of ancient usage and ancient judicial thought".[1] Meanwhile, in the interval between the publication of these two works Maine had had first hand opportunity to pursue his study of India during his time as Law Member of the Viceroy's Council, when he was always ready to underline the importance of ensuring that official policy was informed by a sound knowledge of Indian society.

But the career of Henry Maine is only one of the many links between India, anthropology and imperialism. Another, equally important, is the stimulus given to British officials by the Revolt of 1857 to look more closely at the structure of Indian society in an effort to discover how it was being changed by imperial rule. In some cases the knowledge was put to direct use in framing government policy. More rarely it was employed in an attempt to construct a theory of Indian social development based on the methods to be found in the works of the early anthropologists. It was no accident that it was the decade which saw the publication of

---

[1] *Village Communities in the East and the West*, London 1871, p. 22.

*Ancient Law* and J. P. McLennan's *Primitive Marriage*, as well as the founding of the Anthropological Association in 1863, which also saw the first attempt at a "scientific" study of Indian society.

A central figure in this two-fold process of using the study of society both as a guide to the formulation of policy and as the raw material for the development of theory was Sir Alfred Lyall (1835-1911). His importance lies in three related directions. First, not only was he a close friend of Maine but he was also one of the first men to employ many of the ideas to be found in *Ancient Law* in a specifically Indian context. Second, Lyall was the author of a series of articles, later collected together in one work, *Asiatic Studies: Religious and Social* (First Series, 1882), which were a serious, although not very well sustained, attempt to analyse the structure of Indian society. Third, as a result of *Asiatic Studies*, and also of the important posts he came to hold at the end of his Indian career, Lyall became one of the most influential men within the Empire, someone whose advice was sought on many major issues. He was thus in a position to make sure that his ideas did not go unregarded.

Unlike Maine, who is usually remembered as a writer on the sociology of law rather than as an Imperial administrator, Lyall is regarded first and foremost as an official who also happened to produce a few books. However, as I hope to show, his career is, among other things, a good illustration of the misleading distinction between writing and governing. I will begin with a description of his investigations into Indian religious and social organisation while on service in the Central Provinces (1865-73) and in the Rajput States (1874-78). There will then be a brief account of certain works written by Lyall after his retirement in 1888 when he had an opportunity to return to his early studies of the development of Indian society. Finally, I will conclude with an assessment of the influence of Lyall's thought on the policies pursued by the British in India and elsewhere.

## 1. Lyall and the role of religion in the development of Indian society

Alfred Lyall was born in 1835, the son of a well-to-do clergyman.[2] He was educated at Eton and then at Haileybury, from where he set out for Calcutta in November 1855. Once in India he asked to be sent to the North West Provinces. He was posted to a town not

[2]For details of Lyall's life, see Sir H.M. Durand, *Life of Sir A. C. Lyall*, London 1913.

far from Meerut and within a little more than a year found himself
in the thick of the fighting which marked the first stage of the sepoy
mutiny. It was the events of this period which first seem to have
aroused his interest in questions relating to the British government
of India. As he wrote home in 1859:

I always find myself diverging into Indian politics, for I am
interested heart and soul in the affairs of the country, and am
always thinking of the probable future of our Empire and trying
to conceive it possible to civilise an enormous nation by the
mechanical process of the present times by establishing schools
and missionary societies. Also, having civilised them, and taught
them the advantages of liberty and the use of European sciences,
how are we going to keep them under us, and to persuade them
that it is hoped for their own good that we keep all the high
offices of government.[3]

Such preoccupations were to continue for the rest of his life.

After writing this letter Lyall spent another six years in the North
West Provinces before being transferred to a district in the Central
Provinces in 1865. It was here that his interest in the effects of
British rule on Indian society took a more constructive form, when
he was forced to pursue his habitual observation of Indian social
and religious organisation in a disciplined way as a result of the
need to contribute to, and later to edit, some of the first gazetteers,
those vast compendia of information about the geography and ethnography of each particular district under British control. Lyall
spent some years editing the Gazetteer of the Central Provinces,
sifting through the large amounts of data provided by the magis-
trates, collectors and others and trying to reduce it to manageable
proportions. Later, he was the sole editor of the Gazetteer for West
Berar, or the so-called Hyderabad Assigned District, which first
appeared in 1870.

It was the information collected and edited during these years
which formed the basis for much of Lyall's thinking about the
development of Indian society. But before giving a brief analysis of
the major tenets of his thought it would be useful to say something
about the influence of Maine, McLennan and the other early anthropologists on his whole approach to the subject. As he freely
acknowledged, it was they who provided him with the methods by
which random observations could be ordered and by which different
social groups could be analysed.

[3]*Ibid.*, p. 89.

To begin with, Lyall, like Maine and McLennan, was a firm believer in the utility of what was then known as the "comparative method", the basis of which consisted in the recognition of certain similarities between the political and social institutions of contemporary "primitive" peoples and those of the communities which had existed in Europe many centuries before.[4] Given the prevailing assumption that human progress could be seen as a linear movement from "barbarism" to civilisation, it was then supposed that it was possible to undertake the systematic classification of different societies with the object of constructing a hypothetical sequence illustrating the historical development of mankind. Two implications followed. *One,* just as Maine and McLennan regarded it as legitimate to assume that you could learn much about Europe's past by looking at Asia's present, Lyall believed that you could also use this process in reverse and fill in certain gaps in India's recent history by studying developments in Europe many centuries before. *Two,* the comparative method provided a means, not only of classifying different societies in different parts of the world, but it also suggested that it was possible to "rank" different social groups within India itself, according to the level of development they had reached.

Lyall's second debt to the early anthropologists can be seen in the way in which he used McLennan's theories about the central role played in a "primitive" society by the rules governing the choice of marriage partner. For Lyall, the analysis of such rules was basic to his efforts to understand the role of caste and clan in Indian life and also to his attempts to explain the way in which these institutions had developed.[5]

Finally, Lyall seems to have been greatly influenced by the ideas of Maine and other Positivist thinkers that the belief system of a particular society was moulded by its communal needs, and thus that, as needs changed, so too did beliefs. In Maine's words:

. . . the usages which a particular society are found to have adopted in its infancy and its primitive seats are generally those

[4]For the use of the comparative method at this time, see G. Lienhardt, *Social Anthropology,* London 1964, ch. 1; E. E. Evans-Pritchard, *Essays in Social Anthropology,* London 1962, ch. 1; and T. K. Pennman, *A Hundred Years of Anthropology,* 2nd edn., London 1952, pp. 152-4.
[5]Lyall's debt to McLennan can be seen clearly in his section of the *Berar Gazetteer* devoted to the study of local marriage in terms of McLennan's concept of "exogamy", *Gazetteer for the Hyderabad Assigned Districts, commonly called Berar,* Bombay 1870, pp. 187-9.

which are best suited to promote its physical and moral
well-being; and if they are retained in their integrity until new
social wants have taught new practices, the upward march of
society is certain.[6]
Lyall also followed Maine in his assertion that, though men were
led to match beliefs with needs, they often did this without properly
knowing what they were doing.[7] Hence, although they observed
customs of obvious social utility they were incapable of understanding why they did so, with the result that they were left to invent
false, superstitious reasons for their activity. In the words of J. W.
Burrow, Maine regarded man as "an incompetent sociologist".[8]
Lyall, on the other hand, whose interest was mainly with Indian
religions and which, unlike Maine, he regarded as more than mere
"superstitions" and central to the ordering of Indian society, sometimes changed the emphasis a little and was more ready to regard
man as "an incompetent scientist".[9] As he saw it Man's efforts to
come to terms with his horrible fears of a dark, capricious universe
led him to personify or to deify natural forces and thus, of course,
to a completely "unscientific" approach to what was actually taking
place in nature. "Here in India, more than any other part of the
world," he wrote in that section of the *Berar Gazetteer* devoted to
"Religion and Castes",

> do men worship what they understand least, Not only do they
> adore strange phenomena and incomprehensible forces—being
> driven by incessant awe of the invisible power to propitiate every
> unusual shape or striking natural object—but their pantheistic
> piety leads them to invest with a mysterious potentiality the
> animals which are most useful to man, and even the implements
> of his profitable trade.[10]

It is now possible to return to Lyall's own theories about Indian
society, based on the observations he made in the Central Provinces.[11] One is of particular importance and lies at the root of almost all he was to write about India in the years which followed:

[6]*Ancient Law*, London 1861, p. 15.
[7]*Ibid.*, p. 16.
[8]*Evolution and Society*, Cambridge 1966, p. 167.
[9]This is also Burrow's phrase. *Ibid.*
[10]*Gazetteer of the Hyderabad Assigned Districts*, pp. 189-190.
[11]Lyall's principle theories based on his Central Provinces experiences can
be found in three articles first published in the *Fortnightly Review* in 1872
and then republished in *Asiatic Studies*, 1st ser., London 1882, as "Religion
of an Indian Province" (ch. 1), "Our Religious Policy in India" (ch. 8)
and "The Religious Situation in India" (ch. 9).

his belief that Indian society had in-built divisive tendencies. Of these by far the most important was religion, acting through the agency of caste. Using Max Müller's three-fold classification of the formation of Indian castes—ethnological, political, and professional —he went on to add a fourth, the sectarian, "meaning the castes which are produced by differences of religion, by new gods, new rites, new views, and new dogmas".[12] It was castes organized on this last, religious basis, with strict rules forbidding marriage or even the sharing of food with outsiders which, according to Lyall, acted constantly as a wedge upon Indian society, subjecting it to "perpetual morcellement" by splitting existing groups into smaller subgroups and by creating more and more new divisions. Some of the ways in which this process took place are described in the *Berar Gazetteer* and in his article "Religion of an Indian Province". One which he mentions is that a man might break the matrimonial rules of his caste and be forced to leave it. Later, in the course of time, he, or perhaps his children, might draw together with others in a similar position and a new sub-caste would be formed. Alternatively, the excommunicated man might seek to vindicate himself by preaching a new doctrine and so, by this method, gather a group of followers around him. Another way in which, according to Lyall, new castes were formed stemmed from the Hindu practice of setting up tutelary deities without number who watched over the interests of special classes and callings, and who were served by special rites peculiar to their shrines. New deities of this type were constantly being recruited from the ranks of hermits, ascetics, and even men who had been known for one particular virtue in a worldly career. After death a shrine would be established at their grave—they were not cremated as other men—and, gradually, a group of people would collect round it, eventually forming a new caste of its own.

One of the most important effects of British rule, however, was to diminish the vitality by which fresh secretarian divisions were constantly being created: and, according to Lyall, this tendency was certain to increase as the years went by. As evidence for this he was later to cite the introduction of new laws, for example the Native Marriage Act as it had existed before amendment by Maine in the 1860s, which made illegitimate the children of people expelled from their caste. By increasing the penalties for leaving a particular

---

[12]"Religion of an Indian Province", p. 5. For Müller's analysis of the origins of caste, cf. his *Chips from a German Workshop*, London 1867, ii, pp. 319-46.

caste, the law automatically increased the hold which it possessed over its members and inhibited the formation of new sub-groups.[13] Again, more importantly, the British were engaged in the task of transforming the whole Indian environment, with their trains which reduced journeys to a fraction of their former length, their schools where children could obtain a European education, their public works, and their emphasis on law and order. This in turn was bound to have far-reaching effects on Indian religious beliefs and social organisations. It was not merely a question of the rational, sceptical, questioning attitude of mind which the British had brought to India and which, as Lyall asserted, had produced among the Indians "an advanced party of those who are easily inculcated with the Voltairian spirit, with contempt for irrational beliefs and for institutions which seem absurd on the face of them".[14] But as a country's religion was always so intimately connected with its political organisation, its system of laws, and its material condition, any radical change in these latter would inevitably involve the former. "The beliefs of the multitude," he wrote

are the reflections of their social and political history through many generations. Now that the Hindus have been rescued by the English out of a chronic state of anarchy, insecurity, lawlessness and precarious exposure to the caprice of despots, they will surely introduce, at least, some ideas of our rule, organised purpose, and moral law, into their popular conceptions of the ways of their gods towards man. It seems certain, at any rate, that wider experience, nearer and more frequent intercourse with the outside world, and the general education of modern life, must soon raise even the masses above the mental level that can credit contemporary miracles and incarnations, however they may still hold to the prodigies of older tradition. And this will be enough to sever the tap-root of a religion which now, like the banyan tree which it venerates, strikes fresh roots from every branch, discovers a new god under every mystery and wonder.[15]

What was to replace the old beliefs? Here Lyall's answer is less certain. Although he was sure that the small group of western-educated Indians would give up religion altogether, there could be no question of the great majority of the people abandoning their traditional faiths. Just as he believed that higher education could lead only to atheism,[16] he was also convinced that the harsh nature

[13]"Sir Henry Maine", *Law Quarterly Review*, iv, 14 April 1888, p. 133.
[14]"The Religious Situation in India", p. 302.

of the Indian environment would always demand some kind of
spiritual response from those who continued to live outside the large
towns.[17] One possibility he sometimes seems to have put forward
was that there might be a move up to the religious scale, that is
away from "naturalism" towards "supernaturalism". Evidence for
this comes from his assertion that British rule was leading to the end
of "simple Paganism" and idolatry.[18] On the other hand, his account
of the religious situation in Berar, in which he attempts to classify
the beliefs of different groups in an ascending order from the wor-
ship of sticks and stones to that of "the supreme gods of Hinduism",[19] leaves the reader in doubt as to whether he supposed that
all people could be expected to progress naturally from the "lower"
to the "higher". Indeed, there is one passage in which he seems to
be suggesting that any movement up the religious scale was inevitably followed by a counter movement downwards. Describing the
founder of a sect called the Manshaus, he wrote:

Men of this temperament have constantly come forth in India,
who, by their creative intellectual originality, joined to a spiritual
kind of life, have stirred up great movements and aspirations in
Hinduism, and have founded sects which endure to this day: but
it has almost invariably happened that the later followers of such
a teacher have undone his work of moral reform. They have
fallen back on evidences of miraculous birth, upon signs and
wonders, and a superhuman translation from the world: so that
gradually the founder's history becomes prodigious and
extra-natural, until his real doctrines sink into mystical secrets
known only to the initiated disciples, while the vulgar turn the
iconoclast into a new idol.[20]

What is more certain is that Lyall was convinced that any new
religious movement would spread very much more widely than in
the past. Previously, before the coming of the British, the political
confusion, the division of the sub-continent into separate states and
the difficulty of getting from one part of India to another had prevented the growth and expansion of the numerous sects which had
kept springing up. Now however all that had changed, and the
barriers which had previously prevented such a movement from
gaining adherents from over a large area had almost totally dis-

[15]"Religion of an Indian Province", pp. 28-9.
[16]Cf. his letter to his mother, 22 February 1856, Lyall Papers, India Office
Library, MSS. Eur. F.132/2.
[17]Cf. his review article, "Christianity and the Brahma Samaj" (n.d. 1873?), a
copy of which is in Lyall Papers MSS. Eur. F.132/49.
[18]"Religion of an Indian Province", p. 29.
[19]Ibid., pp. 7-27.

appeared.[21] Thus once again, so he believed, the effects of British rule was to unify, to break down divisions, and perhaps ultimately to produce the very thing which it had most to fear—a religious movement incorporating the vast majority of the Hindu peoples.[22]

Lyall left the Central Provinces on leave in March 1873. Soon after his return, 18 months later, he was made Home Secretary of the Government of India, promotion which he felt he owed in part to his articles on Indian religion.[23] However his stay in Calcutta was of only short duration for in 1874 he was posted to the Rajput States as Agent to the Governor General, a kind of British Resident. It was during his service in Rajputana that Lyall continued his examination of Indian political and social development. The result of his thinking can be found in two articles, "The Rajput States of India"[24] and "On the Formation of some Clans and Castes in India"[25] which do much to provide an historical context for his earlier theories about the rôle of religion in shaping the structure of Indian society.

The article on the Rajput States provides a brief sketch of India's political development during the previous two or three centuries. According to Lyall the Mughals had destroyed all the centres of existing political power in those areas of North India which fell under their direct control. Only Rajputana and one or two other states had been able to resist Muslim pressure. Hence the British had come upon a land without long-seated ruling dynasties or an ancient aristocracy, and this was one of the reasons why they had been able to conquer it without difficulty. Again, with the exception of the Rajput States, all the dynasties and principalities which existed in India in the 1870s had been established during the chaotic conditions of the 18th century. The majority of them owed their preservation to British rule without which they would certainly have disappeared, being unfitted by their primitive institutions to resist the professional armies of peoples like the Marattas and the Pathans.

Lyall was anxious for political reasons that the British continue their protection of these states. But in the case of Rajputana there was also an additional reason: the fact that it provided a window

[20]*Ibid.*, pp. 26-7.
[21]"The Religious Situation in India", p. 301.
[22]Cf. Lyall to Morley, 1873, in Durand, *Life of Lyall*, pp. 164-5.
[23]*Ibid.*, p. 162.
[24]First published in *Edinburgh Review*, July 1876. Republished in *Asiatic Studies*, 1st ser., ch. 8.
[25]First published in *Fortnightly Review*, January 1877. Republished in *Asiatic Studies*, 1st ser., ch. 7.

onto a system of political and social organization which had been superseded almost everywhere else in India. It is a description of this system which forms the subject matter of "On the Formation of some Clans and Castes". According to Lyall there was a period in the history of all peoples, whether European or Asiatic, when the dominant institution was that of the tribe. In India this period had not yet come to an end in areas like the Rajput States which were never subject to strong government from outside. It followed that an examination of the social institutions of Rajputana would reveal 'the roots from which society has grown up all over India". What were these institutions? Lyall believed that, in general, they ranged themselves along two lines: those of kinship (clans) and those of religion (caste). Both had much in common. In particular they were each defined by certain basic rules about whom their members could could not marry. These marriage rules were to be seen most clearly in an institution Lyall calls the "pure clan". All its members believed themselves to be descended from one common ancestor, all were subject to a tight system of rules which forbade marriage either to certain members of their own family or to those outside the clan. In McLennan's phrase, they formed a large "circle of affinity".

Such clans, so Lyall believed, owed their origin to the success of some chieftain in using his power to form a kinship group out of some of the "irregular tribes" inhabiting Central India, which, lacking a well-formulated system of rules or a common ancestor, were neither "pure clans" of descent nor castes. Once formed there was a tendency for such clans to move "upwards", as a result both of success in war and also of the influence of Hindu laws which imposed more and more rigid rules on any group which managed to maintain its social cohesion and its political power over a certain period of time. But as in the case of castes "downward" movement was also possible. In Lyall's view the very strict rules which distinguished the "pure clan" of descent were too rigid for a "good working institution", while the tendency for the leaders of such groups to become an aristocracy, soon "shackled by luxurious vices", led to a decline in their warlike capacities. Hence, such clans might find themselves pushed aside by "impure" clans pressing upward from below. Then as time went on the newcomers would also become more particular and more orthodox in their turn, as they were exposed to "the increasing pressure of the Brahmanical atmosphere" with its heavy emphasis on social regulation.

Castes, like clans, were also formed as the result of developments

within tribal society. In the more settled areas, where the hold of
tribes over their members tended to dissolve, the separate family
groups would begin to take different occupations and to inhabit
different places.

Then the trade, or the profession, or the common ritual becomes
the bond of union instead of descent or political association;
and thus the mixed population of India may have re-arranged
itself into castes, propelled into those grooves of the archaic and
inveterate exclusiveness of primitive Asiatics regarding marriage
and food.[26]

Once again the rôle of religion was all important, the result of the
influence of the Brahmins over the marriage law which, according
to Lyall, lay at the "foundation of society". Yet powerful though it
was Brahmanism had never attempted any reform of tribal customs;
it had not acted to crush out the innumerable sects of heathendom,
as had Christianity in Europe after the fall of the Roman Empire,
or Islam in North India. Its rôle was not that of an agent of change,
rather it "registered and confirmed" changes which had already
taken place. Thus when Lyall speaks of religion as being the
"cement" of Indian society he does not mean that it imposed a
straightjacket on Indian social evolution; what he means is that it
provided the framework inside which that evolution could take
place. Once tribal groupings began to break down, it was the institutions of clans and castes, their structure determined by certain
religiously-sanctioned rules, which served as an alternative form of
social organisation. Again so pervasive was the influence of Brahmanism that, as a group began to develop, its customs and sentiments, which may originally have been formed according to
"practical needs and experiments", inevitably tended to harden into
laws. However you might choose to look at it, religion was the key
to the understanding of Indian society.

## 2.  Lyall and the "arrested state" of Indian development

Lyall left the Rajput States in 1878 to take up the post of Foreign
Secretary of the Government of India. This was followed in 1882
by six years as Lieutenant-Governor of the North West Provinces,
and it was only after his retirement in 1888 that he seems to have
found time to continue his early studies of Indian social development. In particular he returned to the problem, raised over and
over again in *Asiatic Studies*, of trying to explain how India had
come to be in what he believed was "an arrested state of develop-

[26]"On the Formation of some Clans and Castes in India", p. 177.

ment".[27] Why had the tribal groups of which it had once been
composed not gradually amalgamated and fused into larger political entities inhabiting well-defined territories, as they had in
Europe? What had kept Indian society as a "mere loose conglo-
meration of tribes, races, and castes"? Lyall's provisional answer to
these questions is to be found in a number of articles and in two
works of history, *Rise and Expansion of British Dominion in India*
(London, 1894) and the chapter on "The Moghul Empire' which
he wrote for the *Cambridge Modern History*, Vol. VI. In brief, what
he believed was that India's "backwardness" was due to its failure
to develop the political institutions which in Europe had paved the
way for the emergence of a strong, stable nation-state by acting as
a counter-balancing force to the powerful centralising tendencies of
the monarchy. As he described the process:

> In Asia a new kingdom is almost always founded by some able
> leader with a genius for military organisation, who can raise and
> command an effective army, which he employs not only to beat
> rivals in the field but also to deal with all minor chiefships, to
> disarm every kind of possible opposition within his borders, and
> generally to level every barrier that might limit his personal
> authority. But he who thus sweeps away all means of resistance
> leaves himself no supports, for support implies capacity to resist;
> and the very strength and keenness of the military instrument
> that he has forged renders it doubly dangerous for his successor.
> If the next ruler's heart and hand fail him, there is no longer any
> counterpoise to the overpowering weight of the sword in the
> political balance, and the state of the dynasty is upset.[28]

The Moghul Empire was a good illustration of this thesis. Founded
by soldiers of genius, it lasted only so long as there were men
strong and skilful enough to rule its wide dominions. Meanwhile no
alternative centres of political power could be allowed to develop.
The great towns of India never achieved any municipal autonomy.
Most of the nobles owed their position to the Emperor and could
be removed at will. The religious corps had little independent influence of their own. Finally the army was not a locally-recruited force
as in Europe, with men of all religions in its ranks, but consisted
almost entirely of Muslims, many of them foreign mercenaries

[27]My attention was drawn to this point by E. T. Stokes. Cf. his "The
Administrators and Historical Writing on India" in C. H. Philips ed.
*Historians of India, Pakistan, and Ceylon*, London 1961.
[28]*Rise and Expansion of British Dominion in India*, 5th edn., London 1910,
pp. 321-2.

whose loyalty could not always be relied on. In such a situation there was nothing to prevent a collapse when the supreme authority passed into "feeble hands".[29]

Without political stability there could be no religious or social stability either. Long dominion by foreigners arrested intellectual development. It also kept the Hindus in a dislocated and disorganised condition, for their priesthood was never able to achieve any great degree of mastery of the constant movement and change in ritual and belief.[30] But it was not just a question of the Muslims disorganising Hinduism without substituting any strong religious edifice of their own; the basic factor in the situation was the way in which their presence had inhibited the development of strong nation-states in the sub-continent. As Lyall had written in 1872, the formation of nations "aids powerfully the concentration of religious beliefs", by providing a framework inside which the stronger sects gradually absorb the others.[31] Again, it assisted the formation of a formal ecclesiastical organisation with a well-defined theology.[32] Other aspects of India's "arrested development" could also be explained in this way. Lacking the protection which a stable state afforded, people were forced to create a system of social cohesion for themselves out of caste and clan.[33] Kinship ties refused to narrow down to encompass simply the restricted family. Polytheism persisted. Only with the coming of the British was progress possible.

### 3. The policy implication of Lyall's analysis of Indian society

The various articles in *Asiatic Studies* (First Series), as well as those written after his retirement contain a number of hints as to the policy implications of Lyall's analysis of Indian social development. It goes without saying that for him, as for every other Englishman, India's numerous political and religious divisions were a source of British strength. If the Mutiny had taught them one lesson it was that anything which allowed the Indians to combine was dangerous, while anything which kept them apart was to Britain's benefit. But in Lyall's case his anxiety about the speed at which the old barriers between different sections of society were crumbling was accentuated by the conclusions he had drawn from

[29]"The Moghul Empire", *Cambridge Modern History*, Cambridge 1909, vi, pp. 525-6.
[30]"Natural Religion in India", *Rede Lecture*, 17 June 1891. Cambridge 1891, p. 12.
[31]"The Religious Situation in India", p. 292.
[32]*Ibid.*, p. 292.
[33]"Sir Henry Maine", p. 132.

his reading of De Tocqueville's *Ancien Régime* and from his study of the causes of the break-up of the Moghul Empire. In each instance a great state had prepared the way for its own downfall by its passion for uniformity, which had led it to level out all smaller centres of local power upon which in other circumstances it might have relied for support.[34] Lyall was too much of a realist to imagine that the processes set in train by the British in India could be reversed. But he did urge that nothing be done to accelerate the amalgamation of India's many different political and religious groups. In the case of the Rajput States, for instance, the British might well be about to destroy a central feature of their political arrangements—the method by which the power of their chief was balanced by that of "turbulent and reactionary nobles"—in the interest of helping the former to create a uniform institution over his whole territory. This would be to begin the decay of an institution which had existed for many hundreds of years. It would be a pity to see it destroyed before understanding how the void it would leave was to be filled.[35] He was equally anxious about any policies which might put an end to religious division. "Caste", he observed, might look "unnecessary and burdensome"

. . . but these things will tumble quite fast enough without our knocking out their keystones by premature legislation. It is hardly in our interest to bring them down with a crash. We have ourselves to overcome the rather superficial contempt which a European naturally conceives for societies and habits of thought different from those within the range of his ordinary experience; but also to avoid distilling too much of the destructive spirit into the minds of Young India, remembering that for English and natives the object is how to preserve social continuity.[36]

This in an Indian context was a classic statement of the conservative position, with its concern lest old social institutions be swept away before new ones were created, with its accent on the need to maintain difference rather than to attempt to create uniformity. As such, it was a point of view which carried great weight, and its influence on official opinion was considerable. In the first place, in the 1870s, it was used to counter the arguments of a number of powerful administrators who maintained that concern for the fate of traditional ways should never be allowed to provide an excuse

[34]Cf. the letter to his mother, 11 July 1859, *Lyall Papers*, MSS, Eur. F.132/13.
[35]"The Rajput States of India", pp. 225-7.
[36]"The Religious Situation in India", pp. 302-3.

for holding up the introduction of necessary reforms. One important exponent of this latter view was James Fitzjames Stephen (Law Member of the Government of India, 1869-72) whose writings contain a closely-reasoned defence of his efforts to create a new code of law, regardless of the disruption it might cause within Indian society. Indeed so long as it was not politically explosive he seems to have welcomed such disruption, for it was only by destroying the old ways, so he believed, that moral and material progress along European lines could take place.[37] A good example of this is his attack on those who sought the preservation of the traditional Indian village community. Such a community he argued might well have existed for many centuries, but this only showed that India had long been in a stagnant position, "unfavourable to the growth of wealth, intelligence, political experience, and the moral and intellectual changes which are implied in these processes". And he went on:

> The condition of India for centuries past shows what village communities are really worth. Nothing that deserves the name of political institution at all can be ruder and less satisfactory in its results. They are, in fact, a crude form of socialism, paralysing the growth of individual energy and all its consequences. The continuation of such a state of society is radically inconsistent with the fundamental principles of our rule both in theory and practice.[38]

Lyall, for his part, while agreeing with many of Stephen's assumptions about the long term necessity of introducing such European values as belief in law and order and unrestrained competition was always ready to stress the dangers this posed to the British position in the short run. All policies had to be judged in terms of their possible effect on Indian society. Measures which had worked well in Europe might have opposite effects in Asia. It was arguments of this type which Lyall's writings provided for those who wished to oppose the influence of latter-day Benthamites like Stephen.

Secondly, in the early 1880s, Lyall used his theory of Indian social development as the basis for a strategy by which the British could maintain political security while at the same time introducing a number of much-needed concessions to local opinion. His ideas on the subject are spelled out in detail in an anonymous article,

[37]Cf. Stephen's chapter on law in Sir W. W. Hunter, *Life of the Earl of Mayo*, London 1875, 11.
[38]*Ibid.*, pp. 165-6.

"Government of the Indian Empire", published in 1884.[39] After an opening section in which he outlined the main elements in the changing situation which then faced the British in India as a result of such factors as the spread of western education, the emergence of a new middle class in the cities and the activities of a hostile press, he went on to state that the problem was one of steering a middle course between "innovation" and "conservation". While it was impossible for the government to stand still, while it was necessary to make some concessions to the demands of western-educated Indians for a greater share in administration, it was vital that this be accompanied by a policy designed to strengthen the main pillars upon which British rule was based. Of these, much the most important was the multiplicity of India's divisions. "At present the 240 millions of India are separated into social compartments by differences of blood, caste, and religion; and they are also politically intersected, to a material degree, by the native states." However, "as the old social prejudices decay, there is a tendency, already perceptible among the leading classes, to a kind of political fusion, to that gradual subsidence of gentile and religious distinctions that ultimately produces the level of modern society."

In these circumstances and with these prospects, it is clear that the Viceroy's present policy of decentralisation and of discarding class privileges is an appropriate adaptation of administrative measures to change that must be recognised. The old inequality and variety of laws, customs, and personal status parcelled men out into groups, and did thus provide some sort of local self-government, some distribution of authority. Now that these sub-divisions are vanishing, it is in accordance with natural expediency to substitute other administrative and territorial groupings, and to prevent authority from being fixed and concentrated in aristocratic bureaux as in Russia. Otherwise the English dominion in India may drift towards that condition of over-centralised isolation, with shallow foundations and inadequate support which renders an Empire as top-heavy as an over-built tower, and which is unquestionably an element of political instability.

Other recommendations followed. It was important that men of local influence were associated with British rule wherever possible. Great care should be taken when it came to efforts to reform insti-

[39]*Edinburgh Review*, clix, 325, January 1884. Attributed to Lyall by Durand, *Life of Lyall*, p. 477.

tutions which "no foreigners can be expected to understand accurately or exhaustively". Finally, it should always be remembered that it was in "the content and confidence of the land-owning class" that the government found its essential element of stability.

As for the practical application of this strategy it is first necessary to look at Lyall's own approach to the drafting of the three most important bills passed during his term as Lieutenant-Governor of the North West Provinces: the local-government bill, the Oudh rent bill, and the bill to establish a provincial Legislative Council. Let us consider them in turn.

The local-government bill owed its passage to an initiative by the viceroy, Lord Ripon, whose general aim was to provide a political outlet for the ambitions of the growing number of western-educated Indians. One method by which he hoped to do this was to breathe fresh life into the existing machinery of local administration. In two resolutions (30 September 1881 and 18 May 1882) he invited the provincial governments to examine ways and means of raising the numbers of non-official members on municipal and local boards until they comprised at least two-thirds of the total membership. It was also proposed that non-official members be elected wherever possible. Lyall, for his part, was quite content to carry out these proposals as they stood where they applied to the municipal boards in the North West Provinces; but when it came to changes in the composition of the boards in districts and sub-districts he made strenuous efforts to limit their effect. In his first scheme all new members of such boards were to be nominated rather than elected, and it was only after pressure from the viceroy that he suggested a compromise by which an electoral body of government nominees was to choose who was to sit on the sub-district boards from among their own number.[40] A second dispute involved the question of whether the district boards should have an official chairman, as Lyall thought necessary, or a non-official one, as Ripon believed was vital to his whole policy. Once again a compromise was reached, by which the non-official members were to be allowed to elect a chairman of their own choosing, provided at least three-quarters of the board were present at that particular meeting. This was something to which the viceroy agreed with the greatest reluc· tance. As he wrote to Lyall on 8 May 1883, the official members could always prevent such a move by staying away en bloc. Further-

[40]Lyall to Ripon, 10 November, 12 December 1882, *Lyall Papers*, MSS. Eur. F.132/42.

more:

> I must say that the introduction of such a provision renders the
> while proceeding little better than a sham. If the proposal
> emanated from a person in whom I had less confidence than you,
> I should say that it was an elaborately-prepared device for
> taking away with one hand what was seemingly given with the
> other.[41]

It has been pointed out that Lyall's cautious approach to the viceroy's proposals was in some measure justified by the disturbed conditions in parts of his vast province, particular in Oudh.[42] But it is
also clear from the long correspondence between the men that
they were in fundamental disagreement about the whole purpose
of the reform. Whereas for Ripon, local self-government was to be
an instrument of political and popular education and a means by
which educated Indians were to be allowed to take a great step
forward in the management of their own affairs,[43] for Lyall it
appeared very much more as a useful instrument of administrative
devolution and, as he wrote to the viceroy, a way of bringing men
of "position, influence, and character" into district administration.
One aimed at a limited enfranchisement of the new middle class,
the other at associating the landed aristocracy with British rule.
What Ripon attempted to effect in accordance with his liberal principles and his experience in Ireland, Lyall tried to modify in terms
of his conservative approach to problems of Indian social change.

The influence of Lyall's analysis of developments in Indian
society can also be seen at work during the preparation of a bill
aimed at reforming the conditions of tenancy in Oudh. While he
was as convinced as Ripon that some measure was necessary to
protect the peasants of this over-crowded area from what was often
an annual demand for increased rent and from the summary evic-
tion which might so easily follow, he was also anxious to ensure
that nothing was done to alienate the local land-owners, the talukdars. For this reason great care was taken to ensure the agreement
of the talukdars at every stage and on a number of occasions Lyall
attempted to modify provisions in the draft bill in their interests.[44]
As a result the protection afforded the peasants was less than it
would otherwise have been. But this was justified by the fact that

---

[41]*Ibid.*
[42]S. Gopal, *The Viceroyalty of Lord Ripon* 1880-1884, London 1953, p. 103.
[43]*Ibid.*, pp. 84, 93.
[44]Cf. Lyall to Dufferin, 8 May 1886, *Dufferin Papers,* India Office Library,
   MSS. Eur. F. 130/42A.

ther were "important political considerations" involved.[45] As Lyall
wrote to Lord Dufferin, Ripon's successor as viceroy:

There is no doubt at this moment that the talukdars, as a body,
still adhere to the old-fashioned notion that it is their duty and
their interest to submit to the clearly declared wishes of the
government so long as they can rely upon the government
treating them well and considering their interests. And it is, of
course, very expedient politically to give them no reasonable
grounds for abandoning this notion, especially since even in
Lucknow a good many persons are already anxious to convince
the taludkars that their ideas are obsolete, and that the only way
of meeting the Government is by opposing it.[46]

The third, and last, important measure passed in the North West
Provinces during Lyall's governorship was the introduction of a
Legislative Council. Unlike the local-government reform and the
tenancy bill this was the result of his own initiative. But, like them,
he was ready to justify it in the most direct political terms.

What is wanted in these provinces is to bring forward our
leading native gentlemen and to encourage them to take some
responsible share in the higher administration. They have been
rather kept in the background since the Mutiny. The events of
1857-59 left a lasting impression on the generation that saw and
suffered by them; and the higher classes became little accustomed
to come forward in public affairs, or to show an independent
interest in politics as may be noticed (for example) among some
of the prominent men in the Punjab. Any step towards drawing
out these classes and enlisting them in support of local
administration will to my mind be a measure of conservative
policy.[47]

But Lyall's strategy for strengthening the British position during
the process of reform was not applied in the North West Provinces
alone. Elements of it are to be found in many of Lord Dufferin's
policies, especially those aimed at encouraging the Princes, and at
a further decentralisation of the financial administration.[48] Its influence can also be seen outside India in much of what Lord Cromer
attempted to do in Egypt. It was Cromer's opinion that, "every

[45]Lyall to Dufferin, 2 September 1886, *Dufferin Papers*, MSS. Eur. F.130/
MSS. Eur. F.130/42A.
[46]*Ibid.*, 8 May 1886, *Dufferin Papers*, MSS. Eur. F.130/42A.
[47]*Ibid.*, 12 July 1885, *Lyall Papers*, MSS. Eur. F.132/46.
[48]Cf. S. Gopal *British Policy in India* 1858-1905, Cambridge 1965, p. 156
and Sir A. C. Lyall, *The Life of the Marquis of Dufferin and Ava*, London
1905, ii, p. 154.

European who occupies a high position in the East should study
Sir Alfred Lyall's work",[49] and there is considerable evidence that
he, himself, often took Lyall as his guide.[50] Like the author of
*Asiatic Studies* he was concerned to strengthen British rule by
stressing Egypt's many internal divisions. Like him too he was
anxious to incorporate the conservative classes, notably the rural
land-owners, into the machinery of government. Finally, strategy
apart, it is likely that Cromer's awareness of the dangers of popular
discontent arising from ignorant assaults on local traditions came
from his friendship with Lyall and his reading of Lyall's works. As
he wrote of the Egyptian Ministry of the Interior in 1895, there is
no department in which "the zeal of the earnest reformer is more
to be deprecated. The habits and customs of an oriental people
must not be trifled with lightly."[51]

## Conclusion

Lyall's whole working life is yet another illustration of the close
links which have always existed between anthropology and imperial
government. Several of these links have been described in what has
gone before. First, when the Rebellion of 1857 first drew attention
to the urgent need to study the changes which were being produced
in Indian society by British rule, it was the early anthropologists
who seemed to provide a method by which these changes could be
analysed. However, second, it was not merely a question of men like
Lyall borrowing ideas from academic writers like Maine and
McLennan; the process also worked the other way round. In the
days before 'field' work the anthropologist in England had to rely
almost exclusively on British officials for his information about
Asian societies. In Lyall's own case, as he once pointed out in a
letter, Maine's 1875 Rede lecture (on "The Effects of Observation
of India on Modern European Thought") contained one or two
"leading" ideas taken from his own "Religion of an Indian Province".[52] This was just one of a large number of borrowings of a
similar kind. Third, the fact that much of the early anthropological
writing about India was the work of British officials meant that it
often directly reflected what might be called the administrative

[49]Cf. my "The Influence of Lord Cromer's Indian Experience on British
    Policy in Egypt 1883-1907", *St. Antony's Papers No. 17*, London 1965.
[50]Cf. *ibid.*, pp. 123-4, *The Earl of Cromer, Modern Egypt*, London 1908, i,
    p. 231n.
[51]"Annual Report for 1894", *Parl. Papers* 1895, cix, p. 12.
[52]Lyall to Barbara Lyall, 31 August 1875, *Lyall Papers*, MSS. Eur. F.132/16.

point of view. In the case of Lyall and Maine for example it is interesting that they should have stressed the institutional aspect of custom in India rather than, as Tyler and Robertson-Smith might have done, its ritual character.

Lastly, there is the whole question of the direct influence of Lyall's writing on British imperial policy. Reference has already been made to the way in which his study of Indian society could be used to make a powerful justification for Britain's presence in India by stressing the argument that it was only the arrival of the British which allowed Indian society to emerge from its state of "arrested development". Just as important is the point that his analysis also pointed the way to a political strategy aimed at confronting many of the problems faced by the Government of India in the last quarter of the 19th century. Beyond this Lyall's writings were also important for the way in which they both reflected and then, in turn, reinforced the fundamentally conservative position of the British administration. The inherent conservatism of anthropologists' policy recommendations has already been noted by a large number of writers.[53] In Lyall's own case his detailed knowledge of the social institutions to be found in the Central Provinces and in the Rajput States led him continually to lay greater emphasis on the disruptive nature of British-induced change and on the need to preserve old forms than he would otherwise have done. At a time when the reformers like Stephen seemed likely to carry all before them, Lyall was one of the most important men who pointed to the danger of applying, wholesale, measures that could only be justified because they had worked well in Europe. Legislation had also to be judged in terms of its probable effect on India, and this could only be done by starting from the position that Indian society was governed by more than a mere collection of outworn, obscurantist social ordinances; that it was not static and immutable as many had supposed, but subject to its own laws of development like any other. It is a measure of his influence that he was able to persuade so many officials that this lesson, drawn from the study of Indian society, should be taken seriously to heart.

[53]Cf. L. Mair, *Anthropology and Social Change*, London 1969, p. 2.

# THE INDIGENOUS CRITIQUE OF COLONIALISM:
## A CASE STUDY
### Roy Willis

## I

What is now happening is the re-emergence of a dialogue between Western and non-Western societies and cultures, a dialogue which was brutally interrupted by the colonial period. We seek a deeper understanding of what is called colonialism, and this search leads to an increased awareness of the subtle dialectic between social theory and practice, particularly in the special and interesting case of the relation between anthropology and the colonial system. Here is no simple matter of naïve anthropologists unwittingly (for the most part) serving the interests of metropolitan imperialism. Though there was plenty of that too.[1] But before fieldwork was invented there were anthropological giants about; and it was the grandiose anthropology of 19th century Britain which produced the essential legitimizing *mythos* for the colonial enterprise. The renowned self-confidence and unshakeably paternal authority of Britain's colonial administrators expressed a deep awareness of their country's awesomely responsible position at the top of the social-evolutionary ladder. Without Spencer, Tylor and Frazer there would have been no Sanders of the River.

In the inter-war years, anthropologists got quietly on with their job under the protective umbrella of the colonial system. The equi-

[1]Cf. Banaji, J. 1970 "Anthropology in Crisis", *New Left Review*, p. 64; Goddard, D. 1969. "Limits of British Anthropology", *New Left Review*, 58; Gough, K. 1968. "Anthropology: Child of Imperialism", *Monthly Review*, 19, 11.

librium model of the functionalists fitted well with Lugardian indirect rule to establish a neat division of labour. But I think it is true
to say that anthropology during this period made little impact outside the restricted bounds of its own discipline: the works of Malinowski, Radcliffe-Brown, Firth, Fortes and Evans-Pritchard were in
no way part of the intellectual furniture of cultivated folk in Britain
as those of Spencer, Tylor and Frazer had been. It is also problematic, a matter for investigation, how far the solid output of anthropological monographs during the inter-war years was of practical
assistance to colonial administrators. Indeed it is only recently, with
the virtual extinction of classical colonialism, that the substantial ad-
vances achieved by anthropologists during the colonial period in
human self-knowledge have begun to penetrate the consciousness of
non-anthropologists.[2] The analytic and synthesising labours of Lévi-
Strauss represent, I suspect, only the first wave of a massive resur-
gence of the primitive, mediated through the theoretical constructs
of social anthropology.

The case study offered here is intended primarily as a contribution
to the intellectual history of the small-scale societies who were on
the receiving end of colonialism. So far the literature of the "protest" of the colonised has dealt with armed revolt against the colonisers, with the more devious expression of discontent in spirit possession cults and independent churches, or with the rebellious
writings of Western-educated évolués.[3] The case under discussion
differs from all these in containing a formal critique of Western colonialism and what was perceived by a non-literate African people as
the value-system inherent in it. Properly to appreciate this critique,
it must first be placed in the context of the history, sociology and
basic values of the people concerned.

## II

In the middle 1840s, about the time that Karl Marx, as a refugee in
Paris, was working on the crucial *1844 Manuscripts* and writing the
*Theses on Feuerbach*, the people of Ufipa, in what is now south-
west Tanzania, were undergoing the ordeal of foreign occupation.
The Ngoni under Zwangendaba had invaded and conquered the
country about 1842. Before that Ufipa had been disturbed for many

---

[2]Thus, Evans-Pritchard's study of the Azande, published in 1937, is just
beginning to make its mark for what it really is: a contribution of the
first importance to the comparative sociology of knowledge.
[3]See, for example, *Protest and Power in Black Africa*, eds. Robert I. Rot-
berg and Ali A. Mazrui, O.U.P., 1970.

years by internecine struggle between the related dynasties, called Twa, which ruled the rival Fipa states of Nkansi and Lyangalile. Fortunately for the Fipa, the Ngoni domination was relatively short-lived. In the late 1840s, Zwangendaba died and in the disputes over succession which followed, the Ngoni split into several factions which almost immediately moved out of Ufipa to other parts of East and Central Africa. The Twa in Nkansi and Lyangalile re-established the structures of state power but they never fought one another again. Instead the two countries devoted most of their energies to economic progress and by the later 19th century had achieved a high level of prosperity in relation to most other parts of East-Central Africa. This condition obtained most particularly in Nkansi, the larger and more populous northern state which also had the advantage of lying across one of the main trans-continental trade routes between the mineral-rich empire of Katanga and the East African ports.[4] Between about 1860 until the definitive end of Twa sovereignty with the establishment of a German force there in 1898, Nkansi enjoyed a period of peace and affluence which contrasts markedly with the turbulence and impoverishment suffered by Africans over a wide area during this same period. The contrast was very apparent to the few European travellers through Ufipa during this time. For Joseph Thomson, who stayed at the capital of Nkansi in 1880, there was "no more peaceful race in all Central Africa":

> They are more of a purely agricultural race than any other tribe I have seen. To the cultivation of their fields they devote themselves entirely. They never engage in war, although they will, of course, defend themselves.[5]

The English Protestant missionary Edward Coode Hore reported seeing "vast fields" of many different food-crops when he visited the Lake Tanganyika domain of Nkansi in the same year. When he left his boat's crew was "discontented at leaving the land of plenty".[6] Entering Lyangalile fourteen years later, one of the first Catholic missionaries, Père A. van Ost, noted:

> As soon as one arrives in Ufipa one recognises in the crops an

[4] It was in Nkansi that I did most of my field research in Ufipa, between 1962 and 1964 and again in 1966. In Lyangalile my work was confined mainly to the collection of oral traditions. I wish to express my gratitude to the Emslie Horniman Anthropological Scholarship Fund and to the Wenner-Gren Foundation for Anthropological Research for making this work possible.
[5] Thomson, J., *To the Central African Lakes and Back*, 1881, I, p. 221.
[6] "Voyage to the South End of Lake Tanganyika in 1880", (unpublished manuscript.)

industrious people. The least patch of reasonably fertile land is cultivated. . .[7]

This material abundance was the visible product of a specific social order, a complex structure of institutional forms and cognitive patterns, which must be grasped in outline before we can understand the Fipa perception of Western capitalism and colonialism. Technologically, Fipa agriculture reposed on a vigorous and sophisticated iron-working industry, which also supplied its military force with hardware. A recent authority describes this industry as "the strongest in the Corridor region".[8] The range of iron implements produced included, besides spears and arrow-heads, various kinds of hoe, large and small axes, scythes, chisels, wood-files, pincers, tongs and nails. The Fipa are not shifting cultivators, like the majority of the inhabitants of what Vansina calls "the savanna region"—the broad belt of grassy upland stretching across Central Africa south of the equatorial forests of the Congo.[9] Instead, a shortage on the Fipa plateau of trees (lopping and burning the branches of which fertilises the gardens of the savanna cultivators) has led the Fipa to adopt a method of compost fertilisation involving the construction of large mounds called *intuumba*. These mounds are themselves planted with beans. The result, according to a former Director of Agriculture in the Tanganyika Government, Mr. A. H. Kirby, "is an interesting example of the empirical use of green dressings for improving tilth and adding nitrogen, and the symbiosis of a leguminous plant and its nodule bacteria, also for increasing soil nitrogen".[10]

Although there are no figures to back this up, there seems little doubt that this method of agriculture gives a substantially higher return in food products in relation to area of land cultivated than the "slash and burn" techniques of the savanna peoples, since the Fipa have escaped from what must be a tedious necessity common to these latter peoples of constantly changing village sites as nearby land becomes exhausted. The Bemba, for example, change their village sites every four or five years.[11] An important consequence of

[7]"Voyage au Rukwa", *Chronique Trimestrielle de la Société des Missionnaires d'Afrique (Pères Blancs)*, 64, October 1894, p. 613.
[8]Christopher St. John, writing in R. Gray and D. Birmingham (eds.), *Precolonial African Trade*, 1970, 206. The "Corridor" referred to is the region between Lake Tanganyika and Lake Malawi. This writer is, however, wrong in implying in the same article that the Fipa iron industry died out during the colonial period. To my knowledge at least one well-known smith was still in active production in 1964, and I heard of others.
[9]Vansina, J., *Kingdoms of the Savanna*, 1966.
[10]Official Memorandum dated March 14th, 1927.
[11]Richards, A. I., *Land, Labour and Diet in Northern Rhodesia*, 1939, p. 19.

this difference in productive techniques between the savanna peoples and the Fipa is that the immobile Fipa village is, on average, two and a half times the size of the average settlement in the adjacent eastern savanna region—250 inhabitants against 100.[12] These Fipa settlements are tightly concentrated, with huts packed closely together. It is consistent with the differences in productive technique and the status of the village in the savanna region and among the Fipa, that whereas in the former region man's dependence on wild nature is emphasised in cosmological beliefs which assign the highest mystical prestige to hunting,[13] among the Fipa hunting is considered a mundane activity of no special account and man, centrally organised in the village, is seen as dominating the surrounding, peripheral world of nature.

There is a further significant difference between the people of Ufipa and the peoples of the Eastern savanna which must be taken into account when considering the Fipa view of man and his relation to nature. Bemba villages consist of clusters of kin gathered round one ambitious man who is the founder and headman, and when he dies the village usually breaks up. Elsewhere small localised lineages provide the core of settlements, with the lineage head also being the village headman.[14] Neither of these conditions apply to the Fipa: there the headman is the elected representative of the village residents, and it is he who is identified with the village rather than *vice versa*, as among the Bemba. There is no lineage system among the Fipa, and therefore no headmanship by right of descent, nor any relation between descent groups and ownership of villages or land. The Fipa village is an association of (theoretically) equal individuals who, by right of residence, participate in the village's collective ownership of surrounding land. Rights and duties associated with communal labour apply equally to all residents.

This distinctively Fipa type of social organisation is consistent with a view of man as a being who discovers or constructs himself through interaction with his fellows in pursuance of the collective purpose of human domination of nature. Fipa hold that it is through practical activity aimed at changing or transforming the world that

---

[12]The eastern savanna figure is taken from Vansina, *op. cit.*, 28. Villages in the western savanna are larger—between 150 and 200 or more inhabitants (*ibid.*). The Fipa figure is based on a preliminary analysis of data from more than a hundred settlements in central Ufipa, and probably errs on the conservative side.

[13]See Vansina, *ibid.*, p. 24. A particular example are the Lele as described by Mary Douglas in *African Worlds* (ed. C. Daryll Forde), 1954, p. 1-26.

[14]Cf. Vansina, *op. cit.*, p. 26-8.

man constitutes himself, and that such activity is necessarily social, a function of the relation between the self and interacting others. Such a world-view inevitably emphasises the primacy of verbal communication as the ground of that mutual understanding which is the basis of common action, and the concentrated settlements of the Fipa effectively meet this primary need. Thus, for about 30 years in the later 19th century, while their centrally controlled military force held off the imperialisms of the Nyamwezi to the north and the Bemba to the south, the people of Nkansi built an essentially humanist society: in the sense that man saw himself as a being alone, unmediated by any such time-transcending entity as a clan or lineage, constructing himself in social interaction with his fellows, as part of the continuing process by which human society controlled and dominated external nature. Such a world-view was itself the outcome of a long and conflictful historical process, recorded for Fipa themselves in their massive corpus of historical traditions. Its cardinal discoveries are preserved in a large body of stories and proverbs through which, in a still largely non-literate society, the accumulated knowledge of the past is transmitted to the young. It was this historically shaped and developed world-view, with its institutional basis and framework, that accounts for the pacific, orderly and industrious characteristics of the Fipa which so impressed 19th century European observers. Not that they had always been so: in 1798 the Portuguese traveller Lacerda noted that the Fipa settlers near Kazembe's country in what is now north-west Zambia were, like the Bemba, "mortal enemies to, never sparing, the Cazembe's people".[15]

By 1880, the Fipa had completely shed these aggressive and zenophobic characteristics. Joseph Thomson's characterisation of the Fipa as pre-eminently peaceful and hard-working has been invoked already. He was also under the impression—probably mistakenly—that capital punishment was unknown in Ufipa: but the impression is nonetheless signficant.[16] E. C. Hore was particularly struck by the suave, unruffled manner in which the Lake Tanganyika villagers re-

---

[15]Lacerda, F. J. M., *Journey to Cazembe in 1798,* 1873, trans. R. F. Burton, p. 99. Burton, after Lacerda, calls these people "Mussucumas" and evidently equates them with the Sukuma of the Lake Victoria region, who speak a language closely akin to Nyamwezi. In fact the "Mussucumas" are a people of the central plateau of Ufipa, whom the Fipa call *aSukuma,* and their language is one of several main dialects of what is now generally called *ciFipa,* the language of the Fipa, and which is grouped by linguists with Bemba.

[16]Thomson, *op. cit.,* II, p. 222.

acted to the sudden appearance in their midst of a complete stranger
such as himself, writing:

Here in Fipa more than anywhere else the people most wonder-
fully disguised their surprise on seeing me—one would think white
men were as common as black among some whom I knew had
never seen one before.[17]

So far in fact from repelling foreigners, the society constructed by
the Fipa in the second half of the 19th century seems positively to
have welcomed them. Arab and Swahili traders from the East African coast were known from the 1850s onward, according to oral
tradition, and the Nyamwezi traders traversed the country much
earlier on their way to Katanga.[18] By the time of Thomson's visit in
1880, a considerable number of Arabs and Swahilis had become
thoroughly integrated into the structure of Fipa society, as Thomson
attests.[19] He was, however, almost certainly wrong in assuming that
the leader of this immigrant community, an Arab called "Ng'oombesasi", "the rich in cattle", wielded disproportionate power in
Ufipa to the extent of having the legitimate ruler of Nkansi, the Twa
chief Nandi Kapuufi, "very much under his thumb".[20] For ten years
later, in 1890, we find the same "Ng'oombesasi" (his real name was
Shinkambi Khamis[21]) being removed from the royal capital by
Kapuufi and transferred to the governorship of Kirando, a Lake
Tanganyika port on the very edge of Fipa territory.[22]

The culturally instilled attitude to strangers current in Ufipa in the
later 19th century was that, no matter how bizarre their outward
appearance, they were people with whom business might profitably
be done—an attitude summed up in the proverb "Young man, don't
hurt the black snake—it may bring forth an abundance of (edible)
black fish".[23] Ethnically the population of Ufipa was by this time
extremely diverse (as it remains to this day). From about the end of
the 17th century or the beginning of the 18th there appears to have
been a migration into Ufipa of small groups from the Zambian

[17]Hore, op. cit.
[18]Livingstone records meeting an old man in Tabora, central Tanzania, in
1872 who remembered as a small boy accompanying his father on a trading
journey through Ufipa to Katanga. (Livingstone, D., Last Journals, 1874,
II, p. 180.)
[19]Ibid., p. 217-8.
[20]Thomson, ibid.
[21]See the "History of Ufipa" written by Sir John Lamb in the Sumbawanga
District Book, c. 1927.
[22]Reported in Chroniques Trimestrielles, May 1890, p. 130.
[23]"Unndumeendo, utaci ucuum" insoka induku, utamanyile cikulufyaal"
ikambaale".

plateau and the south-eastern highlands of the Congo; one of the earliest of these groups established the ritually important chiefship of Milansi in central Ufipa.[24] Other groups entered Ufipa from the north, coming from central and North-western Tanzania; this category included the ancestors of the politically dominant Twa chiefs of Ufipa, who were quite probably of Tutsi origin. This long process of immigration into Ufipa of heterogeneous alien elements, and their absorption into Fipa society, was accelerated in the 19th century by the turbulent conditions created first by the Ngoni depredations in Zambia and northern Malawi, and later by the imperialistic expansion of the Bemba state to the south of Ufipa and the Nyamwezi empires of Mirambo and Nyungu-ya-Mawe to the north.[25] The very violence attending these movements of refugee groups into Ufipa, and the social disruption wrought in Ufipa by the Ngoni conquest and occupation, may well have contributed to the shaping of the peculiarly Fipa social order, based on the co-operation of self-acting individuals joined in the collective enterprise of human domination of external nature which emerged in the latter half of the 19th century.

## III

We come now to the encounter between Fipa society and culture and Western colonialism, an encounter which may be said to have begun with the first organised European missionary expedition into Ufipa—that of the Société des Missionnaires d'Afrique (the White Fathers), whose representatives were entertained at the royal capital of Nkansi by Nandi Kapuufi in 1886. As a result of this visit, this missionary society set up its first station in Ufipa, at the Lake Tanganyika port of Kirando, in 1888.[26] Two years later the Anglo-German Agreement of July 1890 assigned Ufipa, together with what is now the rest of Tanzania, as a German sphere of influence. The last nominally sovereign ruler of Nkansi, Nandi Msuulwa, committed suicide in 1898, after "seeing his authority pass almost entirely

[24]See Willis, 1964, and the same author's chapter on Fipa history in A. Roberts (ed.) *Tanzania Before 1900*, Nairobi, 1968.
[25]The destruction and terror wrought by Bemba slave-raiding forays into the territory of the Mambwe and Lungu, whose territory borders Ufipa to the south and south-west, is vividly described by several authorities including V. Giraud, *Les Lacs de l'Afrique Equatoriale: voyage exécuté de 1883 à 1885*, Paris, 1890, p. 531 ff. On Mirambo and Nyungu-ya-Mawe and the aggressive expansion of these two Nyamwezi chiefs see Aylward Shorter, 'Nyungu-ya-Mawe and the "Empire of the Ruga-Rugas",' *Journal of African History*, IX, 2, 1968, p. 235-59.
[26]*Vide* Lechaptois, A., *Au rives du Tanganyika*, 1913, pp. 272-3.

into the hands of Europeans".[27] Three days after the succession to office of Msuulwa's heir, Kapele, a German force entered the country and took formal possession of it in the name of the Kaiser.[28]

The interesting question is how this change in political sovereignty, and the radical changes in the economic and ideological spheres which accompanied colonial domination, were perceived by the Fipa. We have seen that the social order which took definitive shape in Ufipa after about 1850, predisposed the people to admit, and then assimilate, foreign people and exotic ideas and products.[29] There was, however, that in the world-view of Western capitalism which challenged the very basis of Fipa culture, which assumed the social order to be built on the reciprocal interaction of autonomous human beings. Fipa consciousness of the essential differences between the world they knew in the later 19th century and the forces shaping society and the individual under Western colonialism is expressed in a myth in which old and new worlds are explicitly contrasted. This myth, which I transcribed from Fipa informants during field research in Ufipa, I have called "The Story of Kaswa" after the principal actor in it.[30]

The myth begins by introducing the central figure, the prophet Kaswa, sitting with a group composed of "elders" and "equals". The myth has already identified one of the fundamental contradictions in Fipa society—that between the assumption of equality between the reciprocally interacting, autonomous individuals composing the human community, and the arrogation of authority and power by a minority of "elders". The resolution of this contradiction is to be one of the main themes of the myth. But the position of Kaswa is made clear only two lines later: it is solely to the "equals" (*aniina*)[31] that Kaswa addresses himself:

And, being seated, he speaks to these comrades saying . . .
—And what he says is patently mysterious, to the effect that "some-

[27]Lechaptois, *ibid.*, p. 65.

[28]*Vide* Lamb, *op. cit.*

[29]Thus, before the colonial period Ufipa had a flourishing weaving industry, producing a warm and durable cloth. But as soon as European clothes began to arrive in the country, the people of Ufipa, led by the chief Kapele and his courtiers, began to wear the new style of clothing. Within a few years the indigenous industry was virtually extinct. (*Chroniques Trimesrielles*, 1900, 87, pp. 401-2.)

[30]A literal and a free translation of this extraordinary text, together with the vernacular original, first appeared in "Kaswa: Oral Tradition of a Fipa Prophet", published in *Africa*, July 1970, pp. 248-56.

[31]S., *unniina*—variously meaning, according to context, "sibling of the same sex", "fellow", "friend", "comrade", etc.

thing is coming, creeping, from the east—something with god-like powers". These two lines gain their force not merely by reference to a historical process—it was from the East coast, along the east-west trade route, that European missionaries, explorers and armed expeditions penetrated into the East African interior—but also because they evoke a proverb well known to Fipa, according to which anything that can be formulated by the human mind, however improbable, will eventually come to pass.[32]

The myth says that Kaswa's hearers admit to having tried but failed to understand him, and so he goes on more explicitly:

There are coming monstrous inventors,
Bringing war, striking you unawares, relentlessly.
'O you people, you are going to be robbed of your country—
You won't even be allowed to cough'.

There follows, in the second part of the myth, an account by Kaswa of the main changes in the structure of Fipa society which are to ensue from colonial domination. The younger generation, breaking away from the authority of their fathers, are not even present when the old ones come to die. As for the Twa ruling dynasty, it will disappear altogether.[33]

Kaswa goes on to characterise the changes in man's perception of himself and his relation to others which are to be introduced by Western capitalism. Man becomes isolated from his fellows: he cannot "see" them nor can he be himself "seen". The myth makes Kaswa express this "disappearance" of man as an autonomous but reciprocally interacting social being by saying that "a person clothes his whole body, even his eyes are clothed". In this state men are unable to communicate meaningfully one with another:

Those born in that time are devoid of manners,
Incapable of civilised utterance.

As for material things, everything will be measured in money—even natural products like grass and earth:

Everything becomes currency (ifyuuma)[34]—grass and the very earth itself.

In this alarmingly transformed world, the products of man's social labour take on a frightening life of their own, so that the motor-cars

[32]"*Caatakwa, cisuulwa, kwiisa*".
[33]This prophecy has been virtually realised: the Twa in Ufipa are now a tiny and diminishing group with scarcely a trace of their old authority.
[34]This word refers to the pieces of unworked iron, each sufficient to make a medium-sized hoe, which functioned as currency in Ufipa in the later 19th century. Cf. Marx (1964, p. 169): "Money . . . confounds and exchanges all things".

of the Europeans, the "monstrous inventors", have "protruding eyes" (headlamps), while their anuses (exhaust pipes) exude fire. Alienated and reified human labour has itself become a monstrous force in this image of the prophet Kaswa.

In the third and final part of the myth, an attempt is made to resolve the tension generated by the juxtaposition of two incompatible world-views. The narrative invokes the original unity of the Fipa universe, in which man dominates the world of nature. Kaswa himself acts out this human role, which is shown as consisting in a combination of action and intellectual control:

Then he arose and went all over the country,

Teaching people the names of every thing:

Mountains, rivers, trees, and so on.

Then Kaswa returns to the contradiction in the Fipa social order between an ideal of human equality and the privileged position of a minority of elders—the problem which had been posed in the beginning of the narrative. In an almost brutal symbolisation of the dissolution of bonds between the generations, he seizes the children's carrying-cloths—the pieces of goatskin or calico with which Fipa mothers bind their infants to their backs:

Then he steals the carrying-cloths of the children,

And returning, he went to a place called Loss of Mind.[35]

Then he said: 'You people:

I am going with these cloths of your children!'

There follows a vivid image which again recapitulates the structural unity of the Fipa cosmos. Kaswa raises his hands "high towards heaven" ("*fí umw'iyulu*")—then sinks into the ground. (In Fipa cosmology "sky" is conceived as analogous to the dominant intellect or "head", and to organised human society, in relation to "earth", which is analogous to both "wild nature" and to the properly subordinate lower body or "loins".[36])

The myth ends, no doubt appropriately, in an ambiguous manner, for the resolution of the problem posed by the conjunction of Fipa

[35] *Nkooswa n'Ilaango.* There is said to be a place of this name in the uninhabited bush in central Ufipa. The name may indicate that it was once a cult centre involving spirit possession. But the name also fits into a pattern running through the whole myth in which conscious human control of the world is contrasted with a converse state in which the (real) products of the human mind control man and annihilate his freedom and consciousness.

[36] Cf. Willis, R. G., *The head and the loins: Lévi-Strauss and Beyond* (*Man*, 1967, II, p. 4); and Willis, "Pollution and Paradigms" (*Man*, 1972, VII, p. 3).

and Western cultures is a matter for the future. The people react to
the disappearance of Kaswa with reasoned and co-ordinated action:
   They say: 'Let's dig and seize those cloths of our children!'
   They found but a stone . . .
That is, Kaswa has gone for ever, and the Fipa are left alone with
their historical heritage and their present condition.

## IV

   Obviously not every non-literate society would or could have
produced such a critique of modern Western culture as is contained
in the Kaswa myth. These oddly familiar ideas could be generated
by the Fipa because their society and culture shares with the West a
sense of having developed, and as still developing, through time.
Such a historical consciousness has been lacking in many literate
civilisations and anthropological research has shown it to be lacking
in many, and perhaps most, non-literate societies. Another significant and related feature of Fipa culture, that again recalls a characteristic of Western civilisation, is that it sees itself as changing
through absorption of new people, ideas and products from outside.
From the particular conjunction of the Fipa geographical and ecological situation, and their conflictful and often violent history up to
the middle of the 19th century, there emerged a peaceful, industrious and orderly society devoted to the "domestication" of nature
and external humanity. But towards the end of the 19th century, the
Fipa came to realise that what they had caught in their net was a
monster—something, in their terms, at once sub- and super-human.
   Evidently the rather close parallelism between Fipa and Western
world-views, a structural similarity which enabled the Fipa to express such oddly familiar ideas as those contained in the Kaswa
myth, poses a problem of explanation. This is not the place to pursue it.[37] For us at this time the signficance of such testimonies as the
Kaswa myth, and of the social anthropology that was born out of
the colonial system, may well lie primarily on the light they, and it,
can shed on the dark aspects of our own social selves.

[37]For a fuller statement of this problem see Man and Beast: a comparative
analysis of animal symbolism in three African societies (Willis, in press).

# SOME REMARKS FROM THE THIRD WORLD ON ANTHROPOLOGY AND COLONIALISM: THE SUDAN
## Abdel Ghaffar M. Ahmed

With the abolition of the slave trade, African Studies could no longer be inspired by the economic motive. The experts in African Studies therefore changed the content and direction of their writings; they began to give accounts of African society which were used to justify colonialism as a duty of civilisation. Even the most flattering of these writings fell short of objectivity and truth. This explains, I believe, the popularity and success of anthropology as the main segment of African Studies.
(Kwame Nkrumah, quoted in D. Brokensha, *Applied Anthropology in English-Speaking Africa*, 1966, p. 15.)

The first phase of contact between Europeans and Africans was marked by the establishment of the slave trade on a large scale. The second phase was dividing Africa between the dominant European powers seeking the exploitation of the area. The goal announced by these European powers when appealing for the help and support of their masses was to establish law and order among the 'savages' and to stop them from killing each other. "Now that he (the savage) was no longer to be carried off to civilisation, it might be right that civilisation should be carried to him."[1] In this process the ways of life and the systems of thought of the "natives" had to be studied so that alternative ways of introducing civilisation to them, or introducing them to civilisation with the least possible cost, could be found.

[1]V. G. Kiernan, *The Lords of Human Kind*, London, 1969 (Pelican edition), p. 213.

Nkrumah, though he might not have been fully justified, was saying aloud what many other African nationalists were thinking. It was typical of much contemporary thought in new nations. "Most African intellectuals are at best indifferent to, or mildly tolerant of, social anthropology, and frequently they have strong feelings of hostility to the subject and its practitioners. This attitude is reflected in the small number of Africans who study the subject; when Kenyatta, Azikiwe, or Busia were students of anthropology in the 1930s, there was a very different climate, and it was not thought strange or inappropriate that they should concentrate on anthropology. But today African anthropologists face a difficult time, with little understanding or encouragement from their own society."[2]

Anthropologists are regarded as reactionaries by the majority of the African intellectuals; and hence statements to the effect that "most social anthropologists held and still hold radical or liberal political views"[3] hardly find much sympathy among African intellectuals. The basic argument of the African intellectual here is that in the colonial period anthropological studies did not reflect the liberal political ideals of their authors. While it remains true that "in their personal capacity anthropologists, like everyone else, have a wide spectrum of political views. Some are known 'conservatives'; others lean far to the 'left',"[4] it has also been argued that "classical functionalism prevented [liberal anthropologists] from effecting a fruitful conjunction between their political commitments and their sociological analysis."[5] That is really what counts in this situation, and therefore the attribution of "invidious political motives" to such anthropologists cannot be dismissed as mistaken or unjust.

In this paper I shall make some remarks on the relation of anthropology to colonial rule on the basis of the Sudan experience. I shall touch—though without drawing firm conclusions—on an issue which is mostly neglected in anthropological analysis: the anthropologist's initial attitude towards the people he is studying. Such attitudes are mostly the products of the anthropologist's own society, and are the results of the judgement that arose from the first contact between the colonial powers and the populations of the colonies.

[2]D. Brokensha, *Applied Anthropology in English-Speaking Africa*, 1966, p. 16.
[3]T. Asad, *The Kababish Arabs*, London, 1970, p. 10.
[4]V. Turner, (ed.) *Colonialism in Africa 1870-1960*, Cambridge, 1971, p. 1.
[5]T. Asad, op. cit., p. 19.

## II

The case of the exploitation of African workers from former French colonies that was to be investigated by the International Labour Organisation—at the request of the United Nations Economic and Social Council—during the first week of August 1972 led to many comments which reflected the persistence of European attitudes towards the population of their ex-colonies. (See, e.g., *Newsweek*, August 14, 1972.) At the same time a comment on the issue, given by a British anthropologist on BBC radio, elaborated on the definition of slavery giving comparative ethnographic material from a number of societies studied by anthropologists.[6] His whole exercise, by obscuring the meaning of slavery, amounted to an indirect justification of the exploitation of African workers in Europe. This shows how the anthropologist might use his knowledge to justify certain attitudes held by his own society towards other people.

The whole issue has a long genealogy. European attitudes to the outside world in the imperial age had—and still have—a great influence on the thinking of many European scholars in various fields of knowledge. Kiernan gives an extensively documented account of some of these attitudes and how they developed and varied considerably between the seventeenth and twentieth centuries. Some basic ideas held by some Europeans about the "natives" who came under their domination have remained in currency, e.g., that the European is a superior human being in relation to the "native" who is hardly human in every respect. On the basis of such ideas a number of drastic measures taken against "natives" were justified. For example, "as the slave-trade grew and prospered, it suited Europe to think of Africa so unmitigatedly barbarous that no removal from it could worsen the lot of its inhabitants".[7] The assumption has aways been that since Europe is the home of civilization it is the mission of the European—who makes this assumption himself—to lead "barbarians" and "savages" in the rest of the world towards "civilization". By doing this the European, whether a trader, an administrator, or a missionary, was trying to set a course for the European exploitation of areas that came under his power. In confirming this much of the literature on the people of the colonies accounted for different customs and values that projected them as "not much better than animals", or, at best second rate human beings. Even in the fifties it was not unusual for a

[6]This commentary on the news was given by Anthony Forge.
[7]V. G. Kiernan, op. cit., p. 203.

European child on meeting a black man in the street to rush "to his mother's arms [crying] : 'Mama the nigger is going to eat me'."[8]

Taking the Sudan case, many examples of such attitudes may be cited. In forcing the population to do compulsory work that the government felt necessary for its own purposes, a European administrator who played a major role in the establishment of the Anglo-Egyptian Condominium justified the policy as follows : " 'The nigger is a lazy beast', said Sir Rudolph Slatin of the Sudan, 'and must be compelled to work—compelled by the government.' Asked how, he replied: 'With a stick'." Another example is Churchill's description of the Mahdists first published in 1899. While Gordon was pictured as a leader of a civilizing mission, the Mahdi and his men who led a revolution to free their land from Turkish rule were represented as a "savage mob". It must be admitted that Churchill, albeit with an air of superiority, had something good to say of the Mahdi: "It should not be forgotten that he put life and soul into the hearts of his countrymen, and freed his native land of foreigners. The poor miserable natives, eating only a handful of grain, toiling half-naked and without hope, found a new, if terrible, magnificence added to life. Within their humble breasts the spirit of the Mahdi roused the fire of patriotism and religion."[10] Dignity is assumed, by Europeans, to be normally a virtue of "civilized" people in ordinary life and hence it is almost conventional to see the native behaving in a dignified way only in defeat or at the moment of his death. Describing the end of the Khalifa, Churchill wrote that "Osman Sheikh-ed-Din was wounded, and as he was carried away urged the Khalifa to save himself by flight; but the latter, with a dramatic dignity sometimes denied to more civilized warriors, refused."[11]

The attitudes of superiority embodied in such statements were later expressed in an explicit way by one of the most able administrators in the British Empire , Sir Harold MacMichael. Discussing anthropology and its relevance to administrators, especially when it studied social structure, customs, beliefs and ways of thought of the "races of mankind", he said: "Some understanding of these will be conceded to be an essential equipment of the administrator

---

[8]Fanon quoted in Wallerstein, I. (ed.) *Social Change, the Colonial Situation*, 1966, p. 78.

[9]V. G. Kiernan, op. cit., p. 242-43.

[10]W. S. Churchill, *Frontiers and Wars, His Four Early Books Covering His Life as a Soldier and War Correspondent*, London (Pelican edition), 1972, p. 162.

[11]W. S. Churchill, op. cit., p. 378.

responsible for the tutelage of primitive races whose mental processes are not as ours. Between the mind of the educated European,
with its heritage of some centuries of occidental [?] and that of
the primitive savage a great gulf is fixed which the former can
bridge hardly and with patient study only."[12]

With these attitudes, developed over a period of time and firmly
held by administrators as well as missionaries,[13] it is hard to see
how the anthropologist, who shared the administrator's and missionary's culture, could avoid the influence of such attitudes in his
work. What makes this influence more probable is that in all
situations it was the administrator or the missionary—or both—
who introduced the anthropologist to the people whom he wanted
to study, and acted as intermediary in the early stages of the study,
suggesting informants and giving advice and information. It is true
that "anthropologists are trained over almost as many years as
doctors to collect a certain kind of information as "participant
observers" which will enable them, whatever may be their personal
views, to present as objectively as the current level of their discipline's development permits, a coherent picture of the sociocultural
system they have elected to spend some years of their lives in
studying, and of the kind of processes that go on in it."[14] But it is
also true that the institutes that give the anthropologist his training
are influenced by ideas current in the society to which they belong.
It is these training institutes which are responsible for planting in
the minds of their students a number of questionable Euro-centric
assumptions as if they were accepted facts; e.g., that "It is a fact of
history that it was the European peoples who discoverd the others,
[ . . . ] and not vice versa."[15]

Such assumptions have affected the kind of terminology adopted
by anthropologists as well as the emphasis put on certain topics in
the field of their studies. It is unfortunate that up to the 1960s
European anthropologists found it convenient to use terms such
as 'primitive' that express their assumed superiority. It is hard to
see how a European anthropologist can escape being influenced by
ideas in his own society, and to insist that he can avoid this influence would be to minimise the importance of socialization empha-

---

[12]H. MacMichael, Letter dated 10th Jan. 1929, *No. C.S./17/M/1 Financial
Secretary, S. G. Khartoum, GGC/296-99 File 18.D.7,* Sudan Law Project,
University of Khartoum.
[13]M. Forsberg, *Land Beyond the Nile,* New York, 1958.
[14]V. Turner, op. cit., p. 1.
[15]L. Mair, *Primitive Government,* London, 1962, p. 1.

sized by anthropology as a discipline.

## III

"Social anthropology has never been *merely* an aid to enlightened colonial administration, nor should it be viewed now as *merely* an aid to development in new states."[16] The emphasis as it was put by Lewis here confirms the fact that anthropology—beside other things —was an aid to colonial administration. The feeling among intellectuals of ex-colonies is that though it was not *merely* an aid to colonial administration, it played—more than any other human science—a major role in introducing to the administration the people of the colonies and in showing ways by which their social system could be controlled and hence exploited. It is true that anthropologists were not policy makers. "Anthropology had grown under the wing of the colonial office in Britain, and academics were restrained when dealing with overseas policy. Administrators received training in anthropology, and had a fairly good idea of the limitations on its practical use; they learned the local language and kept close to people, so that much of what the anthropologist had to say was not strange to them."[17] The administrators by combining their general knowledge with the anthropologist's special knowledge of specific peoples were able to develop their policy over time. But it can be legitimately argued that anthropologists, being in such a position, did at least indirectly contribute to policy making.

This association gave anthropology a conservative reputation and in recent years has led to many debates among anthropologists themselves when some of them tried to evaluate the influence of the subject and the rôle of its practitioners during colonial rule. The most recent of these was Sir Edward Evans-Pritchard's angry letter to *The Times Literary Supplement* dismissing Kluckhohn's statements regarding the positions held by British Anthropologists in the Foreign Office.

> Sir,—In going through some notebooks I find a quotation from the late Clyde Kluckhohn's widely circulated *Mirror for Man* (1949). He says:
>
>> During the recent war applied anthropology blossomed. British anthropologists held important posts in the Foreign Office, the Admiralty, the British Information Service, the Wartime

[16]I. Lewis, Comment on "Social Responsibilities Symposium" in *Current Anthropology*, vol 9, No. 5, pp. 417-18.
[17]G. Cochrane, *Development Anthropology*, Oxford, 1971, pp. 4-5.
[18]*The Times Literary Supplement*, March 10, 1972.

Social Survey, and in the field. One man was political adviser
for the whole Middle East, another carried the main
administrative burden for the vast Anglo-Egyptian Sudan,
still another handled liaison problems in Kenya and Abyssinia.
This makes us look pretentious, stupid and vulgar, and I think it
should be stated, in case this should get into the history of our
subject, that it is, at any rate in my opinion, complete rubbish.
Who these people holding "important posts" were I cannot
imagine. However, as I have sometimes been asked if I was
"political adviser for the whole Middle East" I have a right to
reject this imputation. I would wish to put it on record that I
was nothing of the kind—I was just an insignificant captain who
held no important position whatsoever. With regard to the
anthropologist who is supposed to have "carried the main
administrative burden for the vast Anglo-Egyptian Sudan", I
can only suppose that the late Professor Nadel is referred to.
In fact, he had nothing to do with administration of the Sudan.
For good measure I may well add that the statement (page 176)
that British anthropologists "created the principle of 'indirect
rule' " is also nonsense. Who were they and how and when and
where did they do it?

                                        E. E. EVANS-PRITCHARD
All Souls College, Oxford.

In spite of this the fact that anthropology had been a great help to
administrators was acknowledged by many of them, no matter
whether the anthropologist in the situation was appointed by the
colonial government or was working from a British University.[19] In
the words of Sir Edward Evans-Pritchard himself writing two
decades earlier: "The value of social anthropology to administration has been generally recognised from the beginning of the century and both the Colonial Office and colonial governments have
shown an increasing interest in anthropological teaching and research. For a good number of years past colonial cadets, before
taking up their appointments, have received, among other courses

[19]An example of this is P. M. Larken's statement when referring to Evans-
Pritchard's work on the Zande:
    With his knowledge for a guide, one can now form a just appreciation
    of Zande action and reactions which might otherwise appear incompre-
    hensible or even blameworthy. No doubt many people will, thanks to
    him, escape unjust punishment, and receive a favourable response to their
    often obscure requests.
    My constant regret is that he did not make his visit many years earlier,
    so that I could have had the chance to benefit from his teaching, for I
    should have been a far better D.C. if such good fortune had been mine.
    (Larken quoted in Singer and Street Zande Themes Oxford (1971 opening
    page.)

of instruction, instruction in social anthropology at Oxford and Cambridge, and more recently in London."[20] In fact not only did administrators recognise the role of anthropology, but in a number of cases, they suggested fields of study and produced lists of the kinds of questions that ought to be asked, on the grounds that they were best qualified to point to social problems of special relevance to the stage of development of a particular colony. The colonial governments, through lack of finances, could not afford the luxury of supporting research on topics that did not contribute directly to their main interest—maintenance of 'law and order'.

Considering the Sudan situation, many intellectuals nowadays connect the fact that most social anthropological studies were focused on the southern region of the Sudan to colonial government policy towards the south. But in my view this is a mistake, mainly because the discussions and publications as well as the events of the last twenty years have proved, beyond any doubt that the colonial government lacked a consistent policy *towards the South*. To explain why the northern Sudan did not have a fair share of anthropological studies, when compared with the South, we have to consider a number of points. First, it was financially difficult to support anthropological studies. Secondly, since the main focus in the early stages of the administration was on the maintenance of law and order, the administrators in the north, most of whom were very competent and highly qualified, thought that there was not a great deal that anthropology could do there for them. Their own contribution in the field of cultural history and social organisation of the people among whom they worked laid the basis for the limited series of objectives they had in mind.[21] It is apparent that even when anthropologists, who were willing to work in the area, appeared, they were directed to places where the Government lacked information or did not have enough or enough competent administrators — namely the south (e.g. the Seligmans).

The development of anthropology and its increasing contribution to the administration of other colonies gradually convinced the leading administrators in the Sudan Government that they should make use of it. The value of anthropological research especially in relation to the administrative problem of the South was stressed. On

[20]E. E. Evans-Pritchard, *Social Anthropology*, London, 1951, p. 110.
[21]The large number of articles on history, beliefs, customs and values that appeared in *Sudan Notes and Records* represent a major part of these contributions. Some other major works include MacMichael's: *A History of the Arabs in the Sudan Tribes of Northern and Central Kordofan*...etc.

this topic MacMichael's letter to the Financial Secretary of the Sudan Government on the 10th January 1929 concerning the employment of a trained anthropologist throws light on the relation between anthropology and the colonial administration in the Sudan. Here and subsequently, I quote, at length, from that letter:

When Professor Seligman proposed Mr. Evans-Pritchard's visit it was made a condition of the grant to the latter that he should give the Sudan Government, within a reasonable time, a report of his studies in a form suitable for the use of administrative officials.

After stressing the importance of anthropology to the European administration of 'primitive' peoples, MacMichael goes on to explain that "the administrative official is unavoidably handicapped in the endeavour to study the cultural anthropology of the people with whom he is in contact." This is attributed to a lack of the necessary minimum of technical anthropological training required to enable him to sift and co-ordinate his evidence or even, in the first instance, to question the native intelligently with a view to the collection of evidence itself:

Illustration of the foregoing arguments and of the effects of the lack of expert knowledge could without difficulty, I think, be cited from the record of this Government's administration of the south, where grave errors have been all too often made through ignorance of local beliefs and habits and insufficient understanding of savage ways of thought, and there can be no doubt but that our troubles with the Nuer, e.g., have been intensified by our lack of knowledge of the social structure of this people and the relative status of the various kinds of chiefs and Kujurs.

I feel strongly that, assuming officials ought to be encouraged by every possible means to acquire a fuller and more intimate knowledge of all that pertains to native modes of thought, their efforts must be based upon scientific research which calls in the first instance, for the services of a trained anthropologist. I would urge that the Sudan Government provide the means for the conduct of this research.

Two alternative decisions were possible:

(a) We might employ a staff of trained anthropologists to make a complete comprehensive and elaborate anthropological survey of the Sudan. Such anthropologists would be appointed for an indefinite period and their work be comparable to that done by the Geological Survey.

(b) Alternatively we might employ a trained anthropologist or a series of trained anthropologists for field-work, each for a limited period and for a specific objective or objectives, on the same lines as those on which we are engaging a language expert.

I am personally strongly in favour of the adoption of the latter alternative because it is not ultra-ambitious nor ultra-expensive. I feel too that we should get practical results in a shorter time and have more chance of avoiding the danger to which one is always liable in dealing with the scientific expert, viz: that he will sink the practical in the recondite and lapse into over-elaboration.

The sum of my proposal is therefore that a properly qualified man be employed as from next winter, on the same lines as Mr. Evans-Pritchard, to study a given tribe or series of tribes. It should certainly be a part of his terms of reference that he should within a given time furnish the Government with a report of the results of his fieldwork in the form of a monograph or series of monographs couched in easily comprehensible terms and dealing with those social and cultural aspects of the subjects of his study a knowledge of which is essential to the administrator. He might be given as a guide a short questionnaire covering these essential points, such as that which was drafted for Mr. Evans-Pritchard in 1926 and to which, as illustrating my arguments, I would draw particular attention.

The immediate field of study should probably be the Nuer. It is possible that Mr. Evans-Pritchard himself is the right man, and might be willing to undertake the work. The period of his present engagement ends in April next and he will then wish to spend some months in England collecting and preparing his material. If he does not wish to return upon our terms, I am certain that Professor Seligman, whom I consulted when last in England, could suggest a suitable alternative.

The Appendix mentioned in MacMichael's letter consisted of the following questions:
1. Names of tribe.
   (a) Used by the tribe itself
   (b) Used by neighbouring tribes
   (c) Used by the Arabs and the Govt.
2. Habitat and boundaries. Nature of country.
   (Plains, hills, forest, swamps, rivers.)
3. Relations with neighbouring tribes, raiding, intermarriage, alliances, trade.
4. Language. If possible give the first ten numerals and a few common words such as fire, water, man, woman, child, sun, moon, etc. etc. and names of all game animals.
   (a) With which other tribes are they mutually intelligible?

(b) Can any relationship with other languages be traced?
e.g. Shilluk and Anuak are mutually intellibible. Shilluk and Dinka are not mutually intelligible, but are related.
5. Divisions.
(a) Political e.g. chieftainship acting together politically and in war.
(b) Social e.g., clans, totemic and otherwise tracing descent from a common ancestor. Age grades.
6. Chiefs. Paramount and sub-chiefs. Political and religious chiefs, such as rainmakers. Are these identical? What are their powers? How appointed?
7. Numbers, as far as ascertainable of tribe and sub-sections. How many villages?
8. Economic Life.
Pastoral or agricultural or both? Nomadism. What animals are kept? Size of herds. What plants are cultivated. Hunting and fishing. Crafts such as iron working, pottery and basket-making. Are these professional? Carried on by men or women?
9. Weapons used for war, hunting and fishing. Dress and ornaments.
10. Distinguishing customs relating to
(1) birth
(2) marriage
(3) death and burial
(4) inheritance
(5) circumcision
(6) naming
(7) initiation
11. Religious beliefs and specially cults, organisation of cults, secret societies.

One cannot say whether Sir Edward Evans-Pritchard actually supplied answers to these questions directly to the Sudan Government: the fact is that they were available in the classic monographs on the Nuer.

Other examples of how the relationship between anthropology and administration, based on the same principles, continued could be seen in Nadel's appointment to make a study of the Nuba and in Arkell's appointment as a government anthropologist.[22] It is right to emphasise the fact that anthropology was not "*merely* an aid to enlightened colonial administration" but such an emphasis is an attempt to avoid the question about the extent and influence of that aid. The Sudan case shows that the indirect role of anthropologists —whether they were aware of it or not—was great; and that the reactions of intellectuals in the country towards the subject are based on findings filling a large number of files in the Sudan Government Archives.

At the same time one would like to see anthropology aiding development in new states especially when the anthropologist in-

[22]K. D. D. Henderson, *The Making of the Modern Sudan*, London, 1952, pp. 79-80.

volved is a "native". Since I have this attitude, I would like to make it clear that I am not condemning the involvement of anthropologists with administration in the Sudan during the colonial period. I am merely establishing and documenting this involvement. I believe that no branch of social science can or should be neutral and these anthropologists conform with my view. One feels that they were doing what they thought was right and adopted the current ideologies of their time. This invites a more systematic re-valuation of their contribution seen within the context of the colonial framework (similar to Magubane)[23] which this paper, though condemning the ideology of colonialism, falls short of making.

## IV

To sum up, though my remarks might seem a little incoherent, I try to make the point that the cultural heritage, education and socialisation of the anthropologist as a member of a human group which has developed certain images of "natives" must have carried some of these images with him to the field. How much this influenced his work is a different question; and the answer varies from one individual to another, especially in relation to training and character. By going into such questions I hope to cast some doubt on issues taken for granted rather than to reach firm conclusions.

The only reference to the relations between anthropologists and administrators in colonies appeared in brief acknowledgements in prefaces to anthropological monographs. The administrators on their side stated their views on the subject through their own channels. After independence the intellectuals of new nations gained access to state archives and so learned many things about the history of the subject and its practitioners. They took anthropologists to be equally responsible for the inadequacies of development in these countries during the period of colonial rule and thus became hostile to them and to their subject.

[23]B. Magubane, "A Critical Look at Indices Used in the Study of Social Change in Colonial Africa", *Current Anthropology*, vol. 12, No. 4-5.

# BIBLIOGRAPHICAL ESSAY
## Philip Marfleet

This short article will review the substantial contributions to the debate over anthropology and colonialism. It will attempt to give an initial orientation to the themes of the discussion, which will provide a basis for the consideration of later contributions, and a number of reference points for the literature cited as bibliography throughout the book. 'Substantial contributions' include all those dealing in whole or part with the anthropology/colonialism relationship as a specific and particular question.

Anthropologists have long been aware of a relationship between their discipline and colonialism. Such an awareness was however largely restricted to an acknowledgement of the colonial system as simply part of the given order. Anthropologists may have been aware, for example, of certain problems created by imperial administrations, but it is reasonable to suggest that by and large they were uncritical of colonialism as a system, as constituting a problem in itself. It is when colonialism came to be regarded in these terms that the relationship with anthropology was brought into question.

In the late 1940s came a first isolated attack from Gregg and Williams in their paper "The Dismal Science of Functionalism" (1948). Although later described as "frequently incorrect in fact and ethically entirely too wild and presumptuous" (by Marvin Harris in his *The Rise of Anthropological Theory*, London 1968 p. 534), this article anticipated many later critical reviews especially of the British method. They saw the 'dismal science' consisting in a perspective largely borrowed from the laissez-faire doctrines of neo-classical economics. Its 'primitive' world was peopled with a socially rational man motivated by self-interest to gratify the needs generated by inborn physical mechanisms. But like the classical economic analysis of capitalist society, such a perspective makes all social interests appear right and good by definition. This individual-ising bio-psychological analysis, argued Gregg and Williams, was placed in a context which made the 'primitive' community function-ally organised and perfectly integrated, and thus an unchangingly proper and seemingly naturally just 'organism'. The sterile func-tionalism which articulated such a view was to be seen as merely another apology for the status quo, for the social organisation of capitalism, with its "depressions, imperialism, and war". The activi-ties of anthropologists in the British colonial administration or in the American military establishment, reflected the utility of anthro-pological theory in maintaining society as it is.

This type of radical and forceful attack upon the anthropological establishment, here with a detailed, if patchy examination of func-tionalist theory was not to be repeated for nearly twenty years.

The next positive comment on the colonial relationship was made by J. R. Hooker in "The Anthropologist's Frontier; The Last Phase of African Exploitation" (1963). This historical study des-cribed the changing position of the anthropologist in relation to the gradual breakdown of colonialism. Initially the hand-maiden of colonial governments, the anthropologist found himself increasingly in sympathy with African interests, and by the anti-colonial period was even actively engaged against the administration. African sus-picion of the discipline remained however and despite his personal concern the anthropologist has found himself rejected. He has not been able to overcome the stigma of involvement in a study seen as so closely related to the colonial system.

Hooker's article was closely followed by a paper from a Belgian anthropologist Jaquet Maquet whose "Objectivity in Anthropology" appeared in 1964. Maquet noted the irony of a situation in which the anthropologist, seeing himself, as Hooker had noted, as liberal-minded and sympathetic toward 'primitive' societies, was nevethe-less responsible for the development of ideas ideologically useful to the exploiting powers. Maquet located the anthropologist as not merely a member of the dominant white ruling group, but as a representative of its middle classes—those most completely involved in the colonial system. This paper also contained one of the first of many prophesies of the coming disintegration of anthropology. With the disappearance of the 'primitive' world, and of the colonial relationship, argued Maquet, anthropological subject matter would be divided between history and sociology. Then at least a more objective body of theory might be assembled.

At this stage it remains convenient to consider contributions to the debate chronologically, and it is Worsley's paper "The End of Anthropology" (1968) which comes under review. This article made a more indirect criticism of the colonial relationship in the course of an analysis of the theoretical state of the discipline, and noted that the anthropologist had traditionally seen his concern as with the 'primitive' world. But emergent social relationships in post-colonial society are increasingly of the 'modern' type—a universal society is in the making. Unhappily, the anthropological desire for universalism is negated by sterile theoretical formalism and relativism. There must be a developmental, processual perspective which will allow for the consideration of a world developing outside the old imperial frame. For Worsley only a rapid reorientation to dynamic study could provide an alternative to anthropology's dissolution and fragmentation.

Claude Levi-Strauss in "Anthropology: Its Achievements and Future" (1966) reinforced Worsley's doubts. He saw the developing world's hostility toward anthropology as an understandable reaction to a discipline which had been part of the appallingly violent process of domination which established and maintained colonialism. For 'native' cultures ever to view anthropology as legitimate, it must undergo a transformation, to disengage itself from the colonial system. It must become a study of society from the inside, breaking down into a number of other disciplines. Anthropology will survive in a changing world "by allowing itself to perish in order to be born again in a new guise".

Published in the same year (1966), Onwuachi and Wolfe's "The Place of Anthropology in the Future of Africa" also noted the rejection of anthropology in a continent where the old imperial power relationships had been destroyed. Africa had once been merely an extension of Europe; in now asserting its own identity it rejected an anthropology which had not redefined its own perspective. As the science of man, anthropology should work within the broadest context, yet the traditional, and now damaging interest in small-scale societies was still dominant. Anthropology might have a future in Africa, but only after a genuine and careful reorganisation.

Isolated articles written over a period of three years to 1966 may now be seen as elements in a pattern of criticism which was to become more sharply defined, and to assume the proportions of a major debate. Since 1968 there has been a growing interest in the problem of the colonial relationship; contributions have appeared more frequently, and have assumed a more intense and polemical character. These more recent contributions may be conveniently viewed in four groups—those constituting the radical American critique, the British New Left critique, those of the African anthropologists, and the general reviews by Firth and Leclerc.

## The American Critique

The three initial papers of the American critique fall together by virtue of their simultaneous appearance in the *Current Anthropology Social Responsibilities Symposium* of 1968. Berreman's Is Anthropology Alive? is primarily concerned with the ethical position of the American anthropologist. The continuing currency of the myth of a value-free science he argues has lead the anthropologist to allow the utilisation of his research material by those whose interest is not for people but like the U.S. military establishment and the CIA, for power. 'Scientific unaccountability' has merely disengaged the anthropologist from his real moral responsibility. This must be reasserted. Although expressed in an intense polemic against the American anthropological establishment, Berreman's position is, we are warned from further to the Left, merely "a model for seductive left-liberalism in the guise of a radical alternative." (Moore 1971. See below.)

Gjessing in "The Social Responsibility of the Social Scientist" expresses a concern for anthropology as having had a more general relationship with Western colonialism. He notes the development of the discipline as a response to certain imperial demands, and the nature of its theory as being ideologically useful to the dominant powers. Like Berreman he points out the dangers of acceptance of the idea of scientific neutrality. He argues for a realisation of the true nature of the anthropological perspective, especially of its Western middle class orientation. The anthropologist Gjessing asserts must be able to look outside this framework by asking questions which may be subversive of the wider system. Primarily he must define his overriding responsibility by making a real personal commitment to the cause of the oppressed.

The third of these symposium papers—Kathleen Gough's "New Proposals for Anthropologists"—has the most critical and militant tone. It locates anthropology as "the child of Western imperialism", a discipline which has interpreted the non-Western world in terms

of the absolute values of capitalist society. The socialist states of the
developing world have largely been ignored, and the problems posed
by the growth of revolutionary struggles confronting Western, and
primarily American imperialism, left unattended. Yet these are
issues of the greatest importance. Anthropologists must make a
rapid reassessment of their personal positions in relation to the discipline. If not able to assert themselves in favour of their individual
moralities, they should first ask how they may free themselves from
the limitations imposed by their own system.

A related but later American criticism has come from John
Moore. His "Perspective for a Partisan Anthropology" (1971) traces
the development of both British and American anthropology in
relation to the changing needs of the two imperialisms. The former
aided the colonial administration as well as providing the rationales
needed by an exploitative system. The latter, when involved in the
colonisation of Amerindian lands provided a similar set of settler
ideologies. Later during the neo-imperial period it has been explicitly tied to the capitalist ethic, and responsible for research into
the efficiency of the very techniques of exploitation. In an intensly
critical paper Moore argues for a truly revolutionary or 'partisan'
anthropology to provide the only alternative for a discipline com-
plicit in exploitation and oppression. This genuinely radical perspective will contrast with the mere 'liberalism' of White, Harris and
Berreman.

This set of papers from the United States emphasised the immediate and practical character of the anthropological relationship
with imperialism. The main concern was to assert the need for individual responsibility in the light not only of the discipline's relationship with an exploitative system, but of its continuing involvement in, for example, the Vietnam conflict. By contrast the British
critique put greatest emphasis upon theoretical and particularly ideological aspects of the relationship.

## The British New Left Critique

The first of the British Contributions, Anderson's "Components
Of the National Culture" (1968) was an attempt to expose the ideological nature of the whole of British intellectual life under capitalism. In Britain, Anderson argued, the development of the total
social idea was proscribed by a ruling class careful to avoid the
possibility of social theory becoming subversion. The notion of
totality was displaced onto the colonial world, where the concept
of 'the primitive' could be elaborated within the classically totalising perspective of functionalism at no risk to the domestic political
scene. A flourishing, indeed 'brilliant' anthropology was allowed to
develop, which played the dual role of administrative advisor and

ideologist for the imperial system. David Goddard's "Limits of British Anthropology" (1969) contained the most careful analysis of the theoretical shortcomings of anthropology in relation to its colonial setting. Goddard saw the relegation of human identity to that of 'the primitive' to be related to a limited self-conscious borrowing from the work of Durkheim, (and to a lesser extent from Maine) which emphasised the rule-governed nature of society. Applied in the oppressive colonial situation this resulted in a study of social 'things'—real of de facto aspects of behaviour—to the exclusion of a consideration of the most important part of the Durkheimian heritage—its 'metaphysical' aspect. This emphasised the analysis of phenomena into their constituent parts, and implied the importance of an analysis of the non-normative elements of social life—conflicts, interests, and the like. In ignoring this area of Durkheim's work anthropology remained theoretically sterile, and unaware of the crudity of the system within which it developed.

"The Crisis of British Anthropology" by Jairus Banaji (1970) suggested that during the post-war period anthropology has unsuccessfully faced two problems. First, the development of a world in which economic and national change and revolutionary struggle make traditional subject matter and fieldwork less and less viable bases for the formation of theory. Born out of imperialism the discipline cannot now adapt to an anti-imperial world. Second, faced with the growth of structuralism as a partial alternative to stagnant functionalist theory, anthropology has ignored the new scheme or 'naturalised' or 'defused' it. Now in crisis, functionalism is offered but one solution, that of historical materialism with its theory of 'social formations'. Marxist anthropologists must expose the cruelty of the imperial system, and substitute new theory in conjunction with real political practice on behalf of surviving 'primitive' groups.

The British New Left perspective has been phrased in less personal and immediate terms than the American critique. It has been less wide-ranging, and less militant in tone, though it has utilised a more recognisably Marxist form of analysis.

## The African Anthropologists

The third group of most recent studies consists in two articles by African anthropologists. These are not classified together by virtue of the social origin of their authors, but in relation to the perspectives adopted, which are critical of certain categories and assumptions which have been the planks of functionalist theory in Africa.

Mafeje's "The Ideology of Tribalism" (1971) notes that there has often been no indigenous word for 'tribe', and that it has been the colonial authorities, aided by the anthropologist, who have "created" these entities. 'Tribalism' has an ideological basis, and it reflects the power of the European ruling class, or that of the new African elite. It is merely a fiction in the false consciousness of supposed tribesmen, it obscures the realities of exploitation and control, and as such is ideology in the original Marxist sense. The real history of Africa will only be rewritten when the importance of regional particularism, of culture, and of class formation, are asserted against the imperialists' mystifications 'tribe' and 'tribalism'.

"A Critical Look at Indices Used in the Study of Social Change in Colonial Africa" by Bernard Magubane (1971) is a detailed examination of the way in which anthropologists have misinterpreted the true nature of 'Westernisation' or 'modernisation'. The ruling imperial powers attempted to obliterate the independent African personality. In the urban situation, where the African was most subject to the pressure to conform to petty European standards (related to dress, education, occupation, and the like) the anthropological study made him human only in so far as he approximated to a set of status indices determined in relation to the values of the dominant culture. A complex of status hierarchies was made to overlie the reality of an extractive, two-class system. But the ideological complicity of the anthropologist could not complete the process of eradication of the African identity, which has reasserted itself to expose the crude nature of colonial sociology.

The two articles by Mafeje and Magubane have been among the most interesting studies of the anthropology/colonialism relationship. Each is concerned with the way in which one area of anthropological theory has been related to a specific part of the colonial system. Each makes an analysis in terms of the legitimacy that functionalist categories have had for the subjected sector of colonial society. An attempt has been made to expose ideology 'from the inside'. Hooker and Levi-Strauss among others had made an appeal for such a form of analysis. It is worthwhile noting that of all contributors to the recent debate only these two authors have been in a position to draw on the indigenous African experience.

## Firth & Leclerc

The final set of contributions are those most recently published. By 1972 the issue had become one of real importance, and two general statements appeared. Leclerc's book *Anthropologie et Colonialisme* pinpoints classic functionalism's principle failing to have been an inability to distinguish colonial reality as merely one among others. The imperial system bred an uncomprehending, ideological discipline. Certain trends in anthropology, notably American cultural anthropology, supported in France by Griaule and others, stressed the importance of cultural relativism, and thus gave assistance to the anti-colonial movement. But anthropology today is still a mirror of existing colonial attitudes, and it has been rejected both by Third World intellectuals and Western radicals. Even the anthropology of a decolonised world, structuralism, is condemned as being ideological. Anthropology is unable to escape its origins. For Leclerc an anthropology more closely related to the founding spirit of the Enlightenment—anti-colonial, liberating, and universal —will provide a genuine alternative to today's stigmatised discipline.

The first argued response to the radical critics of anthropology has come from Raymond Firth, a leading figure of the British school. His paper "The Sceptical Anthropologist? Social Anthropology and Marxist Views on Society" is partially devoted to a response to the 'gut-Marxists' and others who have sought to expose the discipline as having supported an exploitative system. Much of their criticism, claims Firth, is 'a travesty'. "Anthropology is not the bastard of imperialism, but the legitimate child of the Enlightenment." Anthropologists have sought to gain respect for the peoples they have studied, and have often received appreciation in response. They have recorded the disruptive effects of colonialism, and examined the system itself as a social type. Conflict as well as integration has been stressed, and cognitive as well as behavioural aspects of social life examined. Firth responds to Gough's analysis of the personal crisis faced by the contemporary anthropologist by suggesting that the delineation of priorities is often difficult, and that critics frequently simplify alternatives within complex situations.

Firth's reaction to the radical attack, from a self-defined position as 'a liberal anthropologist of socialist interests', relies upon assertion rather than argument and example. So certainly do many of the articles to which he responds.

Anderson, P., "Components of the National Culture", *New Left Review*, 50, 1968, pp. 3-57.

Anthropologie et Imperialisme: Symposium, in *Les Temps Moderne*, 27, Dec. 1970-Jan. 1971, pp. 1061-1201.

Balandier, G., *The Sociology of Black Africa*, London, 1970.

Banaji, J., "The Crisis of British Anthropology", *New Left Review*, 1970, pp. 71-85.

Batalla, G. B., "Conservative Thought in Applied Anthropology: a critique", *Human Organisation*, 25, 2, 1966, pp. 89-92.

Berreman, G. D., "Is Anthropology Alive? Social Responsibility in

Anthropology", *Current Anthropology*, 9, 1968, pp. 391-398.

Copans, J., "Pour une histoire et une sociologie des études Africaines", *Cahiers d'etudes Africaines*, 11, 1971, pp. 422-47.

Firth, R., "The Sceptical Anthropologist? Social Anthropology and Marxist Views on Society", Inaugural Radcliffe-Brown Lecture in Social Anthropology, 1972. (Pamphlet)—from the *Proceedings of the British Academy*, Vol. LVIII, Oxford University Press, London, 1972.

Gjessing, G., "The Social Responsibility of the Social Scientist", *Current Anthropology*, 9, 1968, pp. 397-402.

Goddard, D., "Limits of British Anthropology", *New Left Review*, 58, 1969, pp. 79-89.

Gough, K., "New Proposals for Anthropologists", *Current Anthropology*, 9, 1968, pp. 403-407.

Gregg, D., Williams, E., "The Dismal Science of Functionalism", *American Anthropologist*, 50, 1948.

Harris, M., *The Rise of Anthropological Theory*, London 1968.

Hooker, J. R., "The Anthropologist's Frontier: The Last Phase of African Exploitation", *Journal of Modern African Studies*, 1, 1963, pp. 455-59.

Leclerc, G., *Anthropologie et Colonialisme*, Paris, 1972.

Lévi-Strauss, C., "Anthropology: Its Achievements and Future", *Current Anthropology*, 7, 1966, pp. 124-7.

Mafeje, A., "The Ideology of Tribalism", *Journal of Modern African Studies*, 9, 1971, pp. 253-261.

Magubane, B., "A Critical Look at Indices Used in the Study of Social Change in Colonial Africa", *Current Anthropology*, 12, 1971, pp. 419-430.

Maquet, J. J., "Objectivity in Anthropology", *Current Anthropology*, 5, 1964, pp. 47-55.

Manners, R. A., "Functionalism, Realpolitik & Anthropology in Underdeveloped Areas", in R. A. Manners & D. Kaplan (eds.), *Theory in Anthropology*, Chicago, 1968.

Moore, J., "Perspective for a Partisan Anthropology", *Liberation*, Nov. 1971, pp. 34-43.

Onwuachi, P. C., Wolfe, A. W., "The Place of Anthropology in the Future of Africa", *Human Organisation*, 25, 1966, pp. 93-95.

Worsley, P., "The End of Anthropology?", Paper for Sociology and Social Anthropology Working Group, 6th World Congress of Sociology, May 1966.

# Index of Names

# Notes on Contributors

**Talal Asad** MA Edinburgh, B Litt & D Phil Oxford is a lecturer at the University of Hull. He has published a book and several papers on the Kababish Arabs of Sudan and on political anthropology.

**Abdel Ghaffar M Ahmed** BA & MA Khartoum, Ph D Bergen is a lecturer at the University of Khartoum. He has published several papers on the Rufa'a Arabs of Sudan.

**Richard Brown** MA Cambridge is a lecturer in African History at the University of Sussex. He has published a number of articles on the history of the Ndebele and on modern Rhodesia, and co-edited with E T Stokes *The Zambesian Past* 1966.

**John Clammer** BA Lancaster, DipAnth & D Phil Oxford has carried out field work in Fiji. He has published articles on theoretical topics and is a lecturer at the University of Hull.

**James Faris** BS New Mexico & Ph D Cambridge is associate professor at the University of Connecticut. He has published a number of books and papers on his work in Newfoundland and on the Nuba, Sudan.

**Stephan Feuchtwang** BA Oxford & MA London is a lecturer at the School of Oriental & African Studies, London. Several articles on his work in Chinese religion are in the press.

**Peter Forster** MA Econ Manchester is a lecturer at the University of Hull. He has published papers on the sociology of religion.

**Wendy James** B Litt, MA & D Phil Oxford is lecturer in Social Anthropology at Oxford. She has conducted field research in Port Sudan and on the Sudan-Ethiopian border, particularly among the Uduk speaking people on which she has published various articles and a book is in preparation. She is co-editor with Ian Cunnison of *Essays in Sudan Ethnography* 1972.

**Helen Lackner** BA London is working on the theory of economic anthropology. She is interested in contemporary Middle Eastern affairs and is a member of the Gulf Committee.

**Philip Marfleet** BA Hull is preparing for field work in the Middle East. He is interested in political anthropology.

**Roger Owen** BA & D Phil Oxford is lecturer in the Recent Economic History of the Middle East and Fellow of St Antony's College Oxford. He is the author of *Cotton and the Egyptian Economy, 1820-1914: a Study in Trade and Development* & editor with Bob Sutcliffe of *Studies in the Theory of Imperialism*.

**Roy Willis** B Litt & D Phil Oxford is a lecturer in the Department of Social Anthropology, Edinburgh. He is the author of *The Fipa and Related Peoples of South-West Tanzania and North-East Zambia* (Ethnographic Survey of Africa) 1966, and several papers.